Land Use
and
Living Space

Frontispiece 'London going out of town – or – the march of bricks and mortar' by George Cruikshank, 1829

Land Use
and
Living Space

Robin H. Best

METHUEN
London and New York

First published in 1981 by
Methuen & Co. Ltd
11 New Fetter Lane, London EC4P 4EE

Published in the USA by
Methuen & Co.
in association with Methuen, Inc.
733 Third Avenue, New York, NY 10017

Typeset by Inforum Ltd, Portsmouth
Printed in Great Britain by
Richard Clay (The Chaucer Press), Ltd
Bungay, Suffolk

British Library Cataloguing in Publication Data
Best, Robin H.
Land use and living space.
1. Land use
333.7   HD111
ISBN 0-416-73760-9
ISBN 0-416-73770-6 Pbk (University paperback 747)

Contents

Tables

Figures

ERRATA

In Figure 8 the vertical shading in the counties of Cumberland, Durham and Northumberland is indistinct and seriously affects the impression which is intended.

In Figure 9 the vertical shading in the top section of the key (0.2-0.3+) is indistinct, also in the maps 1950-55 in the Home Counties, in 1955-60 the London area, and in 1960-65 and 1965-70 the South Wales area.

Acknowledgements

The author and the publishers would like to thank the following for permission to reproduce certain material and figures:

National Farmers' Union, Table 18; Agriculture Economic Development Council, Table 22; Land Service of the Ministry of Agriculture, Fisheries and Food, Table 23; A.G. Champion, Figures 4 and 14; The Editors of *Urban Studies*, Figures 5 and 6; M. A. Anderson, Figure 17; British Museum, Frontispiece.

Measurements

Metric measurements are used throughout the text, except in a few isolated instances. Note in particular that areal measurement is expressed in hectares (abbreviated to ha). One hectare equals about $2\frac{1}{2}$ acres (see conversion table in the Appendix).

Preface

A Britain paved and built over from end to end is not an appealing prospect. It is not a very likely one either – or not in the foreseeable future. Yet apprehension can fuel the imagination to such an extent that what is a barely credible, distant fantasy can become a real and immediate threat in many minds.

It is not, then, so surprising that student and other groups, with little or no previous instruction in land-use matters, consistently give an inflated total when questioned about the extent to which England and Wales are built-up. Most answers place the proportionate coverage of urban land within the range of 15 to 30 per cent, or even higher, though the actual figure at the present time is much smaller than this – not more than 12 per cent. Undoubtedly, the tendency to exaggerate the sprawl of urban areas is rife, and probably reflects the inherent dislike and even fear of urbanisation which is felt by many people in this country.

For those who experience such disquiet when viewing the apparently inexorable growth of our cities and towns, it may be some consolation to realise that the construction of a continuous brick and concrete carapace over the entire surface of Britain, at the current rate of converting rural land to urban use, would take well over a thousand years. With England and Wales alone, where the speed of change is greater, the outlook is not quite so good. Nevertheless, it would not be until around the year 2800 that, at present rates of transfer, the last piece of rural land south of the Border might finally pass into urban use. Only then, by piecemeal ingestion, would we have achieved the unenviable ultimate environment of a completely urban country in physical form as well as in social structure.

Another eight centuries or more is a long way ahead on the human time-scale, and it is obvious enough that many distorting elements will influence the scale of urban growth and rates of expansion over that period. Certainly, we should be extremely cautious of the exaggerated claims so often expressed nowadays that most of the countryside will disappear without trace in the next few decades. It will not. But even with a slowing increase in population and the better use of derelict and vacant land within urban areas, new green-field sites will still be required for development, and particularly for housing, if all our people are to have homes fit to live in with an adequate provision of space for their legitimate needs.

Too often now, as in the past, illogicalities pervade the discussion of land-take for urban growth and improved living space. It was Bertrand Russell who recalled the frustration of trying to make one of his older relations see that it was inconsistent to declare, at one and the same time, that everybody should be well-housed and yet that no new houses should be built because they were a blot on the landscape. You do not have to search far to find such contradictory and unhelpful attitudes still persisting today.

If this is true for urban development, it is equally apposite for agricultural land losses, which, to a large extent, are the other side of the coin. Indeed, the consternation over farmland transfers sometimes assumes obsessive proportions. Pessimism about potential shortage of food supplies and loss of countryside is not just a recent event, however; it is a chronic affliction. It has dominated British thinking for nearly two hundred years and goes right back to Thomas Malthus in 1798 and his exposition of how population growth would outrun the likely increase in home food production. George Cruickshank's nightmarish cartoon in 1829 of 'London going out of town – or – the march of bricks and mortar' (Frontispiece) shows unmistakably how the whole idea of a threat to the countryside and farming was catching on. And a century after Malthus, in 1898, the scientific world was still pursuing the same topic. In that year a respected scientist, Sir William Crookes, in his presidential address to the British Association, predicted famine in the western world by the 1930s because of shortages of wheat. But, in reality, the 1930s, far from seeing wheat shortages, were, ironically, years of vast oversupply when cereal crops were being burnt, dumped or otherwise disposed of simply because they could not find a market.

Despite such wrongful forecasts, pessimism about land and food supplies has continued unabated to the present day. Not many years ago, Lord Rothschild, former head of the government's 'think-tank', was even incautiously predicting that Britain could face food rationing if the take-over of farming land for urban development continued at its current rate. Alice Coleman, a Cassandra of this depressing land-use future, has coupled her fears for food supplies with a controversial indictment of land-use planning in a special issue of the *Architects' Journal* (in 1977). In it, she roundly contends that good agricultural land is being turned over to urban use at an 'increasing and alarming rate' and that, because of this alleged 'galloping consumption', the country is 'rapidly running out of productive land'.

The evidence presented in the following chapters does not support this view: indeed, to a large extent a completely contrary assessment is arrived at. If anything, transfers of agricultural land to urban use have tended to decline; and this has been particularly true since the mid-1970s as recession has bitten deeper into the economy, and mortgages and credit have become more expensive to obtain. Less land was converted to urban use annually at the close of the 1970s than at any other time since the end of the last war, and land loss, at the rates sustained in recent decades, should not be any real worry for the farming industry in the foreseeable future.

In fact, one of the main problems now facing British and EEC agriculture is the actual or potential over-supply of many foodstuffs rather than any shortage of production. The beef, butter and barley mountains, the milk and wine lakes, are constantly recurring dilemmas of Community agricultural policy. So why such gloomy prognostications? And why should they be made not only in Europe, but in North America as well, where – completely unlike so many of the developing countries of the world – nutritional worries are most frequently associated with the over-eating of the relatively cheap and liberal supplies of readily available foods? There may be many answers to this question, often more emotional than logical or reasonable. They can probably be seen as part of what John Maddox has called 'the Domesday Syndrome'.

This is perhaps an appropriate moment to face up to what has become an increasing confusion in the minds of many environmentalists towards the countryside. None of us (or, at any rate, not many) takes pleasure in seeing attractive rural areas built on or dispoiled by urban intrusions like power lines and rubbish dumps. Over the years, the author himself has had his own house in the countryside progressively surrounded by new estates. He does not like it, but he does not thereby assume that the 100 per cent urbanisation of his surrounding world is repeated across the entire face of the country, or that the loss of farmland which has been entailed has had a noticeable effect on the agricultural economy of Britain. Moreover, the personal dislike of this development by himself and his family has also to be set against the satisfaction and enjoyment of several hundred other people in their new and better homes. As Fraser Hart, in the United States, has perceptively remarked, 'the psychological impact of urban growth may be far more important than its physical impact'.

The real point is that we should not allow our own emotional reactions to confuse and distort wider resource and social considerations. An individual Briton may find the environment of the Netherlands somewhat claustrophobic, and an American may feel the same about England; but this does not mean to say that the economy of these densely developed countries suffers either industrially or agriculturally, or that their social structure is any the less stable. This is not to imply, of course, that what we like or dislike about the environment, and particularly the aesthetic aspects of a situation, should have no part to play in determining our attitudes towards it. On the contrary, such preferences must assume a vital role in formulating policy. But what they should not be allowed to do is to confuse the issues. Just because we dislike to see productive farmland eaten into by houses and roads, it does not follow automatically that this loss of land is a 'bad' thing for agriculture and the nation as a whole, or that food supplies will necessarily suffer in the process.

At the outset, therefore, it should be made quite clear that this book is not dealing with personal preferences about land use – of whether we like or do not like what we see. Rather it is concerned with the *amounts* of land and space that are available for various activities, and whether changes in the land-use structure are likely to have any decided effects on our land resources and life-styles, particularly where food supplies are concerned. Unfortunately, we know only too well that tracts of farmland or forest, just as much as housing estates, can in certain cases be visual disasters, whereas others, by contrast, are highly attractive and desirable. Not infrequently, this has relatively little to do with the amounts of land involved: more often than not, it is simply an outcome of man's discrimination or insensitivity in design, technology and aesthetic appreciation. One badly sited and designed house, pylon, barn or stand of trees can more effectively urbanise or mar a rural landscape than a well-located and perhaps more extensive encroachment on to a greater area of land.

In their attempt to get more precision and less subjectivity into the discussion of land use, some of the following chapters are quite substantially loaded with quantitative material – with facts and figures. In this respect, it is inevitable that certain parts of the book are heavier-going than others and it may, therefore, be of some assistance if a few suggestions are made on approaching the text. This is proposed with a little hesitation for it may seem rather a presumptuous thing to do: nevertheless, experience has shown that many people would often welcome some indication of how to make the best use of a book for specific purposes with reasonable economy of effort and time. After all, knowledge is required at many different levels for many different purposes. According to what you do and who you are, your requirements and approach will vary radically.

At the one extreme, you may simply require a few general figures on land use in Britain. If this is so, turn to Table 8, which is the basic table in the book. It shows the existing structure of land use at various dates during the course of the twentieth century, and the information is recorded graphically in Figure 2. Table 15 and Figure 7 carry this information further by giving the transfers of agricultural land to urban use over several decades. In addition, Tables 29 and 31 indicate the situation for other countries in comparison with that in the United Kingdom.

For someone who wants rather more than just the bare bones of land use, a summarised version of the main themes, with a brief analysis and interpretation, is presented in the last chapter. The student and more specialist reader, however, will no doubt require a much fuller and detailed account. In this case, he or she might like to read the last chapter first to gather a brief overview before tackling the rest of the text in a selective way. It should be noted that Chapters 3 and 5 on land-use structure and transfers of farmland provide the core of the book, and selective progress will be assisted by reference to the fairly full summaries of the chief points and statistics which conclude most of the chapters. It is hoped that these summaries, when taken together, will provide the student with a reasonably comprehensive set of basic notes. Chapters 4, 7 and 8 are more specialist in character, referring specifically to urban, regional and rural aspects of land use, respectively. Referencing in such a potentially wide field has been kept strictly in rein, so that mention is made of only the most pertinent, useful or interesting publications. Frequently, these references themselves record further publications which, if so desired, can be used to widen the coverage of the subject.

The statistical content of the book raises one other matter which calls for brief comment. A perusal of the tables and the data in the text may give a somewhat dated impression. No estimate of the national structure of land use is given for later than 1971, and much of the other material recorded refers to the 1960s and even to the 1950s. This situation simply reflects the gaps in time before satisfactory and fairly complete land-use information becomes available. Even the most recently published Agricultural Statistics refer to the mid-1970s, and the last woodland census was in 1965 (a new one is being carried out at the present time). Urban data are even worse. Although several estimates of the coverage of urban land were made for the 1960s and 1950s, only the development plans gave a reasonably comprehensive yet detailed statement of urban land-use structure and provision in about 1961. With the advent of structure plans in the 1970s, no similar urban figures are likely to be available in the near future, unless remote sensing techniques can help to fill the gap. Consequently, a delay of ten years or so is nothing exceptional when dealing with land-use information and patterns of land use. Fortunately, over such a period the overall land-use structure of a country does not normally alter very fundamentally.

It is a daunting prospect after working for so many years in the subject of land use to look back and recall all those who have given me so much assistance, consideration and kindness. Research at Wye College into land use was started and stimulated in 1954 by Gerald Wibberley with the help of Counterpart Funds. At this early stage, as well as in later years, I was also given much encouragement and practical advice by Dudley Stamp and Terry Coppock, both of whose work in land use is seminal. The research and teaching grew in volume and scope until, in 1970, the Countryside Planning Unit was instituted with the aid of generous support from the Cook Trust. Subsequent development into the Department of Environmental Studies and Countryside Planning in 1979 has seen the continuance and strengthening of this work.

Over nearly three decades, several government departments have provided many basic and essential data and facilities. A great deal is owed to the Ministry of Agriculture, Fisheries and Food, and particularly to its Agricultural Censuses and Surveys Branch at Guildford; to the Forestry Commission and its officers, especially Michael Locke and Arnold Grayson; and to the Department of the Environment (and its predecessors) where, if one division were to be singled out, it would be the Library, which has provided bibliographical assistance in so many ways. Consistent financial support for various parts of the research, in the form of studentships and specific research grants, has been given by the Social Science Research Council, though other organisations have also made awards in the post-graduate sector.

Many additions to land-use research at Wye College over the years have been made by post-graduate students or research assistants working with me. In chronological order, they are Michael Bruce, Tony Champion, Alan Rogers, Maurice Mandale, Tim Shaw, Guy Swinnerton, Allan Jones, Paul Cloke, Dorothy Wilkinson and John Hansen; and I am indebted to them all. Their contributions are recorded at the appropriate places in the text, and a number of them have passed on to posts in higher education and are developing land-use or other investigations in their own right. Tony Champion has not only allowed me to draw on his work, but has also kindly let me adapt some of his original maps for my own use.

My present departmental colleagues at Wye have chivvied and urged me to bring this book to completion and I am sincerely grateful to all of them, particularly Margaret Anderson who has also undertaken that onerous yet vital task of reading and commenting on much of the script. Sue Briant has done most of the typing from my disordered manuscripts with creditable care and accuracy. Helen Best has spent time off from her vacation studies to draw or re-draw skilfully many of the maps and diagrams in the following pages. Yet, of course, far more than academic assistance alone is needed to write a book, so perhaps I may be allowed a very personal, if somewhat different, note of appreciation to my wife Jean for all her support and understanding.

R.H.B.
Wye College
January 1981

1
Living space and environment

To a large extent, the physical form and the habits of the earth's vegetation and its animal life have been moulded by the environment. Considering the whole span of earthly time, the opposite effect, in which life actually modifies its surroundings, has been relatively slight. Only within the moment of time represented by the present century has one species – man – acquired significant power to alter the nature of his world.

(Rachel Carson: *Silent Spring*)

No more than three hundred years ago, Britain was relatively empty of people. Over many thousands of years, right up to the mid-seventeenth century, the inhabitants of this country never totalled more than a few millions. Their number had oscillated, often dramatically, with the vicious cycle of pestilence, prosperity, famine and war: long-term growth of population was slow and hesitant. It was a Malthusian world.

Yet, at length, as the natural and human environment came more under man's control, the scene was set for radical changes in social and economic structure. The gradual transformation of the feudal society in the Middle Ages, with all its constraints on people and production, and the eventual shift from a largely subsistence type of economy to a fully-fledged commercial one, was accompanied by a spectacular quickening in population growth. Extensions of farmed land and improvements in agricultural techniques, providing food for millions of new mouths, went hand in hand with the upsurge of a new urban-industrial society which has culminated in the technologically advanced economy of the present day.

But although population has increased tenfold in the last three centuries, the total land area of Britain has, inevitably, remained roughly the same in extent. As a consequence, the land surface has had to support and sustain ever more people, until today, in England and Wales, we all have less than one-third of a hectare each on which to live compared with nearly three hectares for every person

Table 1 Changes in population, density and land provision in England and Wales since Roman times

Date	Population millions	Density persons/km²	Land provision ha/person
300–400	0.6	4	25.0
1086 (Domesday)	1.5	10	10.0
1260	2.6	17	5.9
1340 (pre-Black Death)	4.5	30	3.3
1377 (post-Black Death)	2.4	16	6.3
1470	3.0	20	5.0
1545	3.5	23	4.3
1600	4.6	30	3.3
1650	5.2	34	2.9
1700	5.8	38	2.6
1750	6.1	40	2.5
1800	9.1	60	1.6
1851 (Census)	17.9	118	0.8
1901 (Census)	32.5	214	0.5
1961 (Census)	46.1	304	0.3
2001 (estimated)	50.5	333	0.3

in 1650 (Table 1). By the end of the century, the area available may have been reduced even further.

Small though this personal allocation may be when compared with the space enjoyed by our ancestors tilling the open fields of medieval England, the modern individual of the human species does not need nearly so much land to provide him with many of the basic necessities of existence – like food, clothing and fuel. Technological innovation and economic development have allowed growing numbers of people to live and be provided for at vastly improved standards of nutrition, material wealth and general well-being on just the same area of land that was available for previous, and less crowded, generations. In agriculture, for instance, land inevitably features quite strongly as a factor of production; yet despite this, the industry has been intensifying its output immensely – producing more and more from the same piece of ground – so that land is coming to play a diminishing role in the production of all types of food. Indeed, certain farm enterprises concerned with poultry, pigs and beef cattle are actually beginning to assume some of the spatial characteristics of urban uses, with a concentration of animals on land that resembles, or exceeds, the closeness of human beings in cities.

Urban space

Though agriculture began with rather poor and extensive cultivations and grazings and has progressively intensified its use of land over time, urban development started out at the other extreme of the density spectrum. Cities have always been crowded places and could not have fulfilled their primary functions unless this had been so. Until about a hundred years ago, the relatively small size of cities, which permitted ready access to more open surroundings, mitigated many problems of insufficient urban living space. These problems only began to become acute when rapidly increasing populations were clustered together in the very much larger urban-industrial communities of the nineteenth century which failed to provide a significant improvement in density standards or amenities compared with those of earlier centuries. In this way, a spatial stranglehold was inflicted on millions of people who were still too poor and too disorganised to make their needs for more adequate living conditions felt.

Greater personal and public affluence in technologically advanced countries, coupled with vastly improved means of communication, have now caused this straight-jacket to be broken wide open, and the demand for extra room for each person is incessant and irresistible. In addition, urban population numbers may still be expanding at considerable rates. As a result, urban areas are spreading with some rapidity when measured by the growth in previous centuries, though it is easy to magnify unduly the pace and extent of this development and the reduction in densities which is taking place. Some indication of how thick on the ground modern urban man still lives is illustrated by our own country. In a group of 162 English towns, with a large element of suburban development at what would normally be considered fairly low urban densities, there is, in reality, an average urban land provision of only around 0.03 ha per person.[1] This is as little as a tenth of the space (0.3 ha per person) which each inhabitant enjoys in relation to the whole land surface of the country (Table 1).

The truth of the matter is that, even with substantial and necessary improvements in urban space standards, urban uses require relatively little land compared with agriculture and forestry. Take out farm, forest and other rural land in Britain, and there remains only 8 per cent of the surface area on which the entire population of well over 50 million resides and on which, for the most part, it works and plays as well. Not a very large proportion, it might be thought, for one of the most highly urbanised and densely populated countries in the world. Indeed, it is interesting to discover that, by using the very adequate provision of urban land planned for our earlier new towns, the whole population of Europe – not far short of 700 million people – could be settled quite comfortably within the boundaries of England and Wales. Unreal as such a calculation may be in purely practical terms, it nevertheless demonstrates once again just how limited in extent existing urban areas are – not only in Britain, but in every other country of Europe and, in fact, throughout the whole world. In the more extreme cases, where nations are of a very large physical size or populations are relatively small, urban uses can occupy negligible proportions of the total land area: compared with Britain's 8 per cent, the figure in the United States, for example, is only 3 per cent, while in Canada it is less than 1 per cent. Clearly then, from the viewpoint of land availability, it appears that man should have little difficulty in finding all the urban living space he needs in most countries on earth, either now or in the foreseeable future.

In many nations, the physical process of urban growth, as opposed to the social trend towards urbanisation, has hardly progressed beyond its early stages, and, at first sight, the competition between rural and urban uses does not yet seem to assume very meaningful proportions. In practice, however, this can be a much oversimplified assessment. Because of natural or socio-economic factors, sizeable parts of the land surface provide a completely inappropriate location for certain activities. By way of contrast, other areas can be highly suitable for several different land uses. In such circumstances, the effective spatial arena for land competition is reduced while the intensity of conflict is accentuated. Historically, for instance, towns have usually grown up where their immediate hinterlands could provide a ready supply of food and where nodes of communication made for an easy concentration and distribution of products. Hence, land that is most valuable for agriculture, from both a physical and an economic point of view, is frequently the most desirable for urban development as well. Consequently, competing demands on land can arise not only because of an absolute shortage of land, but also because of a relative scarcity of mutually advantageous locations. Under these conditions, the land use with the greatest economic or social viability will not necessarily eliminate the less competitive uses, but will simply displace them to somewhat less desirable locations or, alternatively, stimulate an intensification of activity in the remaining areas.

Urban growth illustrates this process very well. In large or developing countries, the extension of the urban area at the expense of agriculture or other rural uses can be easily compensated for by the bringing into production of new land or the upgrading of existing rural land. With small and heavily urbanised countries like Britain and the Netherlands, however, the situation is far more complicated. Additional productive land is more difficult and costly to reclaim so that adjustments become increasingly confined to the existing area of the major land uses. Moreover, the inroads made by urban growth into agricultural land are relatively greater and begin to warrant closer attention. In spite of this, it would be wrong to imply that a really critical *economic* problem concerning the land allocations for these two uses is arising at present. On the contrary, wherever urban growth is taking place, there are few real signs that it is being inhibited or hindered significantly by a general shortage of land for development or that agricultural production is suffering to a serious degree, if at all. Far more probably, any future retardation of urban extension, leaving aside conscious planning for social and aesthetic purposes, will not come directly from economic restraints but from completely different quarters.

Although human society can adapt itself quickly and easily enough to greatly increased material affluence, it seems that man's mental make-up will not so readily adjust to the ever increasing proximity of ever larger numbers of his fellow human beings. It has been contended that the warning signs of a greater propensity for mental and social disorders are already to be seen where very high numbers and densities of people have built up in technologically advanced societies.[2,3] Whatever may be the apparent sophistication of modern communities, the superficial veneer of civilisation and wealth barely hide a basically unchanged human nature adapted to a spacious environment which has now largely disappeared for many millions of people, or is in the process of doing so. 'Getting away from it all' has become a common catchphrase of our society, but, even by driving out of the towns and into the so-called open countryside, the continual contact with other people is often not substantially reduced. Moreover, it becomes less and less so as the years go by, and as the relatively unmodified 'natural' scene grows progressively harder to find. Under these circumstances, the breaking point in the constantly tightening ratio of man to land may well come not so much because of any shortage of surface area to provide the material requirements of human beings, but rather from the social and psychological tensions engendered by too many people living in too little space.

By no means all authorities, however, would agree with such a diagnosis. Jonathan Freedman thinks that high population density has been much maligned, at least as it affects human beings.[4] With supportive evidence, he maintains that 'people who live under crowded conditions do not suffer from being crowded. Other things being equal, they are no worse off than other people.' So it is evident that no consensus of opinion yet exists on this thorny question. Nevertheless, all these contentions on densities and numbers of people have a built-in assumption that populations will continue to expand. But will they? Already in Britain and some other countries of the western world birth rates have been slumping and total population numbers are faltering in their growth. Conditioned as we are to the exponential population increases of the last two centuries, it is not easy to readjust our thinking to the possibility of zero growth or even decline. Yet should the population curve level out eventually, the urban expansion trend as we see it in Britain would also disappear in time, leaving a completely different but equally contentious set of problems in its wake.

A divided Britain

Although Britain is a fairly small country compared with many others, it has, for so relatively limited an area, a landscape that is incredibly diversified and full of contrasts. The foundations of the land surface, the rocks themselves, range in age and type from ancient Pre-Cambrian to recent Quaternary; from old, hard crystalline strata, through the softer sedimentaries, to the patchy cover of glacial and alluvial deposits. From this rock base comes a wealth of minerals; overlying it, there is a wide variety of soils, from the poorest to the most fertile. In some ways influenced by this diversified foundation, the face of the country alters with remarkable frequency over quite short distances. Moors, woods, farms, villages and towns, industrial sites, roads, railways and airfields, mines and quarries – land uses press upon each other in an intricate and often seemingly inextricable assortment.

Yet one primary division of this complex landscape is normally made. This is the distinction between the north and the south of the country; between the relatively deprived and relatively affluent regions. Geographers, however, generally recognise a rather more sharply defined and physically based duality.[5] If an imaginary line is drawn diagonally across the country from the mouth of the Tees in north-east Yorkshire to the mouth of the Exe on the south coast of Devon, Britain is divided into two broadly contrasting parts of not dissimilar size (Fig. 1). The land to the north and west of the line is composed geologically of old, resistant strata, rich in minerals, which now form a mainly rugged and wild upland area of poor grazings, forests and moors. It coincides very closely with the regions in which a tenth or more of the agricultural area is under rough grazings. The soils are mostly thin and poor, the climate damp; and taken as a whole the area is physically inhospitable except in certain favoured and rather isolated localities. Settlements are generally small and scattered, except around the landward boundary where the old industrial areas are situated. This division is known as Highland Britain and covers an area of some 13 million ha.

To the south and east is the younger portion of the country both geologically and culturally. It lies wholly within England itself. Although diversified by hill lands and escarpments, it is in general rather flat or undulating in character with good soils and a fairly dry, sunny climate. It makes an intrusion into Highland Britain by way of the Cheshire Plain and is altogether more agriculturally attractive. Throughout most of our history, cultural continuity has been less marked in these parts than in the north and west; change has been the dominant characteristic. It is here, in particular, that the population has usually grown the fastest and that we have witnessed in recent times the greatest spread of industry and towns. This division is Lowland Britain and accounts for some 10 million ha.

The distinction between Highland and Lowland Britain has been of profound significance from the land-use point of view throughout most of the history of this island. Lacking the resources of modern science and technology, our ancestors were substantially dominated by the character of the natural environment. Time and again, new incursions of people and cultures from Continental Europe entered and overran many parts, or all, of Lowland Britain only to find their further progress restricted and hindered as they reached the Highland Zone. The Romans, the Saxons, and even the Normans did not penetrate very deeply or very effectively into the northern and western uplands; the new systems and techniques of agriculture or the new features of urban structure which they brought with them

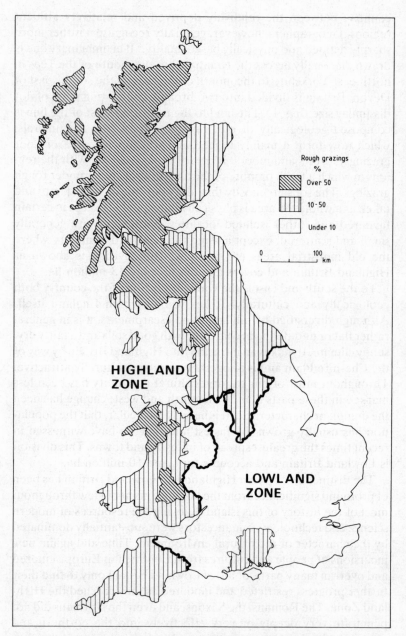

Figure 1 Highland and Lowland Britain defined on a county basis, and the distribution of rough grazings as a proportion of all agricultural land, 1970 (After Best and Coppock, 1962; Edwards and Rogers, 1974)

found their full expression only in the south and east, while the older ways persisted in the north and west.

This situation did not change materially until the end of the eighteenth century. Then, with the development of manufacturing industry based on coal and steam power, the emphasis of population and urban growth shifted to the coalfield areas on the margins of, or actually within, Highland Britain. Since the First World War, however, there has been a relative decline in the importance of the heavy industries concentrated in these areas, while, at the same time, new sources of power, like oil and electricity, have assisted in the spread of manufacturing industry and population away from the older centres. As a result, many of the locational advantages of Lowland Britain for economic growth have reasserted themselves; but, despite this, the tendency for economic development to revert more strongly towards the south-east has been only partly reflected in a similar distribution of urban growth. For reasons to be discussed later, some areas of Highland Britain have also contributed substantially to urban development since the Second World War. Much of the more recent urban growth is centred in and around the major northern as well as the midland conurbations, and extends south-eastwards into the London Region along an axis which runs at right angles to the dividing line between Highland and Lowland Britain. The increasing development along this so-called axial belt may well be reinforced as economic ties with Continental Europe become closer and the volume of trade increases, so that eventually a spine of urbanisation will extend virtually without interruption, except for the English Channel, from Merseyside to the Ruhr.

Early land use

The increasingly urbanised landscape of the present century is the latest phase in a long historical sequence of land-use events extending back to the end of the Ice Age in Europe. Since that time, three main stages of landscape change and land-use development can be recognised:

(a) A forest and woodland cover that dominated the scene for seven to eight thousand years, after about 8000 B.C. In many respects this was not a land use at all, but simply a category of vegetation or type of habitat which, on the whole, was used rather slightly for man's activities over most of the period concerned.

(b) An extending area of agricultural use, cutting ever more extensively into the forest and woodland over a period of some five thousand years up to the present time. However, agriculture has only been a dominant activity across much of the landscape for the past thousand years or so, reaching its maximum areal extent towards the end of the nineteenth century.

(c) The rapid spread of urban land in the last century to become a notable feature of land-use structure. The short time period involved and the continuing, persistent growth suggest that this stage has not yet run its course, though the pace of land-use change in general has clearly speeded up dramatically over the centuries.

To go back to the beginning, it is some ten thousand years ago that the ice sheets of the last glacial phase of the Pleistocene finally receded from the British Isles, and plants and animals moved in to colonise the whole country. The tundra and steppe of the sub-arctic phase gave way to birch and pine, and the open landscape was transmuted into forest. Eventually, as the climate grew more temperate, the forest cover became largely deciduous in character and extremely dense in many lowland areas. By about 3000 B.C. the Highland Zone was dominated by oak and the Lowland Zone by a mosaic of forest types in which lime was probably the commonest tree.[6] In pre-Neolithic times, it is now clear that the blanket of forest and woodland was practically all-pervading, except on particularly unsuitable tracts of land such as the higher mountains, steep rock faces, and stretches of bog and marsh. In total, it occupied about two-thirds of the surface and persisted, though not without change in botanical content and composition, throughout by far the greater part of the post-glacial history of these islands.

Even as late as the Iron Age, tree-cover still took up over half of the land area, and only in the last two thousand years has its extent shown a rapid and marked decline. The contraction is indicated by figures provided mainly by James Fisher, though they must be regarded as very rough estimates (Table 2).[7] Edlin, however, reached similar conclusions and surmised that, by the Norman Conquest, some two-thirds of the original forests in Britain had vanished, leaving only a fifth of the country wooded.[8] This remaining portion was quickly eroded. The diminution of the forest area, of course, did not take place through natural processes, but rather at

Table 2 Decline in the forest and woodland area of Britain since Neolithic times

Period	Forest and woodland million ha [a]
Early Neolithic	16
End of Bronze Age	13
End of Iron Age	10
End of Roman period	8
Norman Conquest	4
About 1700	1
About 1900	1

[a] Total land area = 23 million ha

the hand of farmers, iron smelters, shipbuilders and other human exploiters who cut voraciously into this seemingly inexhaustable resource. But, unfortunately, the trees of the forest were far from unlimited in number; and today, after several centuries of felling and insufficient replacement, we are, somewhat paradoxically, at almost the other extreme, with a lower proportion of woodland than in most other countries of western Europe.

The first farmers came to these islands some five or six thousand years ago, but to begin with their economy of shifting agriculture brought about only a small alteration to the natural landscape.[9] With the establishment of settled agricultural communities, the potential population which could be supported was substantially increased, and the environmental impact also grew considerably. Some measure of the enormous scale of this change compared with non-agricultural societies can be grasped from even the rather tentative figures compiled by Colin Clark.[10] For hunting and collecting economies, as in Palaeolithic times, not less than about 10km² per person was needed to provide an adequate supply of food. In complete contrast, in early agricultural, crop-growing economies, the figures could actually be reversed with a minimum of ten people being supported from each square kilometre of food-producing land. Nevertheless, the inhabitants of Britain remained rather small in number until Roman times.

The conquest of Britain by the Romans came in the first century A.D., and by urban and agricultural development they brought to bear the resources of a far more technically developed civilisation upon the English landscape. Forest was cleared, swamps were drained, large stretches of fertile soil were brought into cultivation

11

and many towns were built, connected by paved roads. But this development of the land surface was largely confined to the Roman Civil Zone which, to all intents and purposes, coincided with Lowland Britain: the Military Zone, to the north and west, still remained relatively untouched. In some districts, the work of the Romans was very extensive and the natural landscape must have been considerably altered and brought into more productive use. Yet, in the country as a whole, the impression they made must not be over-drawn.

During Roman times there may have been about 100 towns and some 2500 rural settlements such as villas, hamlets and isolated farms. According to Dudley Stamp, this probably represents only between 400,000 and 1,600,000 ha as being cultivated and cropped, although a large additional area would also be used for grazing purposes.[11] W.G. Hoskins estimates that the area was even less – under 300,000 ha.[12] Taking the lower end of Stamp's range as encompassing the most likely figure when exports of grain are allowed for, it does not seem very probable that more than 3 to 4 per cent of England and Wales had been cleared and cultivated. Perhaps another 3000 ha were under towns, villa houses and other settlements, but this figure excludes the countrywide network of main roads (over 8000 km). Although this area of urban land is infinitesimal, some of the towns were large by the standards of the time. London, for example, eventually occupied over 120 ha, or more than almost any other Roman city north of the Alps.[13] Conversely, Bath only covered 9 ha.

With the arrival in force of the Anglo-Saxons in the fifth century, the pace of change quickened once again. England now became a land of villages and the beginnings of a rural settlement pattern were laid down that has survived, though with many modifications, right up to the present day.[14] In this way, the newcomers initiated an upsurge of colonisation which was to continue in a fluctuating manner for several centuries with the extension of village lands, the intakes made by individual squatters and the farming activities of monastic houses.

Knowledge of land use and of what the landscape was like in Norman England is derived particularly from the Domesday Book. This book was compiled from information collected during what was, in effect, the first agricultural land-use survey made in this country. It was put in hand by the king in 1086 and revealed that in England to the south of Yorkshire and Cheshire there were some

3.6 million ha of cropland with some 2 million ha sown in any one year.[15] This was something like seven times the area cultivated in Roman times and it amounted to about one-quarter of the whole land surface of England and Wales.

Yet even with this considerable spread of open-field farming and other cultivations during the previous 500 or 600 years, the outstanding impression of the landscape after the Norman conquest was its uncultivated aspect in many areas compared with that of later centuries; though in one sense some of this land was by no means unutilised. For many generations before and after the Norman conquest, the kings and their noblemen hunted wild animals as a recreation; and because of this activity Royal Forests, or more exactly legal hunting grounds, were widely established throughout England. By the thirteenth century, it is estimated that as much as one third of the country may have been covered by them, and even today in Lowland Britain fragments of these forests continue to exist – like Epping Forest and the New Forest.[16]

Modern times

For another 500 years or so after Domesday Book very little is known in any detail of alterations in land use, despite the radical changes occasioned by the Black Death, or bubonic plague. By the seventeenth century, however, there were increasing attempts to estimate and define some major elements of the land-use structure, particularly in the agricultural sector. In 1601, Maxey estimated

Table 3 Changes in the area and provision of cropland since Roman times. The gain in area between 1901 and 1971 was not continuous and, in contrast, cultivated land (crops and grass) has shown a marked decline over the same period

Year	Population millions	Cropland area million ha	Cropland provision ha/person
300	0.6	0.5	0.8
1086	1.5	3.6	2.4
		(2.0)[a]	(1.3)[a]
1696	5.8	4.4	0.8
1901	32.5	4.9	0.2
1971	48.6	5.7	0.1

[a] It is estimated that, at this time, only 2 million ha of cropland were actually sown in any one year

Table 4 The land-use structure of England and Wales in 1696, 1901 and 1971. The figures for 1696 are those of Gregory King, and the over-estimation of the total land area at this time should be noted

Land use	1696	1901	1971
		million ha	
Crops and grass	8.4	11.1	9.7
Cropland	4.4	4.9	5.7
Permanent grass	4.0	6.2	4.0
Rough grazings	4.0 [a]	1.4	1.9
Forest and woodland	2.4 [b]	0.8	1.1
Urban land	0.6 [c]	0.7	1.6
Other land [d]	–	1.0	0.7
Total land area [e]	15.4	15.0	15.0

[a] Heath, moor, mountain and barren land
[b] Including parklands and commons
[c] Including orchards and waste land. Urban land was probably no more than 200,000 ha
[d] Including land unaccounted for, and opencast mineral workings, military land and unutilised rural areas not recorded under other uses
[e] Excluding rivers, lakes and ponds (200,000 ha) in 1696 and inland water (86,000 ha) in 1901 and 1971

that cropland or arable in England and Wales covered 2.7 to 3.6 million ha, or probably less than the Domesday arable area for feeding nearly four times as many people. Not only does this figure not include grazing land but, during the course of the century, the draining of the Fens and other reclamations were to increase the cropland area quite considerably. Hence, by 1696, Gregory King could estimate the arable at 4.4 million ha (Table 3).

It is the estimates of King at the very end of the seventeenth century which, for the first time, provide a quantification of the whole pattern of land use in England and Wales.[17] Unfortunately, his assessment was based on an overestimated total land area, but the use of hectares rather than acres and the rounding of the figures help to absorb the discrepancy (Table 4). Apart from the much reduced extent of forest and woodland, the most outstanding feature was the immense area of barren and wild land, an unknown portion of which was used for rough grazing. These uncultivated tracts extended to some 4 million ha, or more than a quarter of the whole land surface, though W.G. Hoskins believes that this figure is too high (he reduces it to 2.8 million ha). A century later, the Board of Agriculture was able to state that the area had diminished to not much more than 3 million ha, or about one-fifth of the land surface. Urban land probably extended to no more than a third of the 600,000 ha which also covered orchards and waste land.

The effects on land use of the so-called Agricultural and Industrial Revolutions of the eighteenth and nineteenth centuries were perhaps not so dramatic as demographic, economic and social change over this period might at first suggest. Inevitably, towns expanded as population began to concentrate in them; but the urban area was still an extremely small proportion of the total land surface and the new houses and factories, more often than not, were built at high densities on fairly small sites. As a result, the areal extension of towns was still not very substantial. Moreover, the steep increase in urban population was not accompanied by any notable dispersion of settlement. In the days when public transport facilities were primitive and costly, workers had normally to be within walking distance of their workplaces. Consequently, industry, housing and other urban uses were inevitably situated fairly close together.

On the other hand, agriculture continued to extend its sway across the landscape, helping to swell the supply of food needed for the growing number of industrial workers. This expansion of the agricultural area in England and Wales continued to the very end of the nineteenth century when the hectarage of farmland reached a maximum. With some 87 per cent or more of the total land surface then under agricultural use (allowing for farmland not recorded in the official statistics), the virtual limit of extension in such a comparatively small country had been reached in a physical as well as in an economic sense.[18] Part of this land under agriculture, however, was classified as rough grazing and was used in a very extensive or intermittent way. Even so, the cultivated (crops and grass) area in 1891 was officially recorded as being in excess of 11.2 million ha, or 75 per cent of the total land area, for the first and only occasion in our history.[19]

Population had now risen to around 32 million, and the majority of these people were living at high densities in cramped cities and towns where adequate living space and urban amenities were only notable by their absence. Still further compression was quite untenable. As it was, urban land only covered between 4 and 5 per cent of the whole land surface, while forest and woodland took up very little more. In a nation that had become economically dependent on

15

the output of manufacturing industry and whose inhabitants were predominantly urban-orientated, agriculture certainly had more than its fair share of the land available (Table 4).

This is not to imply that agriculture, at the levels of technology and management then existing, had sufficient land to feed the whole population, although by 1870 it seems that some 80 per cent were still largely fed by home production. From Table 1, it can be seen that no more than half a hectare per person was available for *all* needs and uses – urban and rural – in 1900. With cultivated land alone, about one-third of a hectare had to suffice to feed each person, and this was an impossibly small allocation to provide a reasonable level of nutrition. By this time, however, the increasing population did not need to be fed from its own agricultural land. Tropical products had for long been imported to satisfy specialised demands and now the export of manufactured goods and services paid for a growing importation of temperate food as well.

Although the flood of food imports and feeding stuffs from overseas was at first the principal reason for the reduction in the cultivated area from its peak at the end of the nineteenth century, this downward trend in the area of agricultural land began to be accelerated by the growing competition for land from the newly extending land uses of urban development and forestry. There was, then, a fundamental alteration in the direction and speed of land-use change from the last two decades of the nineteenth century onwards. Agriculture, instead of extending its cultivated area as it had done fairly consistently for several hundreds of years, suddenly began a steep and continuous areal decline. On the other hand, the most intensive sector of agriculture – the cropland area – did not follow the same sequence of change. Fluctuations in the cropland hectarage were quite notable with sharp upturns in the two World Wars and its maintenance at a high level since the end of the last war. Increases in population, however, resulted in a continuing drop in the area available per person.

In contrast to this late nineteenth-century arrest and reversal of long-established trends in agricultural land use, or at least of culti-vated land, urban growth and afforestation have made exceptional claims on land resources compared with previous centuries, particu-larly since the 1920s. It is primarily with these last four decades and with the future that we shall now be concerned.

References

1   Best, R.H., Jones, A.R. and Rogers, A.W. (1974) 'The density-size rule', *Urban Studies*, 11 (2), 201–8.
2   Leyhausen, P. (1965) 'The sane community – a density problem?' *Discovery*, 26 (9), 27–33.
3   Best, R.H. (1966) 'Against high density', *New Society*, 8 (271), 787–9.
4   Freedman, J. (1975) *Crowding and Behaviour*, New York, Viking Press.
5   Stamp, L.D. (1946) *Britain's Structure and Scenery*, London, Collins.
6   Rackham, O. (1976) *Trees and Woodland in the British Landscape*, London, Dent.
7   Fisher, J. (1970) 'Conservation in Britain – the background to European Conservation Year 1970', *Journal of the Town Planning Institute*, 56 (3), 87–91.
8   Edlin, H.L. (1956) *Trees, Woods and Man*, London, Collins.
9   Evans, J.G. (1975) *The Environment of Early Man in the British Isles*, London, Paul Elek.
10 Clark, C. (1967) *Population Growth and Land Use*, London, Macmillan.
11 Stamp, L.D. (1955) *Man and the Land*, London, Collins.
12 Hoskins, W.G. (1955) *The Making of the English Landscape*, London, Hodder & Stoughton.
13 Postan, M.M. (1972) *The Medieval Economy and Society*, London, Weidenfeld & Nicolson.
14 Roberts, B.K. (1977) *Rural Settlement in Britain*, Folkestone, Dawson.
15 Maitland, F.W. (1897) *Domesday Book and Beyond*, reprinted in Fontana Library, London, 1960.
16 Darby, H.C. (1948), 'The economic geography of England, A.D. 1000–1250', in Darby, H.C. (ed.) *An Historical Geography of England Before 1800*, Cambridge, CUP, 165–229. See also: Darby, H.C. (1973) *A New Historical Geography of England*, Cambridge, CUP.
17 Barnett, G.E. (1936) *Two Tracts by Gregory King*, Baltimore, Johns Hopkins University Press.
18 Best, R.H. (1968) 'Competition for land between rural and urban uses', in Institute of British Geographers, *Land Use and Resources: Studies in Applied Geography*, 89–100.
19 Ministry of Agriculture, Fisheries and Food, Department of Agriculture and Fisheries for Scotland (1968) *A Century of Agricultural Statistics: Great Britain 1866–1966*, HMSO.

2
Meanings and material

National land-use statistics are, potentially, a meaningless amalgam of
figures based on different classifications applied to dissimilar areal units
with varying degrees of precision. The results are unlikely to be reliable,
and may well prove positively misleading.

G.C. Dickinson and M.G. Shaw[11]

There is no official land-use inventory compiled for Britain as a
whole at regular intervals of time. Only twice has a complete cartographic and quantitative survey of existing land use been undertaken; first by the Ordnance Survey in the last half of the nineteenth
century, and later, in the 1930s, by the First Land Utilisation
Survey. The records of the former, which no longer exist in their
entirety, were compiled for individual parishes and never summarised, while those for the latter have only been available in a published and summarised form for the whole country since 1948. The
Second Land Utilisation Survey, which commenced its work in
1960, does not cover all of Scotland, and has not yet produced more
than a fairly small and generalised amount of statistical material. As
a result, it has been several independent sets of statistics for individual and mainly rural land uses that, in combination, have provided the chief sources of information from which our conception of
the overall structure of land use and the changes in it have been
derived. But before considering these data sources, we need to turn
to the even more basic task of defining the term, 'land use'.

Definition of land use

What, then, do we mean by 'land use'? At first sight the term may
seem to be self-explanatory; but, as so often happens, this apparent
simplicity is deceptive. An urban area, for instance, is a complicated
entity to define. Quite frequently, the administrative boundary of a
town under the old local government divisions before 1974 was
taken as delimiting the extent of urban land; but this definition soon

ran into serious trouble for, in Britain at any rate, it has usually been found that a considerable part of the administrative urban area is composed of land in agricultural use. Hence, the area actually under urban use is normally less, and often quite a lot less, than the area enclosed by the administrative urban boundary.[1] A wealth of bewilderment has arisen from the failure to grasp this simple distinction.

At the other extreme, we are faced with the problem of whether the small village or the individual farmstead is agricultural or urban. Is it possible, just because a farmer or an agricultural worker lives next door to a commuting businessman, that any useful land-use distinction can be drawn between their dwellings when both houses are used as residences in a similar way to houses in a town? Here, at the very outset, problems posed by inadequate definition intrude. They are to plague the whole subsequent discussion of land use.

There are several general definitions of land use. One of the earliest was given in connection with the First Land Utilisation Survey of Britain from 1931 onwards. It stated quite simply that the object of the survey was to discover 'for what purposes the surface of the country is used'.[2] In this definition it is implied, of course, that it is mankind's adaptation of the land surface which is being investigated. Marion Clawson gives more prominence to this situation by confining the term land use specifically to 'man's activities on land which are directly related to the land'.[3] But Dudley Stamp goes further than this. He defines land use or land utilisation as 'literally the use which is made by man of the surface of the land but in sparsely populated areas including the natural or semi-natural vegetation'.[4]

Certain geographers have extended the definition in this way to allow the infiltration of types of vegetation as land-use categories. Once this is done, we can be on dangerous ground. Fox, for instance, takes up a more extreme position than Stamp and even states that 'the study of land use is concerned primarily with vegetative cover, or its lack'.[5] Such an excursion into what, in large part, is basically biogeography can distort the content of land-use studies to an unwarranted degree. This whole approach is diametrically opposed to that of Clawson, who very correctly points out that, in practice, data about land often confuse man's activity and the vegetative cover.

This particular conflict of definitions expresses itself in two distinct concepts: the *functional* use of land for man's purposes (agricultural, forestal, residential, recreational, etc.) as opposed to simply the *form* of ground cover (crops, trees, houses, moorland, etc.). When the two coincide, there is no problem; but if they do not, the possibility of confusion can be considerable. To avoid this, a number of geographers, like Fox, have favoured a classification of land 'use' by form only. This is certainly advantageous in constructing maps, for the form of ground cover is much easier to ascertain and record cartographically than is the function. Trees and heathland, for instance, can be recognised and defined immediately without any enquiry as to whether or not the land in question is used for agricultural, forest or recreation purposes. Remote sensing techniques further underline the problem.[6]

Yet it is difficult to deny that it is very much stretching a point to call some of these forms of ground cover 'uses' of land in any normally accepted sense of the word. Many are quite definitely not 'uses' in the sense of being individually associated with specific and distinct human activities or purposes. Conversely, a true land use, like agriculture, can extend across several vegetation types or forms, such as various kinds of cropland, grassland, heather moor, marsh and even forest. As Symons says, 'it is an arid and valueless exercise to examine the vegetative cover – from the point of view of use – without integrating consideration of the functions it performs'.[7]

Theoretically, then, there is a sound case for maintaining that human activities are central to any study of land use; and, if this proposition is accepted, a general definition of the subject can be given in the following way

> Land use deals essentially with the spatial aspects of all man's activities on land and the way in which the land surface is adapted, or could be adapted, to serve human needs.[8]

Yet however warrantable such a functional definition may be, it is in practice not possible to adhere completely to it. The reason is straightforward enough. The study of a subject has limitations imposed on it by its basic data. Rarely, in the social sciences, are these collected and compiled in a way that is entirely satisfactory in meeting the ideal theoretical requirements. In land-use studies, four major uses are conventionally defined, and this classification has come about very largely because it is for these four categories that statistics are most readily available, or into which they can be grouped with the greatest facility. These major categories are: agriculture, forest and woodland, urban land and other, miscellaneous land. Taken together, they comprise the whole land surface, as the final heading covers land which is unutilised (e.g. mountain-tops, ice fields, deserts, etc.) as well as used land which does not fall under the other three main divisions.

Unfortunately, though, this classification has some deficiencies when land use is defined on a functional basis. Agriculture and urban development raise few problems in this respect; but the forest and woodland division causes more difficulties as it is inherently a formal, biological category rather than a functional one. All land covered with trees is not used for commercial forestry, and the content of this category can range from trees planted and managed for the production of timber right through to completely unused natural, or semi-natural, forest vegetation. In Britain, however, most woodland can be expected to provide some sort of financial return from the timber it contains or else contribute to some other human activity, like giving shelter to adjacent farmland or assisting in the conservation of water supplies, soil resources and wildlife. Nevertheless, it is clear enough that to define the function of wood-land is not always an easy matter. This circumstance, in conjunction with the fact that trees are so simple to recognise as a distinct vegetational type, has led almost unavoidably to a basic classification by form, with function only implied.

It is of special importance in Britain that there is relatively little clash between forest and woodland defined in this way and the other main categories of land use. In particular, woodland in this country is not used very substantially for agricultural (grazing) purposes. This is not so elsewhere; and in the United States, for example, the overlap has to be accommodated by a sub-division of the statistics for forest and woodland into either pastured or non-pastured areas so that the two elements can be disentangled.[9] Where grazing activities merge into woodland, the extensive extreme of agricultural utilisation is being approached. At the other, intensive, extreme of agricultural use there is again the possibility of some formal overlap – with urban land this time. Private gardens and allotments attached to houses in Britain and other developed countries may grow certain intensive crops like vegetables and fruit, but these crops are not produced primarily for sale (or for subsistence) as on farms, nor are they grown on anything approaching a farm scale.[10] Therefore, it would be unrealistic to regard such domestic food-producing land in urban areas as being in agricultural rather than in urban use.

On the other hand, functional aspects should not be so exclusively pursued that they become the criterion for classifying land use according to the occupations of people using land. The *use* of a site must be distinguished clearly from the *user* of that site.[11] The same house can be occupied successively by a farmer, a shopkeeper and a teacher, but its use for all these various occupants remains residential: it does not change from agricultural to commercial and then to educational on change of occupier. Following from this point, it is plainly more suitable for land-use purposes to regard all houses, including those on farms, as urban (residential) land where this is statistically feasible, even though they may be located in what would generally be considered as rural surroundings.[12] There are few statistical complications in following this procedure in Britain, though in other countries the separation of urban and agricultural uses is not nearly so straightforward.

A more complicated situation arises in the case of recreational land use. Some land, such as open space in urban areas (parks, playing fields, recreation grounds, etc.) is given over almost exclusively to recreational activity and forms a major sub-division of urban land use. But there is also much land in rural areas that is in sporadic *de facto* use for recreation while being used simultaneously but more consistently for other purposes. In other words, it is land in multiple use. Unlike the United States, this is so with our National Parks. In these areas, very little land is used solely for recreation and for nothing else: indeed, most of the land is essentially in some form of agricultural or forestal use to which access can be gained for recreational purposes. Therefore, although recreation may be an important element in the activities carried on in such places, much of the land will be classified as being in farming or forest use. In contrast, in the United States, Federal and State parks are used more exclusively for recreational activities and are classified as such, irrespective of the forest and woodland they include. This is also likely to occur increasingly in Britain with the establishment of country parks and other areas where recreation is indisputably the chief activity. Such land will be placed in the major category of other, miscellaneous land.

Form and function, then, have been widely confused by the tendency to equate types of vegetation with actual land use. Yet, as we have seen, it usually happens that a reasonable compromise on these two differing approaches to land-use classification can be reached without undue trouble. Perhaps a more serious complication has been the tendency to employ the term 'land use' as synonymous with 'agriculture'. As a result, so-called land-use surveys or related studies are not infrequently found to deal only, or very largely, with the agricultural use of land. In one sense, the association is understandable: agriculture takes up by far the greater part of the land surface in Britain and is the most extensive single major use in many other countries as well. Consequently, agricultural uses of land are often dominant, where hectarage alone is concerned, compared with, say, urban and even forest uses. Nevertheless, this is no real excuse for either ignoring or under-emphasising non-agricultural uses which may make a far greater contribution to national life and wealth than their areal extent would suggest.

Official statistical sources

This agricultural and rural bias is matched by a pronounced rural weighting in land-use statistics, with the supply of urban data lagging far behind information for rural uses. Agricultural statistics in Britain have been collected continuously for well over a hundred years, while increasingly detailed forestry and woodland data have been available since the end of last century. In great contrast, urban statistics were practically non-existent in any fairly comprehensive form until after the Second World War.

Britain is in no way untypical in this respect, and serious deficiencies in urban land-use data are found in practically every other country which makes any pretence to account for its land-use structure. In the United States, the collection of statistics for agriculture began in the very same year as in Britain, whereas urban use of land is still poorly defined in any overall and quantitative terms.[13] The same is true of the countries of Europe (see Chapter 9). Agriculture, then, is almost without exception the land use which is best provided for from the point of view of statistics, and this situation is clearly demonstrated by Britain.

Land-use statistics in Britain are obtainable from a number of sources, and the definitive work by Terry Coppock provides a fund of information on this subject.[14] If material from the two Land Utilisation Surveys is set aside for the moment, nearly all the other figures are from official sources and originate ultimately from material compiled by the Ordnance Survey, the Ministry of Agriculture, Fisheries and Food, the Forestry Commission and the Department of the Environment (formerly the Ministry of Housing and Local Government). It will be useful to review briefly each of these official sources in turn, giving special attention to the definitions adopted and the deficiencies in the data.

Ordnance Survey   The first overall land-use assessment of this country was carried out by the Ordnance Survey in conjunction with their original large-scale cadastral survey (1853–93) and, after 1925, land uses on the revised 25-inch plans were again abstracted. These records are now very incomplete, however, many having been destroyed during the last war.[15]

Nowadays, the areas abstracted have reverted to land, inland water, foreshore and tidal water only. The Ordnance Survey records, therefore, are of limited value for land-use purposes, except for the all-important purpose of defining the total land area of the country and its component administrative parts. In addition, it is sometimes feasible to use these maps for point sampling purposes in order to obtain rather broad-grain estimates of land-use patterns.

Ministry of Agriculture, Fisheries and Food   The agricultural area under crops, grass and rough grazings in England and Wales is compiled by the Ministry of Agriculture, Fisheries and Food from returns made by farmers in June each year. The composition of these headings can be shown diagrammatically.

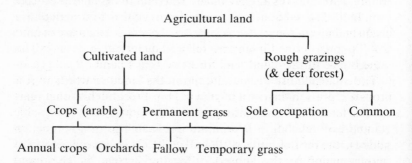

From 1892 until the end of the 1960s, this compilation involved the analysis of returns filled in by individual occupiers of holdings of more than one acre (0.4 ha) in extent. But of the 300,000 such holdings, about one-sixth had very little agricultural production. It was decided, therefore, that as from 1968, some 47,000 holdings with under 10 acres (4 ha) of crops and grass, with no full-time labour and with farm activities accounting for not more than 26 standard man-days (a measure of average labour usage) would no longer be asked to make returns.[16] On the other hand, since 1970, about 2000 holdings of one acre (0.4 ha) or less which have a substantial volume of output (26 SMDs or more), such as intensive horticultural or pig and poultry holdings, have been brought within the scope of the census. From 1973 the limit was raised to 40 SMDs, and well over 70,000 holdings have now been eliminated from the census since 1968.[17] The original 47,000 holdings which were dropped from the census in England and Wales accounted for 83,000 ha of crops, grass and rough grazings, while in Scotland the 16,000 statistically insignificant holdings excluded in 1970 had 383,000 ha of land attributed to them.

The June return is made under about 175 headings (excluding glasshouse crops), but many of these refer to labour and livestock in addition to the land under crops and grass, bare fallow, rough grazings, vegetables, flowers and fruit. The land areas, which include headlands, ditches and hedges, are recorded to the nearest 0.1 ha. The returns also cover rented seasonal grazings and grazing land attached to residential properties, parks, golf courses and so forth. Common rough grazings are estimated by the Ministry. Before 1969, only land specifically growing agricultural crops, grass and rough grazings was included in the returns; but since then, provision has been made for the return of woodland on the holding as well as for the area of land under farm roads, houses, gardens and buildings. The summarised results from all this information are published in the Agricultural Statistics.[18] Similar data are obtained for Scotland, from the returns collected by the Department of Agriculture for Scotland, and for Northern Ireland.

The collection of the agricultural returns for cultivated land (i.e. crops and grass) began on a regular basis in 1866, but for some years the machinery was not working efficiently enough for a reasonable standard of reliability to be attained. Rough grazings were not added to the returns until 1891, and until 1921 they were defined as 'mountain and heathland used for grazing', instead of the present wider definition of 'mountain, heath, moor or down land or other rough land used for grazing'. In Scotland, deer forest has always provided statistical problems.[19] Prior to 1932, the area of rough grazings only included deer forest which was returned as being actually used for grazing purposes: since 1959, the total area of deer forest has been included, although some 600,000 ha may have been virtually ungrazed or very poorly utilised in the 1950s. Such changes in definition of the components of agricultural land have been numerous, but these variations have been discussed in detail elsewhere and no further consideration is called for here.[20]

Except for the period between 1918 and 1921, the collection of the returns was on a voluntary basis until 1926. But even with their compulsory submission, complete enumeration was far from ensured.[21] Occupiers of holdings are legally required to make a return only if officially asked to do so, and the Second World War confirmed that much agricultural land was still escaping the statistics because the holdings in question were not on the Ministry's list. With the introduction of feeding stuffs rationing in 1941, for instance, many persons not formerly making returns found it desirable to draw the attention of the Ministry's officers to the omission. The result was that over 100,000 ha of land previously escaping enumeration were now added to the total agricultural area in that year alone. Similar, but smaller, additions occurred in other years, occasioned principally by rationing, subsidy payments and closer supervision of agriculture during the exigencies of war. This led to a total wartime 'gain' on paper of nearly 200,000 ha of farmland, which was equivalent to over twelve years of actual land losses to urban growth in the subsequent postwar period.[22]

Although omissions still occur, it can now be assumed that the Agricultural Statistics possess a relatively high degree of completeness and accuracy from the point of view of areal measurement at a national level. In any case, it should be recognised that the chief objective of the agricultural returns is to assess crop and livestock *production*; to account for the actual area under agricultural uses is only a secondary consideration. Hence, greater effort has very reasonably been put into obtaining reliable statistics for the more intensively farmed areas under crops and temporary grass. As a consequence, the accuracy of this land-use information tends to decline in moving away from the intensively farmed regions of the country towards the extensively used grazings of the hills and uplands.

Paradoxically, it is the very fact that the Agricultural Statistics have progressively increased in accuracy over many decades that, in some ways, has caused certain incompatibilities to arise in the data. Therefore, the most important point to realise in using these figures is that, because errors in the returns have been continuously rectified over the years, this must to some extent vitiate a detailed comparison of area measurements for different, and especially for widely spaced, dates. Special care needs to be taken at a regional level. Nevertheless, the deficiencies in these data must not be over-emphasised and general trends revealed by the figures are not likely to be called into question.

As a postscript, it should be added that a special part of the agricultural returns, the 'Change in area of holding' section, deals specifically with transfers of agricultural land to and from other major uses like urban development and forestry. These data will be closely examined in Chapter 5.

Forestry Commission Since the end of the last century several calculations of the woodland area of Britain have been made at irregular intervals. The first figures, from 1871 to 1913–14, were compiled by the Boards of Agriculture from statutory returns by woodland owners. With the constitution of the Forestry Commission in 1919, plans for a complete census of woodlands were drawn up. The survey eventually took place from 1921 to 1926, but the statistics were adjusted where necessary to make the census referable to 1924.[23]

The year 1938 saw the initiation of a new census by the Forestry Commission, but war broke out before it had been completed. Widespread wartime fellings and the dated nature of earlier surveys made another early census of woodlands essential once the war had ended. This work was undertaken by the Forestry Commission between 1947 and 1949, the effective date of the survey being taken as September 1947.[24] It was a complete enumeration and covered all woodlands, owned privately or by the state, which were 5 acres (2 ha) or more in extent and one chain (20 m) or over in width. In the interests of completeness, an estimate of the area under small woods of one to five acres (0.4–2 ha) in extent was made by means of a supplementary sample survey in 1951.[25]

It was another eighteen years before the next census of woodlands was carried out. This was undertaken between 1965 and 1967, the operative date being September 1965.[26] The survey, which covered woods down to a minimum size of 0.4 ha, comprised a complete recording of Forestry Commission plantations and a sample survey of private woodlands (62 per cent of the total woodland area but nearer half by the late 1970s). The kilometre grid

27

square was adopted as the sampling unit and the intensity of sampling was 15 per cent of land area. A new woodland census is now under way, and should be completed in 1982. Data for annual changes in the area of woodland, rather than for the total extent of land under trees, will be referred to later in Chapter 5.

Department of the Environment   Under the 1947 Town and Country Planning Act, planning authorities in England and Wales were asked to prepare as part of their development plans a comprehensive statement of existing and proposed acreages under various forms of land use in the old county boroughs and other sizeable urban areas for which town maps were produced.[27] These were usually cities and towns of over 10,000 population. The Ministry of Housing and Local Government (as it then was) extracted and analysed the statistics given for 320 town map areas submitted in England and Wales, and so provided an accurate fund of information for what may be regarded as the 'hard core' of the urban area of the country.[28] The figures obtained in this way were not strictly referable to any one year as this first submission of plans, in practice, was spread over a number of years. Broadly, however, the figures may be taken as reflecting the position in 1951. No similar analysis was made of development plans submitted under the corresponding Act for Scotland.

It was intended that the old-style development plans should be reviewed quinquenially. In the event, the period before revision occurred was more like ten years. Work at Wye College on a sample of 205 reviews and late first submissions for county boroughs and town map areas which had been submitted by 1965 allowed an updating of some of the original Ministry statistics for urban land to an effective date of about 1961 (Chapter 4). Although these statistics from the development plans covered a wide field they were by no means exhaustive. As well as an incomplete coverage of the larger urban areas, there were thousands of smaller towns and villages of under 10,000 population for which town maps, and therefore detailed areal data, were not meant to be provided in any case. In fact, by far the greater part of all urban land in England and Wales fell outside the scope of the development plan statistics. To obtain overall totals for urban land, therefore, estimates had to be made on the basis of these figures.

After 1955, the basic land-use data for reviewed town map submissions were given in a table called 'Changes in land use in town

map area'. In it, the whole area of the town map, including agricultural land, had to be accounted for, and net changes in area between
surveys were entered, together with expected changes to the end of
the next plan stage.[29]

For Department of the Environment purposes, urban land consists of the 'four main urban uses' of housing (net residential area)*,
industry, open space and education, together with the 'residual
urban uses' which are listed as 'railway land, waterways, principal
business and shopping use and public buildings, together (where
applicable) with mineral workings, derelict land, airfields, government establishments, land used by statutory undertakings and other
miscellaneous uses'.[30] In practice, most opencast mineral workings
and military land, in the country as a whole, fall outside the bounds
of measured urban land and therefore come to be included within
the major category of 'other miscellaneous land'.

Important as it is to define what was meant by the urban area in
total, there were also several problems concerning the definition of
individual urban uses. Some variations between planning
authorities occurred in the treatment of land in all of the four main
urban uses. Moreover, the delineation of different land uses could
not, in practice, be carried out, with absolute precision, to the total
exclusion of every non-conforming piece of land, and certain of the
figures given under the various urban headings inevitably contained
some 'impurities'. An added complication was the overlap of two or
more distinct uses, as when, to take an obvious example, a row of
buildings had shopping and commercial facilities on the ground
floor and residential occupation above. In these cases an arbitrary
decision as to the more important component had often to suffice in
determining the land use to be registered.

Finally, it should be noted that by the 1970s, following the Town
and Country Planning Act of 1968, the old form of development
plan had been replaced by the new structure plan with its subsidiary
local plans.[31] At about the same time – in April 1974 to be precise –
the administrative structure of local government under which the
plans are made was also altered. For all the advantages of such
changes, one unfortunate result has been the demise of the formerly
comparable urban land-use statistics for most cities and towns.
Structure plans are much more flexible in character and more
generalised in content and presentation than the former develop-

* The aggregate plot area of dwellings (including gardens) plus any small associated
open spaces and service roads and paths.

ment plans, while in addition, the old county boroughs, municipal boroughs and urban districts have disappeared entirely from the planning scene. As a result, town map areas with their comparable data are now an extinct species. In other words, we possess just one set of detailed, countrywide statistics for urban land use in the 1950s and 1960s (Chapter 4), and it is not likely that such a comprehensive body of data will be compiled again this century by planning authorities.

Land utilisation surveys

In contrast to the last four official data sources which have been discussed, the two land utilisation surveys of Britain were organised by private individuals in London University and were concerned with recording all major land uses, not just one specific use. The idea for the First Land Utilisation Survey was formulated by L. Dudley Stamp at the London School of Economics and was carried out under his direction in the 1930s. The greater part of the field work was completed by the autumn of 1934, by which time some 90 per cent of the country had been surveyed, including nearly all of the main urban areas. The object was to record on six-inch Ordnance Survey maps the existing use of every piece of land in the country. Some 22,000 separate field sheets were involved, and the work of recording was carried out almost wholly by volunteers drawn from universities, colleges and schools. The completed maps were submitted to a central office for checking, editing and reduction to a scale of one-inch to the mile prior to publication.

For the purposes of the survey, seven main categories of land use were distinguished: arable; permanent grass and meadowland; rough grazings, commons, heath and moor; forest and woods; orchards (and nurseries); houses with gardens; and land agriculturally unproductive. The areas under each of these divisions were measured from the one-inch maps, normally from black and white tracings of each particular land use, and the results were recorded in the individual county memoirs which were published to explain and analyse the maps. The figures were brought together in *The Land of Britain – Its Use and Misuse*, written after the war by Stamp, which reviews and summarises the history, results and implications of the project.[32]

The survey admittedly had an agricultural or rural bias in that all but one of the categories of land use it employed were in some way related to food or timber production at a commercial or domestic level. With the exception of 'houses with gardens', which was in part a food producing use, all other urban uses were collected together under 'land agriculturally unproductive'. These two categories in combination provided for the first time a directly measured figure (with small exceptions) for the urban land area at both county and national levels.

The Second Land Utilisation Survey, broadly following the procedures used for the earlier project, was inaugurated thirty years later in 1960 by Alice Coleman of King's College London.[33] Progress was less rapid, however, and only 60 per cent of England and Wales was completed in manuscript form by 1964, although the earliest pilot mapping had started in 1958. The survey was extended to Scotland after this time. The main difference from the first survey was that the final, printed maps were on the 1:25,000 scale ($2\frac{1}{2}$ inches to the mile) instead of the one-inch scale as previously. This increase in scale allowed more detail to be delineated, and thirteen main categories of land use were distinguished: settlement (residential and commercial); industry; transport; derelict land; open space; grassland; arable; market gardening; orchards; woodland; heath and rough land; water and marsh; and unvegetated land. Taken together, the first five uses comprise urban land. The agricultural uses especially were subdivided to a considerable extent, so that, in all, there were sixty-four different land-use divisions.[34]

Again, this tends to result in a marked rural bias, although the greater detail recorded for urban areas than in the original survey certainly enhances the usefulness of the maps. Unfortunately, this advantage is partly offset by the fact that the urban subdivisions do not always coincide very closely with the development plan categories for urban land use. In particular, 'settlement' is employed as an omnibus category which does not distinguish between residential, commercial and educational uses. Similarly, the undivided major category of grassland raises potential problems for comparison with data from the Agricultural Statistics.

The survey of England and Wales was completed by the early 1970s and consisted of 6,500 six-inch field sheets surveyed by volunteers drawn mainly from the ranks of geography teachers. Fifteen per cent of the coverage had been published by 1977 at the 1:25,000 scale. Measurement and analysis of the maps has been carried out at King's College London, using a systematic point sampling method to abstract the required data, but this process has inevitably taken many years because of limited resources. A number of sample resurveys, particularly in south-eastern counties, have also been carried out in the 1970s to try and gain some idea of the trends which are in progress.[35]

References

1   Best, R.H. and Coppock, J.T. (1962) *The Changing Use of Land in Britain*, London, Faber & Faber.
2   Stamp, L.D. (1948) *The Land of Britain: Its Use and Misuse* (3rd edn, 1962), London, Longman.
3   Clawson, M. with Stewart, C.L. (1965) *Land Use Information – A Critical Survey of US Statistics Including Possibilities for Greater Uniformity*, Baltimore, Johns Hopkins University Press.
4   Stamp, L.D. (1961) *A Glossary of Geographical Terms*, London, Longman.
5   Fox, J.W. (1956) *Land-Use Survey – General Principles and a New Zealand Example*, Bulletin No. 49, Auckland University College.
6   Rhind, D. and Hudson, R. (1980) *Land Use*, London, Methuen.
7   Symons, L. (1967) *Agricultural Geography*, London, Bell.
8   Best, R.H. (1968) 'Competition for land between rural and urban uses', in IBG Special Publication No. 1, *Land Use and Resources: Studies in Applied Geography*, 89–100.
9   US Department of Agriculture (1973) *Major Uses of Land in the United States, Summary for 1969*, Agricultural Economic Report No. 247, Washington D.C.
10 Best, R.H. and Ward, J.T. (1956) *The Garden Controversy*, Wye College.
11 Dickinson, G.C. and Shaw, M.G. (1978) 'The collection of national land-use statistics in Great Britain: a critique', *Environment and Planning A*, 10, 295–303.
12 Best, R.H. (1959) *The Major Land Uses of Great Britain*, Wye College.
13 Clawson, M., Held, R.B. and Stoddard, C.H. (1960) *Land for the Future*, Baltimore, Johns Hopkins University Press.
14 Coppock, J.T. and Gebbett, L.F. (1978) *Land Use and Town and Country Planning*, Reviews of UK Statistical Sources, Oxford, Pergamon.
15 Best, R.H. (1959) op. cit.
16 Horscroft, P.G. (1969) 'Changes envisaged in the agricultural census for England and Wales', *Statistical News*, No. 6, 9–10, HMSO.
17 Horscroft, P.G. and Orton, C.R. (1972) 'Reshaping of the agricultural census for England and Wales', *Statistical News*, No. 19, 14–16, HMSO.
18 Ministry of Agriculture, Fisheries and Food, Department of Agricul-

ture and Fisheries for Scotland and Ministry of Agriculture, Northern Ireland (annual or periodic) *Agricultural Statistics – United Kingdom*, HMSO. Statistics for individual counties are given in separate publications for England and Wales and for Scotland.

19   Ministry of Agriculture, Fisheries and Food, Department of Agriculture and Fisheries for Scotland (1968) *A Century of Agricultural Statistics – Great Britain 1866–1966*, HMSO.

20   Best, R.H. and Coppock, J.T. (1962) op. cit.

21   Thomas, E. and Elms, C.E. (1938) *An Economic Survey of Buckinghamshire Agriculture, Part 1, Farms and Estates*, University of Reading.

22   Ministry of Agriculture, Fisheries and Food, Department of Agriculture and Fisheries for Scotland (1968) op. cit.

23   Forestry Commission (1928) *Report on Census of Woodlands and Census of Production of Home Grown Timber, 1924*, HMSO.

24   Forestry Commission (1952) *Census Report No. 1: Census of Woodlands 1947–49 – Woodlands of Five Acres and Over*, HMSO.

25   Forestry Commission (1953) *Census Report No. 2: Hedgerow and Park Timber and Woods under Five Acres, 1951*, HMSO.

26   Forestry Commission (1970) *Census of Woodlands, 1965–67*, HMSO.

27   Ministry of Town and Country Planning (1950) *Town and Country Planning Act, 1947 – Development Plans*, Circular No. 97, HMSO.

28   Ministry of Housing and Local Government (1959) *Report for 1958*, Cmd. 737, App. XXII, HMSO.

29   Ministry of Housing and Local Government (1955) *Town and Country Planning Act, 1947 – First Review of Approved Development Plans*, Circular 8/55, HMSO.

30   Ministry of Housing and Local Government (1959) op. cit.

31   Ministry of Housing and Local Government (1970) *Development Plans – A Manual on Form and Content*, HMSO.

32   Stamp, L.D. (1948) op. cit.

33   Coleman, A. (1961) 'The second land use survey: progress and prospect', *Geographical Journal*, 127 (2), 168–86.

34   Coleman, A. and Maggs, K.R. (1964) *Land Use Survey Handbook* (4th edn), Isle of Thanet Geographical Association.

35   Coleman, A. (1978) 'Agricultural land losses: the evidence from maps', in Rogers, A.W. (ed.) *Urban Growth, Farmland Losses and Planning*, Wye College for Institute of British Geographers.

3
Land-use structure and change

We have huge areas of countryside which most of us never see. At ground-level we realise little of the country which surrounds us . . . It is only from the air that the land-use figures make sense, and we realise that 85 per cent of land undeveloped is not merely a figure on paper but miles of green landscape on the ground.

(Nan Fairbrother: *New Lives, New Landscapes*)

The car journey from the Channel ports to London by the ordinary trunk roads of Kent can all too easily convey the impression of a heavily built-up landscape, though with some sizeable stretches of green countryside interspersed here and there. Fortunately, tourists and most other long-distance travellers are nowadays shuttled along the extending ribbons of motorways. On these newer routes, as on the railways before them, a very different, predominantly rural appearance is presented by the passing scene which is far more in keeping with the conventionally-held concept of Kent as the Garden of England.

In short, the eye alone, particularly at ground-level, can be a very imprecise and distorting instrument for assessing and measuring land use. Visual evaluations of the areal extent of features in the landscape must therefore be treated with care, and even scepticism, for it is often at this point that the foundation of land-use myths is laid and misrepresentation of the national pattern of land use begins. Not until such subjective observations are confirmed or refuted by objective measurement can there be any firm basis for the realistic discussion of land-use problems and policies.

As we have seen, the first attempt to delineate the structure or pattern of land use in England and Wales was made by Gregory King at the end of the seventeenth century (Chapter 1). It will be recalled that the reliability of his data was compromised to some extent by the fact that the figure he used for the total land area was an overestimate. This discrepancy had the effect of calling into question the magnitude of certain of the major land uses which, taken together, accounted for the whole land surface. Inevitably, therefore, the calculation of an accurate figure for the total land area of a country is a prime necessity before a reasonably sound assessment of the existing pattern of land use can be made.

Variations in land area

It is a commonly held view that the total land area of a country is fixed and invariable and that the efforts of man or even of natural processes cannot significantly increase or diminish its supply except over so long a period of time that any consideration of the changes is irrelevant in so far as land utilisation is concerned. Yet perhaps this conception is a little too rigid, for in a country like Britain, which possesses a long sea coast, the land-ocean relationship is never static; there is always continuous change along the coastline, change that is progressively altering the shape and, in the long run, also the total size of the land area.

Superimposed on the natural processes of erosion and accretion that over a very limited period can produce marked local changes, there are also the very slow large-scale movements of the land in relation to sea level that are nationwide in their effects. Since the withdrawal of the ice sheets after the last glacial phase of the Ice Age, isostatic movements of the land and eustatic changes of sea level have combined to produce the most complex geographical effects.[1] But are the resulting changes in the level of the land surface of any significance to us? Fairly recent events suggest that, indirectly, they may be.

Careful tidal observations to establish certain details of mean sea level indicate that a slow sinking of southern England relative to sea level is taking place at a rate of some 3 mm a year. The amount is admittedly small, but taken in conjunction with exceptional tidal and meteorological circumstances it warrants careful consideration. This was emphasised by the disaster which occurred in January 1953 when a great tidal surge breached many of the sea defences along the east coast, inundated over 83,000 ha and caused heavy loss of life and damage to property and agricultural land. London was fortunate on this occasion in escaping the widespread damage caused by the similar floods of 1928, but, nevertheless, serious consequences were only narrowly averted. The new flood barrier being built across the Thames at Woolwich is the latest means of trying to deal with this threat. Since Roman times a change in level of as much as 4.5 m may have occurred along the lower Thames; and over the low-lying areas of eastern and southern England further relative subsidence of the land, even though it be only slight, will obviously give an ever-increasing advantage to destructive natural forces in such special circumstances as have been mentioned and will make attempts to keep out the sea progressively more difficult and costly.

More rapid, if more local, alterations in the coastline are brought about by wave attack and its associated erosive processes and by the accretion of rock material distributed by coastal and estuarine currents. The effects of coastal erosion are well known, for the crumbling of cliffs exposed to wave action is to be observed at many places around the coastline. Looking back over a few centuries, drastic changes are seen to have occurred. The erosion of the Holderness coast of Yorkshire is one of the most notable cases. It has been estimated that, since the Roman period, more than 20,000 ha between Barmston and Kilnsea have disappeared beneath the waves together with the numerous villages that once existed on this land.

Although not so spectacular as coastal erosion, accretion around our coasts is much in excess of erosive loss in area.[2] As with erosion, notable examples of accretion are again very common along the east and south coasts where material for the process is readily available. Areas bordering the Wash provide a good illustration, as do the 23,600 ha of Romney Marsh that have accumulated over the centuries, some 20,000 ha of which are now in agricultural use. But by no means all of the land won from the sea around the coastline is suitable for farming, and reclamations may also be used for afforestation or for industrial purposes.

In favoured situations, then, new areas of land reclaimed from the sea are constantly being brought into use. Quite obviously, however, much of the coastline must be left untouched, for it would be economically and perhaps socially undesirable to interfere with it over long stretches. Nevertheless, figures calculated by the Ministry of Agriculture and Fisheries in 1950 give some idea of the extensive area of land at, or near, sea level which is potentially reclaimable on purely physical grounds. The aggregate figure, comprising potentially useful foreshore areas and saltings in the main estuaries and inlets of England and Wales, amounts to well over 200,000 ha.

The constant subtractions and additions of land along the coastline alter the shape and area of many localities from century to century and even from decade to decade. Nowadays such adjustments in area are carried forward piecemeal into the total land figure for the whole country as Ordnance Survey maps are revised. Just as important, the correction of survey errors on the original maps also have to be recorded. Consequently, figures for the total land area of the country in different years necessarily vary in magnitude to some slight extent. In round figures, though, the total land area of the United Kingdom and its component parts in 1978 can be set out in tabular form:[3]

	ha
England and Wales	15,035,000
Scotland	7,717,000
Great Britain	22,752,000
Northern Ireland	1,348,000
United Kingdom	24,100,000

These statistics are for all land, including saltmarsh, above the high water mark of ordinary tides, but they exclude inland water which covers 86,000 ha in England and Wales, 160,000 ha in Scotland and 64,000 ha in Northern Ireland.

The two countries of England and Wales are usually treated as a single unit for land-use purposes, and it should be noted that their total area is taken as excluding the Channel Islands, the Isle of Man and the Scilly Isles. If Scotland is added to England and Wales, the larger unit which is formed is referred to as Great Britain, or just Britain. The further addition of Northern Ireland, as well as the other islands already mentioned, completes the whole United Kingdom. Should Eire also be attached, the entire grouping is called the British Isles.

It may seem trifling to labour this matter of the sub-division of the British Isles into its component countries. Unfortunately however, it makes an important difference in considering land use. It has happened only too frequently that figures relating to England and Wales, for instance, have been confused with those for Great Britain and the United Kingdom, with a resulting misinterpretation or misrepresentation of data and the conclusions to be drawn from them.

Statistical troubles

With the adequate assessment of the total land area of the whole country, the stage is set to consider how this land surface is apportioned between the different major land uses like agriculture, woodland and urban development. It seems to go almost without saying that the recording of the existing pattern of land use at a particular point (or points) in time is of fundamental importance. Only when the overall situation is known can former or subsequent changes in the extent of the major uses be evaluated in their true perspective. Yet, surprisingly, it frequently happens that information for *changes* in land use is better documented and more readily accessible than data for existing stocks of land in different uses.

Statistics for individual land uses in Britain are normally collected separately and are designed to serve certain specific and circumscribed purposes. In practice, however, the data for rural land uses from the Agricultural Statistics and the Forestry Commission censuses (Chapter 2) have also been used in combination to determine the areal composition of the national land-use pattern as a whole. The first efforts in the interwar period at constructing a complete picture of land use in this country had inevitably to rely solely on these separate rural land-use sources, in the absence of any directly measured urban land-use figures or of the results of the First Land Utilisation Survey. The outcome was that the original, rurally-based, estimates of the structure of national land use compiled by the Ministry of Agriculture passed into general usage and acceptance largely through the agency of official publications. No one at that time appears to have checked or questioned their reliability, which was hardly surprising with the lack of land-use information from urban and other sources.

The publication of the national summaries of the First Land Utilisation Survey and the advent of new data from development plans in the postwar years radically altered this situation. At last it became possible to compare land-use records from different sources and to arrive at some definite conclusions about their respective merits and correctness. Unfortunately, it soon became all too obvious that many serious discrepancies existed, and further investigation of these statistics for land use gave ample cause for emphasising the point that figures are by no means always facts.

The large disparities which occurred and the resolution of these statistical troubles need not concern us for long here, as the subject has been extensively investigated and reported elsewhere.[4] Suffice it to say that the primary problem was the underestimation of the total extent of rural land by the Ministry of Agriculture; more particularly that the area of farmland escaping enumeration in the official statistics was much greater than had been allowed for (see Chapter 2). With the use of a residual calculation in the Ministry of Agriculture's statement of the national land-use pattern of England and Wales for 1937,[5] which was partly based on an earlier calculation for 1925,[6] these rural deficits were carried across into the urban total and incorrectly inflated it by a substantial amount. To be more precise, the Ministry of Agriculture's urban figure for 1937 of 1,684,000 ha[7] was over 50 per cent greater than the more accurate Land Utilisation Survey's urban total of 1,112,000 ha for about 1933.[8] Even allowing for rapid urban growth in the intervening years, the discrepancy must have been of up to half a million hectares – hardly an acceptable margin of error at a time when important policy decisions in relation to urban growth and the loss of rural land were being made. Yet it transpired that the 1925 and 1937 estimates of the structure of land use in England and Wales by the Ministry of Agriculture were accepted as definitive statements on which several others were constructed, and both were submitted in evidence to the Barlow and Scott Committees which reported in 1940 and 1942, respectively.[9]

All these errors and irregularities meant that a new and up-to-date statement of national land use was necessary and desirable in the period following the Second World War. With new data from the Agricultural Statistics, the Forestry Commission and the development plans produced by local planning authorities after 1947, the author was able to construct a more recent estimate for the mid-century situation in 1950. The contrasts with the earlier schedules produced by the Ministry of Agriculture and the First Land Utilisation Survey are set out in Table 5.[10] There were, of course, very definite changes in land use between the 1930s and 1950s and these shifts account for some of the differences which are seen. In particular, the arable or cropland area had extended considerably at the expense of grassland, while urban land had also increased notably – not declined, as a comparison with the Ministry of Agriculture's figure for 1937 would suggest.

A major drawback of the estimates of the land-use pattern in the 1930s was that the entire land surface was accounted for under the three main headings of agriculture, woodland and urban land. This meant that the first of these categories covered not only land which was actually in agricultural use but also land of potential agricultural value and unutilised rural land as well. Therefore, quite apart from

Table 5 Inventories of land use in England and Wales for about 1933, 1937 and 1950. Discrepancies and differences in the figures are discussed in the text

Land use	Land Utilisation Survey (c. 1933)	Ministry of Agriculture and Fisheries (1937)	Wye College [a] (1950)
		'000 ha	
Agriculture [b]	13,056	12,514	12,107
Cropland (arable)	3,697	3,652	5,645
Permanent grass	7,045	6,377	4,248
Rough grazings	2,314	2,202	2,214
Other rural land [c]	–	283	–
Woodland	859	830	960
Urban land	1,112	1,684	1,458
Other land	–	–	503
Total land area	15,027	15,028	15,028

[a] These figures, as originally compiled for 1950, were subsequently revised to some extent to make them referable to 1951 and also to take account of new information (see Table 8)

[b] In 1933 and 1937 includes unutilised rural land and land of potential agricultural value but not so used. In 1950, this land is found under the 'Other land' heading rather than under 'Agriculture'

[c] Excluding woodland

the actual errors in statistics, there was a further element of unsatis-factory classification which helped to build in more distortion. This particular problem was overcome by introducing a new land-use category of 'other' or 'unaccounted for' land into subsequent tables of land use, as in the inventory for 1950.

The inclusion of this category now allowed a statistical home to be found for land that did not fall readily under the other major uses or which, through statistical error, was not enumerated in the existing figures. Therefore, rural land which was not used in any definable way (like the tops of higher mountains and sand dunes) or land that was hard to allocate to the existing major categories because of certain special features (like military training areas not in multiple use and many opencast mineral workings) was all recorded under this new heading. So was the land which escaped enumeration in official data, and especially farmland that was not recorded in the Agricultural Statistics. In this way, it was eventually possible to construct statements of land use which began to bear a closer resemblance to reality than previous estimates had done.

Recent inventories

Further work on land-use structure, and particularly on the extent of the urban area, allowed a new inventory of the national pattern of land use in Britain to be prepared for 1961. In the process, certain of the figures for 1950 needed some small revision, and this was particularly true of the urban area, as will be seen in the next chapter. By the 1960s, many of the previous omissions and inaccuracies in the Agricultural Statistics had been ironed out and, in the middle of the decade, a new census of woodlands was undertaken. With the use of this latest material compiled for 1961, and revised information for earlier decades, it was now possible to construct a series of statements for the whole structure of land use in England and Wales at about ten-year intervals since 1901. An updating to 1971 was also made.[11] The figures are recorded in Tables 6 and 8, and the dates selected have the advantage of allowing a direct comparison with the decadal population censuses.

More recently, the basic land-use statement for 1961 in England and Wales has been complemented by a schedule of land use from another and completely independent source, the Second Land Utilisation Survey of Alice Coleman, which has an effective date of 1963 attached to it.[12] Table 6 sets out in some detail both the Best and Coleman data for comparison, so that it can be seen to what extent they either confirm or diverge from each other. Land-use figures for the 1930s and the 1960s are shown, together with the change over the three intervening decades and the numerical differences between the sets of figures for the corresponding years or periods of time. Differences in definition have been reduced wherever feasible: 'agriculture' here refers only to improved farmland (i.e. cropland and permanent grass), while rough grazings have been relegated to the 'other land' category. Allotments are included under urban land, but in Best's figures only part of the area under mineral workings is recorded in the urban category.

A cursory glance at the table immediately suggests a certain equivalence between the two sets of figures, although often they are not closely similar. But brief reflection will affirm that close correspondence is not to be expected in any case. To start with, the data are for different years, the Coleman figures being the later in time

Table 6 A comparison of land-use data for England and Wales originating from R.H. Best and A.M. Coleman

Land use	Best 1931	Coleman 1933	Difference	Best 1961	Coleman 1963	Difference	Best change 1931-61	Coleman change 1933-63	Difference
				'000 ha					
Agriculture [a]	10,232	10,659	427	9,872	10,163	291	-360	-496	-136
Cropland	3,878	3,991	113	5,522	5,741	219	+1,644	+1,750	+106
Permanent grass	6,354	6,668	314	4,350	4,422	72	-2,004	-2,246	-242
Woodland	840	857	17	1,034	1,213	179	+194	+356	+162
Urban land	1,005	1,117	112	1,490	1,649	159	+485	+532	+47
Other land [b]	2,951	2,359	592	2,631	1,939	692	-320	-420	-100
Inland water	–	130	130	–	160	160	–	+30	+30
Total area	15,028	15,122	94	15,027	15,124	97	-1	+2	+1
				per cent					
Agriculture [a]	68.1	70.5	2.4	65.7	67.2	1.5	-2.4	-3.3	-0.9
Cropland	25.8	26.4	0.6	36.7	38.0	1.3	+10.9	+11.6	+0.7
Permanent grass	42.3	44.1	1.8	29.0	29.2	0.2	-13.3	-14.9	-1.6
Woodland	5.6	5.7	0.1	6.9	8.0	1.1	+1.3	+2.3	+1.0
Urban land	6.7	7.4	0.7	9.9	10.9	1.0	+3.2	+3.5	+0.3
Other land [b]	19.6	15.6	4.0	17.5	12.8	4.7	-2.1	-2.8	-0.7
Inland water	–	0.8	0.8	–	1.1	1.1	–	+0.3	+0.3
Total area	100.0	100.0		100.0	100.0		0.0	0.0	0.0

a Improved farmland, excluding rough grazings
b Including rough grazings

and invariably the larger for the designated land uses. Nevertheless, the magnitude of the discrepancies is generally rather small, amounting in the 1960s to no more than 1.0–1.5 per cent for the most part – with the notable exception of 'other land'. In agriculture, for example, the 1.5 per cent difference represents only 291,000 ha in about 10 million. The larger discrepancy of 2.4 per cent in the 1930s is explained by the fact, already mentioned, that the Agricultural Statistics at that time (as used in Best's inventory) under-stated the farmed area. Because of the land escaping enumeration in the official returns, the total of 'other land' was thereby inflated.

One of the most important causes of lack in comparability, then, lies simply in the dating of the figures. Best's statistics refer fairly precisely to the year 1961, whereas Coleman's data were derived from maps compiled over a period of eight years or more, with a clustering around a median date of 1963 in England and 1966 in Wales.[13] With this discrepancy in mind, allied with some definitional differences especially under urban, other and possibly forest land, the surprising thing is that the figures are so relatively close for the main uses.

The changes in land use recorded by both inventories over the thirty-year period between the 1930s and the 1960s must, of course, also be affected by this inexactness of dating. Problems of consistent definition probably intrude as well, particularly with woodland where Best records a gain of under 200,000 ha (from official sources) compared with Coleman's much greater increase of over 350,000 ha. On the other hand, it should be emphasised very strongly that the discrepancy between the two figures for urban extension over the thirty years is less than 50,000 ha, or the equivalent of only some three years urban growth in the 1960s, which approximates to the likely margin of error associated with dating imprecisions.

From these comments, it is apparent that there is, in reality, little disagreement about the magnitude of the respective land-use figures in the Best and Coleman inventories, for most differences can be accounted for in ways that have just been explained. The real dispute that has arisen in the past few years between the Best and Coleman factions is, therefore, not so much about the validity of the statistics as about their *interpretation* and the indication that they give of the significance or otherwise of shifts in land-use structure.

A further confirmation of the general structure of land use in

Table 7 A comparison of land-use structure in England and Wales for 1961–63 as recorded by Best, Anderson and Coleman

Land use	Best 1961	Anderson 1962	Coleman 1963
		per cent	
Agriculture and other land	83.2	83.3	80.0
Agriculture	79.1	79.1 (77.7–80.5)[a]	n.a.
Other land	4.1	4.2 (3.5–4.9)	n.a.
Woodland	6.9	6.9 (6.0–7.8)	8.0
Urban land	9.9	9.7 (8.6–10.8)	10.9
Inland water	–	0.1 (0.0–0.2)	1.1
Total area	100.0	100.0	100.0

The effective dates given for the three data-sets are approximations

[a] Figures in brackets are 95 per cent confidence limits

England and Wales is given by another independent inventory which has been made by Margaret Anderson.[14] Her figures, like those of Alice Coleman, were obtained by systematic point sampling, but in this case the exercise was carried out on land classification maps as part of a project concerned with amenity areas. Particular care was taken to ensure that the categories of land use recorded during the sampling coincided as closely as possible with the major land uses as defined by Best. Again, the precise dating of Anderson's estimates was not easy because of date variations in the cartographic material, but the modal date for the maps which were used was 1962. The most immediately striking result of the investigation was the marked similarity, indeed almost equivalence, of these figures with those of Best for 1961, and all of Best's figures fell well within the 95 per cent confidence limits calculated by Anderson (Table 7). This must inevitably give much conviction for thinking that the pattern of major land uses in England and Wales is now reasonably certain and circumscribed in quantitative terms.

The changing land-use pattern

We have already seen that, until as late as the end of the nineteenth century, the changing pattern of land use in Britain had been dominated for hundreds of years by the decline of woodland and wasteland as agriculture inexorably extended its frontiers. This long-continued trend has only been arrested and re-directed in any significant way in the last few decades. Quite suddenly, or so it seems in historical retrospect, the whole emphasis has now shifted, and the real key to changes in land-use structure has become growth in urban and forest areas rather than agricultural extension. Perhaps we are too close in time to this fundamental event to be able to gauge its implications at all correctly. But at least it is possible for us to see the turning point in the direction of the trends and to mark the beginnings of new spatial relationships between the major land uses.

A summary and comparative statement of the structure of land use in England and Wales, Scotland, Great Britain and the United Kingdom for 1971 is given in Table 8 (see also Fig. 2). Where available, the pattern for previous decades is also recorded for individual countries, going as far back as 1901 in England and Wales. This table of national land use, in both hectares and percentages, may be regarded as the definitive inventory on which the analyses and discussions of this book are based. The statistics given are not all equally reliable, however, and the figures for England and Wales are probably somewhat more accurate than those for Great Britain and the United Kingdom as a whole.

Towards the end of the nineteenth century, agriculture had reached its maximum extent – perhaps up to some 87 per cent of the land surface in England and Wales (Chapter 1). But although there has subsequently been a fall-back from this figure, farming is still today by far the greatest of all the major land uses. Well over three-quarters of Britain's total area is still recorded as being in some form of agricultural use, though a substantial part of it, perhaps about a quarter of the whole land surface, is slenderly utilised and of low productivity.[15]

Much of this area of poor or very extensive farming, if indeed it is used at all, is found in the Highland Zone and particularly in Scotland, where almost 60 per cent of the surface is under rough grazings, including deer forests. Under these conditions, the agricultural output of the hills and uplands is very small: in the

Table 8 The structure of land use in Britain, 1901–71

Year	Population millions	Agriculture [a]	Cropland [b]	Permanent grass	Rough grazings [c]	Woodland	Urban land [d]	Other land [e]	Total land area
					'000 ha				
England and Wales									
1901	32.5	12,576	4,904	6,232	1,440	748	674	1,027	15,025
1921	37.9	12,496	4,702	5,879	1,915	730	854	949	15,029
1931	40.0	12,383	3,878	6,354	2,151	840	1,005	800	15,028
1939	41.5	12,215	3,616	6,357	2,242	927	1,206	680	15,028
1951	43.8	12,104	5,536	4,365	2,203	971	1,339	614	15,028
1961	46.1	11,880	5,522	4,350	2,008	1,034	1,490	623	15,027
1971	48.8	11,515	5,666	3,965	1,884	1,115	1,646	750	15,026
Scotland									
1931	4.8	5,718	1,235	639	3,844	443	141	1,416	7,718
1961	5.2	6,776	1,387	356	5,033	651	199	91	7,717
1971	5.2	6,226	1,268	417	4,541	738	225	529	7,718
Great Britain									
1931	44.8	18,101	5,113	6,993	5,995	1,283	1,146	2,216	22,746
1961	51.3	18,656	6,909	4,706	7,041	1,685	1,689	714	22,744
1971	54.0	17,741	6,934	4,382	6,425	1,853	1,871	1,279	22,744
United Kingdom									
1971	55.6	18,831	7,227	4,926	6,678	1,908	1,918	1,436	24,093

	millions	per cent							
England and Wales									
1901	32.5	83.7	32.6	41.5	9.6	5.0	4.5	6.8	100.0
1921	37.9	83.1	31.3	39.1	12.7	4.9	5.7	6.3	100.0
1931	40.0	82.4	25.8	42.3	14.3	5.6	6.7	5.3	100.0
1939	41.5	81.3	24.1	42.3	14.9	6.2	8.0	4.5	100.0
1951	43.8	80.5	36.8	29.0	14.7	6.5	8.9	4.1	100.0
1961	46.1	79.1	36.7	29.0	13.4	6.9	9.9	4.1	100.0
1971	48.8	76.6	37.7	26.4	12.5	7.4	11.0	5.0	100.0
Scotland									
1931	4.8	74.1	16.0	8.3	49.8	5.7	1.8	18.4	100.0
1961	5.2	87.8	18.0	4.6	65.2	8.4	2.6	1.2	100.0
1971	5.2	80.7	16.4	5.4	58.9	9.6	2.9	6.8	100.0
Great Britain									
1931	44.8	79.6	22.5	30.7	26.4	5.6	5.0	9.8	100.0
1961	51.3	82.0	30.4	20.7	30.9	7.4	7.4	3.2	100.0
1971	54.0	78.0	30.5	19.3	28.2	8.2	8.2	5.6	100.0
United Kingdom									
1971	55.6	78.2	30.0	20.5	27.7	7.9	8.0	5.9	100.0

Slight discrepancies in some totals result from rounding of figures and conversions from acres to hectares

a In the first part of this century, the agricultural area was seriously underestimated in the official statistics because of the under-recording of rough grazings, especially those held in common, and cultivated land which escaped enumeration. Woodland and other land (buildings, yards, roads, etc.) on farms are recorded under other headings in this table (see also Table 19)

b Arable land, including fallow, temporary grass and orchards

c Specifically including common rough grazings in 1921 and later, and also the area of all deer forests in Scotland after 1931

d Including villages, isolated dwellings and farmsteads, and all transport land

e Includes land unaccounted for, many mineral workings and defence areas in the open countryside, and unutilised rural areas not recorded under other uses. See text for explanation of the substantial increase in this category in 1971

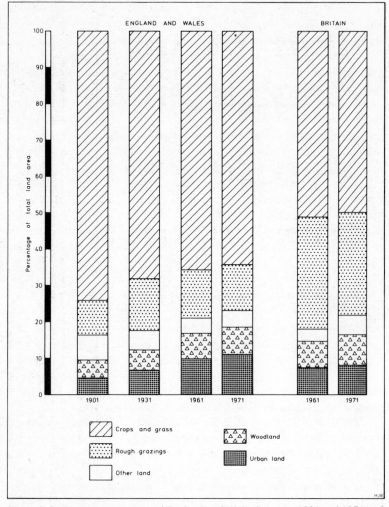

Figure 2 The land-use structure of England and Wales between 1901 and 1971 and Great Britain in 1961 and 1971

1950s it amounted to only 4 per cent of the national total,[16] but by the 1970s the contribution had improved somewhat to around 7 per cent,[17] though at a considerable cost in subsidies of one sort or another. Even so, the contribution made to our food supplies may be more valuable than appears at first sight. This is because the hills and uplands of the United Kingdom provide 20–25 per cent of our cattle and nearly half of our sheep output.[18] In addition livestock, and especially the sheep flock, play an important part in the production of store animals to be fattened in the lowlands.

Nevertheless, the idea has been assiduously cultivated by numerous commentators that, unlike so many other countries, Britain allegedly has a land surface which is carefully and productively used in some way or another over most of its extent. This contention is now seen to be of very doubtful validity where the hills and uplands are concerned. Taking just Scotland alone to begin with, the wide moorland sheep-runs of last century have been increasingly turned into deer forests and grouse moors for sporting purposes. Writing in 1946 about the Scottish moorlands, Dudley Stamp surmised that 'over 1,600,000 ha are unused agriculturally, even for grazing',[19] and by the late 1950s there were still about 600,000 to 700,000 ha out of the total 1,130,000 ha of deer forest which were not grazed at all. The same is largely true of perhaps half a million hectares of crofters' common grazing land, which is partly included in Stamp's figure. There are also around 357,000 ha of country in England and Wales at over 460 m (1500 ft) and 400,000 ha in Scotland at over 610 m (2000 ft) where severe climatic constraints make any sort of land use either impossible or extremely hazardous.

In the aggregate, therefore, between 1.5 and 2.0 million hectares of wild, barren and virtually unutilised land may exist in the whole of Great Britain, or something like 8 per cent of the surface, if not more. A better impression is gained of the truly substantial size of this area when it is realised that it is equivalent to that of the whole urban area or the forest and woodland area of Britain. Although some of this land is clearly unusable in any worthwhile way, it is equally certain that an unknown, but probably considerable, area of rough grazings not included in this total is also under-utilised to the extent of providing no very material agricultural output. A good deal of these combined tracts of unused or barely utilised territory could provide an important reservoir for the extension of forestry and sheep farming, or even the farming of other hardy livestock, if economic and social conditions became favourable. They could also allow for recreational activities and additional nature conservation requirements.

While discussing this poor land, it is relevant to mention again the statistical irregularities associated with it. In reality, the great apparent increase of rough grazings in Scotland after 1931, and therefore in Britain and the United Kingdom as well, came about simply because of the inclusion in the statistics for agriculture of the total area of deer forests, instead of a major part of this land being left as a residual item in the category of other land. On the other hand, the numerical drop in rough grazings between 1961 and 1971 resulted from the decision to exclude from the agricultural returns those basically unproductive holdings with a labour input of less than twenty-six man days (Chapter 2). As a consequence of this reclassification, which applied to more than just rough grazings, this formerly recorded agricultural land was given an unceremonious paper transfer from the agricultural column in the land-use table to that of other land, so causing the sudden rise seen in the latter category in 1971 after decades of decline.

Turning now from the poorer to the far more productive sectors of agriculture, it is found that over 30 per cent of Britain's surface is under relatively intensive crop production, including temporary grass. A large proportion of this area of higher output is concentrated in the Lowland Zone; that is, within England itself. Once again, there are enormous contrasts to be seen between different parts of the United Kingdom, with England and Wales having nearly two-fifths of the land surface under crops while Scotland does not attain as much as half of this figure.

The individual land-use components of farmland in England and Wales have not necessarily followed the overall agricultural trend of almost continual decline in area. Since the 1940s cropland in particular has reached and maintained the fairly high and stable level of 37 to 38 per cent of the land surface. This is its highest point during the present century and compares with only 25 per cent in similar use during the agricultural depression of the 1930s when the economic effects were especially severe on cropland. Conversely, permanent grass now occupies little more than a quarter of the surface in contrast to the 42 per cent reached in the interwar years. If, as seems likely, there will continue to be strong pressure and incentive to maintain the cropland area, then this will be done largely at the expense of permanent grass when land taken for development purposes eats into the cultivated area. This is not to say, of course, that only permanent grass is being and will be taken for urban uses, but simply that cropland also transferred tends to be replaced by the upgrading of pasture.

Non-agricultural land uses on farms and agricultural land outside farms can lead to some confusion and need to be distinguished carefully (Table 9). Agricultural land use outside farms in Britain is

Table 9 Common rough grazings and non-agricultural land on farms in 1971. Unlike common rough grazings, the woodland and other land areas are not included under the agricultural category in Table 8

Land use	England and Wales [a]	Scotland	Great Britain	United Kingdom
	'000 ha			
Common rough grazings [b]	609	503	1,112	1,128
Woodland ancillary to farming	91	48	139	154
Other land on farms (buildings, yards, roads, etc.)	59	26	85	131
	per cent [c]			
Common rough grazings [b]	4.0	6.5	4.9	4.7
Woodland ancillary to farming	0.6	0.6	0.6	0.7
Other land on farms (buildings, yards, roads, etc.)	0.4	0.3	0.4	0.6

[a] The combined woodland and other land figure in England and Wales includes not less than 60,300 ha previously returned as crops, grass or rough grazings (i.e. before 1969)

[b] As this land is used jointly by a number of occupiers it is not part of the area 'within farms' as normally understood

[c] Proportion of total land area

mainly on rough land grazed in common, i.e. common rough grazings. These are included in the Agricultural Statistics, but as this land is used jointly by a number of occupiers it is not part of the area within farms (holdings under sole occupation) as that term is normally understood. Non-agricultural land uses on farms comprise two additional categories – woodland ancillary to farming and farmhouses, cottages, buildings, yards and roads ('other land on farms'). These items are now included in the agricultural returns and are allocated to their appropriate columns (woodland and urban or other land) in the national land-use table. In passing, it is interesting to note that this non-agricultural land on farms accounts for 1 per cent of the Britain's land area.

After cropland, permanent grass and rough grazings, woodland as a rural land use comes a very poor fourth in extent – only some 8.2 per cent of the surface in Britain. The determination of how much land is covered by forests and woods is not always easy to assess accurately because of the long time-spans between censuses. Needless to say, the Forestry Commission update their total area of forest and woodland each year so that the extent of their holding is known precisely at any given date. But with private woodlands such a rolling inventory is not possible; and this creates a major problem in estimating the total area covered by trees between censuses, as between 50 and 60 per cent of all woodland is in private owner-ship.[20] Despite this hindrance to measurement, it is still evident that the forest and woodland area has grown strongly and continuously over much of this century, and particularly since the establishment of the Forestry Commission in 1919. Even so, the United Kingdom has still the smallest percentage of woodland in any country of western Europe, except for Ireland (see Chapter 9).

Occupying almost exactly the same land area as woodland in Britain is urban land, the most intensive land use, though in England and Wales alone, at 11 per cent, it occupies a rather higher proportion. Not by any juggling with statistics nor stretching of the imagination can this use of land be made to appear a very substan-tial one, and taking Scotland by itself it is seen to be far and away the smallest of the major land uses. On the other hand, urban develop-ment has grown persistently during the present century, and it is now sufficiently extensive to form at least a significant part of the land surface. Seen from the air, the spread of urban land a hundred years ago would have appeared far less noticeable, and this is not to be wondered at when it is recognised that, between 1900 and the early 1950s, urban development in England and Wales actually doubled in extent. Yet it is wise to keep a reasonable sense of proportion on this matter. The amount of urban land is still rather limited in extent, at a national level, and there is no possibility at all that, by the beginning of next century, the countryside in general will be completely overwhelmed by the spreading tentacles of a burgeoning urban octopus. However, nothing further will be said about urban use at this point as the subject is dealt with fully in the next chapter.

The last of the major uses is a composite and largely residual category of other, miscellaneous land which comprises a wide vari-ety of land-using activities and non-uses, as indicated earlier in this chapter. Unused mountain-tops, sand dunes and similar areas, in addition to land used exclusively for recreation, are included here, together with what is technically agricultural land but which for one reason or another has gone unrecorded in the official statistics. In the first half of the century, the amount of such unregistered farm-land was substantial, but the decline in the hectarage of 'other land' until the 1950s and 1960s in part reflects the enumeration of this farmland for the first time under its correct heading. The transfer of poorly productive agricultural land in the reverse direction has already been mentioned as the prime cause for the inflation of the figures in the other land category after 1968.

Apart from farmland not included in the official statistics and completely unutilised land, this heading also includes a major part, though not always the whole by any means, of certain land uses which do not fall readily under the other main headings in the land-use table because of their special nature. An important activity of this type is opencast mineral working which has expanded con-siderably since the 1940s. No comprehensive and official figures exist for this use and measurement of its total extent produces profound problems. To begin with, an unknown but probably fairly small part of the total falls within the urban sector. More impor-tantly, opencast sites are often of a transitory nature and pass to another use within a comparatively short space of time, being replaced by acquisitions of land for new workings, again from other uses. Many of these sites, especially for ironstone and coal, have to be compulsorily restored to agriculture. Hence, the total area affected by opencast mining at any given time is particularly hard to assess; but from the limited information available, it was thought very roughly to extend to about 60,000 ha in England and Wales in the 1950s, with an annual net requirement of 1400 ha at that time.[21] In the 1960s, the figure for all the extractive industries and tips has been put at 54,000 ha in England and Wales,[22] while in Britain, over the thirty-five years since the end of the war, a gross area of some 1900 ha a year has been taken just for the opencast mining of coal.[23]

Also predominant among the other, miscellaneous uses is land occupied for defence purposes. The total estate of the Service Departments has waxed and waned dramatically over the years, with a peak being reached during the Second World War when defence requirements rose from an immediate prewar figure in Great Britain of 102,000 ha to the immense total of over 4,650,000 ha. This was more than one-fifth of the entire land area of the country. The greater part of this land was released after the war, and by 1968 the Services only retained about 243,000 ha, the army being the major user.

According to the Nugent Report,[24] the land holdings used in the United Kingdom, rather than Britain, to meet Service needs in 1972 were some 306,000 ha. But a considerable part of this land, probably over 52,000 ha, was in some form of urban use (dockyards, headquarters, depots, etc.), leaving around 254,000 ha in a more rural setting, including some 8000 ha of woodland. By far the largest requirement was for military training areas and ranges which made up about 207,000 ha of the total. Military airfields comprised much of the remainder. Defence lands are still being disposed of, and between 1961 and 1971 some 77,300 ha were released in the United Kingdom.

Both the military training grounds and the airfields are frequently in dual or multiple use, and this inevitably complicates the land-use situation. Of the 243,000 ha held by the Service Departments in Britain in 1968, as many as 112,000 ha, or 46 per cent, were let to farmers.[25] Besides being occupied for defence purposes, therefore, this land was used for some sort of agricultural activity as well, like grazing, grass cutting or even arable cultivation. A good example of such multiple use was on Salisbury Plain where the Ministry of Defence owned 37,000 ha, of which 24,000 ha were farmed in some way or other.

Defence land in agricultural use should, officially, be returned and included in the Agricultural Statistics. Quite a proportion undoubtedly is treated in this way, but it is impossible to say, in practice, just how much of this land is not enumerated. The result is that a reasonably accurate figure cannot be given for the amount of land falling into the other, miscellaneous category which is used exclusively for military purposes and for nothing else; but clearly it should be only a very limited part of the area of defence lands as a whole.

Assessment and summary

Leaving now the consideration of individual land uses and reverting to the overall structure of land use as seen in Table 8, there are a number of important conclusions which may be drawn. The decadal inventories which are set out there are essentially snapshots of the existing pattern of land use at given moments of time. If the extremely significant but unreal 'paper' changes arising from purely statistical machinations are discounted, then it quickly becomes evident that ten years are not normally long enough to allow shifts of any great magnitude in the land-use pattern, though an exception to this generalisation happened within the agricultural sector in the 1940s when, under the exigencies of war, cropland was increased significantly at the expense of permanent grass. But if several decades are taken together, as can be seen in England and Wales, they give a synoptic impression of what is in some respects a quickly altering scene when viewed in historical perspective.

Yet even over one or two generations, the remarkable stability in the substantial area of poorly utilised land in Britain, a good third of the whole surface, is at once apparent. Moreover, we have noted that up to 8 per cent or more of the surface area, or the equivalent of either the total coverage of urban land or woodland, is hardly used at all. Climate, relief, economics and social factors combine to produce this effect over great tracts of the Highland Zone. In contrast, some parts of Highland Britain and many areas of the Lowland Zone show marked alterations in land use across the years. During most of the twentieth century, the outstanding feature of land-use change has undoubtedly been the insistent growth of urban land and, to a lesser extent, of forest and woodland. In recent decades, this urban expansion has been of the order of 1 per cent per decade in England and Wales.

Compared with the increase in urban land, the total area under agriculture appears to have declined rather slowly; and this is doubly strange when it is recalled that afforestation in addition to urban development has been occurring predominantly at the expense of farmland. The discrepancy is largely statistical. As we have seen, a sizeable part of the other, miscellaneous land category in earlier decades of this century was composed of farmland which escaped enumeration in the official returns. The increasing accuracy and completeness of the Agricultural Statistics over the years has led to a spurious 'paper' gain in area from the land not previously accounted for, which has helped to offset and apparently reduce actual losses of farmland to other uses on the debit side of the balance sheet. Since the end of the 1960s, this situation has been reversed with the decision not to record largely unproductive holdings in the official returns.

In reality, then, the agricultural area of England and Wales has fallen more sharply over the first half of the century than the official statistics would suggest. Indeed, the transfer of farmland to all other uses between 1900 and 1950 was probably almost double the decrease of 460,000 ha which the Agricultural Statistics indicate.[26]

Even so, this represents no more than about 7 per cent of the total agricultural area.

On the other hand, the growth of urban land in England and Wales has been quite large, though it has taken place from comparatively small beginnings, from a figure of only 4.5 per cent in 1901. Hence, even a doubling up of the urban area by the early 1950s did not bring the total percentage of the land surface covered by this use into double figures. The structure of urban land and its expansion is, however, a crucial topic in a highly urbanised society like Britain, and this is the subject of the next chapter.

References

1 Sparks, B.W. and West, R.G. (1972) *The Ice Age in Britain*, London, Methuen.

2 Steers, J.A. (1953) *The Sea Coast*, London, Collins.

3 Central Statistical Office (1978) *Annual Abstract of Statistics, 1979 Edition*, No. 115, HMSO.

4 Best, R.H. (1959) *The Major Land Uses of Great Britain*, Wye College.

5 Royal Commission on the Distribution of the Industrial Population (1937) *Minutes of Evidence*, 1 December.

6 Ministry of Agriculture and Fisheries (1927) *The Agricultural Output of England and Wales, 1925*, Cmd. 2815, HMSO.

7 Ministry of Works and Planning (1942) *Report of the Committee on Land Utilisation in Rural Areas* (Scott Report), Cmd. 6378, HMSO.

8 Stamp, L.D. (1948) *The Land of Britain: Its Use and Misuse* (3rd edn, 1962), London, Longman.

9 Wibberley, G.P. (1954) 'The challenge of rural land losses', *Journal of the Royal Society of Arts*, 102, 650–70.

10 Best, R.H. and Coppock, J.T. (1962) *The Changing Use of Land in Britain*, London, Faber & Faber.

11 Best, R.H. (1976) 'The changing land-use structure of Britain', *Town and Country Planning*, 44 (3), 171–6.

12 Coleman, A.M. (1978) 'Planning and land use', *Chartered Surveyor*, 111 (5), 158–63.

13 Rogers, A.W. (ed.) (1978) *Urban Growth, Farmland Losses and Planning*, Wye College for the Institute of British Geographers.

14 Anderson, M.A. (1977) 'A comparison of figures for the land-use structure of England and Wales in the 1960s', *Area*, 9 (1), 43–5.

15 Beresford, T. (1975) *We Plough the Fields: Agriculture in Britain Today*, Harmondsworth, Pelican.

16   Davidson, B.R. and Wibberley, G.P. (1956) *The Agricultural Significance of the Hills*, Wye College.
17   Davidson, J. and Wibberley, G.P. (1977) *Planning and the Rural Environment*, Oxford, Pergamon.
18   Ministry of Agriculture, Fisheries and Food *et al*. (1979) *Farming and the Nation*, Cmnd. 7458, HMSO.
19   Stamp, L.D. (1946) *The Land of Britain and How It Is Used*, London, British Council/Longman.
20   Forestry Commission (1970) *Census of Woodlands 1965–67*, HMSO.
21   Best, R.H. (1959) op. cit.
22   Coleman, A.M. (1976) *Areal Characteristics and Trends of British Land Uses*, SSRC Final Report, H.R. 2705.
23   Anon. (1979) 'Asset stripping', *Town and Country Planning*, 48 (6), 207–9.
24   Ministry of Defence (1973) *Report of the Defence Lands Committee, 1971–73* (Nugent Report), HMSO.
25   *Report from the Select Committee on Agriculture* (1969) Session 1968–69, HMSO.
26   Best, R.H. (1968) 'Competition for land between rural and urban uses', in Institute of British Geographers, *Land Use and Resources: Studies in Applied Geography*, Special Publication No. 1, 89–100.

4
The extent and provision of urban land[1]

I thought it would last my time –
The sense that, beyond the town,
There would always be fields and farms

Philip Larkin's disenchantment with urban growth in his poem 'Going, Going', and his fear that the land still left free is not likely to last a great deal longer, probably reflects accurately the feelings and anxiety of most people about the rapid extension of towns. But is such a strain of impending doom realistic?

One of the most difficult problems about giving a reasoned answer to this vital question is that the actual extent of urban land and its rate of growth have been very imperfectly known. Indeed, it was not until as recently as the 1950s that sufficient data were available to allow even a start to be made on calculating a satisfactory figure for the total area of existing urban land, quite apart from its increasing extent year by year. As we saw in the previous chapter, it was only the advent of new material from the postwar development plans, compiled under the 1947 Town and Country Planning Act, which at last allowed a more definitive figure to emerge.

The urban area, 1951– 71

When grouped data on land use from town maps became available in the 1950s for the old county boroughs and for large and small town map areas, it was at once possible to attempt an estimate of the urban area for 1950/51.[2] The calculation was based on what has been called the density method which uses a statistical relationship between density and population that was later to be termed the density-size rule. In measuring densities of development a figure of persons per hectare is commonly adopted, but for planning purposes it has proved more appropriate and convenient to use the reciprocal of this figure. The measure of hectares per thousand population (abbreviated to ha/1000p) which is derived in this way is called a land provision rather than a density. In essence, then, the calculation of the urban area involved taking the mean urban land provision in hectares per thousand population (ha/1000p) for a representative sample of towns or villages within each defined settlement category (e.g. county boroughs) and multiplying it by the aggregate census population of that category to obtain a total urban area figure.

Like other statistical procedures, the density technique is only as good as its basic data. In particular, at that time there was very little material on the densities of small settlements with populations of under 10,000 and the sample which was eventually used could not be truly random or representative. The estimates for isolated dwellings and for roads and railways in the open countryside also suffered from various limitations. The figures used in the 1950/51 calculation, therefore, tended to become less accurate the further they were down the scale of administrative status and population size to which they applied.

Every effort was made to err on the side of employing generous parameters when a very reliable estimate was difficult to achieve. This was done so that the resulting global figure could not be criticised as being an *under-estimate*. The outcome was that the totals finally calculated for 1950/51 of 1,458,000 ha and 190,000 ha for the urban areas of England and Wales and of Scotland, respectively, were maximum figures. For this reason, any subsequent modification made because of obtaining more precise data would be likely to reduce rather than increase them. As will be demonstrated, this is exactly what has happened.

A source of constant error in calculating the urban area and its extension has been in the incompatability of various definitions of this major land use which have been employed by different workers. For present purposes, however, we have seen that urban land may be defined as the built-up area with its associated open spaces and transport land (Chapter 2). In more detail, it comprises the so-called four main urban uses of housing (net residential area), industry, open space and education, as delineated for planning purposes, together with a number of other 'residual' urban uses which may cover sizeable areas. It should also be noted that farmsteads, along with other isolated dwellings and development in the countryside, are recorded as urban land. The assessments of the urban area in

1961 and 1971, outlined below, are completely in line with this definition; so is the original assessment of the urban area in 1950/51, with the exception that civil airfields were not included under transport uses.

In the course of the 1960s, several significant improvements in land-use data sources allowed more accurate estimates to be made of the component parts of the urban area than could be done for 1950/51. As a result, it became possible to construct a new and more sound estimate of the total extent of urban land in 1961. The computation was again undertaken by using the density method of calculation which had been pioneered in the estimate for 1950/51, but more up-to-date land provision parameters and the 1961 Census figures for population were now employed. The global estimates obtained and the statistical information relating to the contributory parts of the computation are given in Table 10.

The 1961 calculation of the urban area differed in a number of respects from the earlier estimates for 1950/51. In the first place, the growing experience of local planning authorities with the compilation of development plans meant that more precise, and often more reliable, land-use data could be recorded than had been possible in the first submissions. After the mid-1950s, the need to refer specifically in the land-use tables to net areas on the town maps and the requirement to account statistically for the whole area being surveyed, including agricultural and other rural land, left far less scope for errors or omissions than previously.[3] Hence, the first reviews of development plans and new submissions were able to provide a firmer basis for a revised computation.

In 1950/51, there were only grouped data available under urban categories which were fundamentally administrative in character, like county boroughs and large or small town map areas (usually municipal boroughs or urban districts). These divisions reflected population size of settlement, but in only a rather generalised way. In contrast, the 1961 data were ungrouped and could be amalgamated strictly by population size groups, allowing the statistical aspects of the material to be fully assessed.

This investigation was carried out primarily by Allan Jones whose work should be referred to for a detailed statistical analysis.[4] He restricted the analysis to 205 usable, reviewed town maps and late first submissions for England and Wales, mostly surveyed between 1958 and 1962, so that the final figures would have an operative date of 1960/61. The regional distribution of the sample was satis-

The extent and provision of urban land

Table 10 Urban area of Great Britain, 1961

Urban category	Population millions	Land provision ha/1000p[a]	Urban area '000 ha	Urban proportion per cent
England and Wales				
London AC	3.2	9.5	30	2
Over 100,000 [b]	13.5	19.4	261	18
10,000–100,000	18.5	28.1	520	35
Under 10,000 [c]	8.2	34.6	285	19
Isolated dwellings [d]	2.7	50.1	137	9
Transport land [e]	–	–	257	17
Total urban area	46.1	32.3	1,490	100
Scotland				
Over 100,000 [f]	2.7	19.4	51	26
10,000–100,000	0.8	24.5	19	10
Under 10,000 [c]	1.3	28.7	38	19
Isolated dwellings [d]	0.4	50.1	22	11
Transport land [e]	–	–	69	34
Total urban area	5.2	38.5	199	100
Great Britain				
London AC	3.2	9.5	30	2
Over 100,000 [b,f]	16.1	19.4	312	19
10,000–100,000	19.3	27.9	539	32
Under 10,000 [c]	9.5	33.8	322	19
Isolated dwellings [d]	3.2	50.1	159	9
Transport land [e]	–	–	326	19
Total urban area	51.3	32.9	1,689	100

Rounding of figures may cause slight discrepancies in some totals

[a] Hectares per thousand population
[b] Excluding London Administrative County (AC)
[c] Excluding isolated dwellings
[d] Including farmsteads and other isolated development
[e] Roads, railways (BR) and civil airfields outside settlements
[f] Including Clydeside conurbation

factory, and it comprised about one-fifth of both the population and the total urban area within settlements. But forty-three of these town map areas were for populations of under 10,000 people, and they were therefore excluded from consideration in order to avoid overlap with the separate category of small settlements used here. The land provision figures derived for the two urban categories covering settlements of over 10,000 population (excluding London Administrative County) are recorded in Table 10.

It was for small towns and villages of under 10,000 population that available land-use information was the least adequate and reliable. However, this particular deficiency was rectified by the work of Alan Rogers on land use in a representative sample of 260 small settlements in England and Wales, which was drawn from maps of the Second Land Utilisation Survey.[5] From this material, the total number of small settlements in about 1961 was estimated to be of the order of 17,000, while the total extent of their urban land was calculated as 285,000 ha. This compared with the slightly larger figure of 290,000 ha estimated from less satisfactory data for some ten years earlier around 1951.

Outside small settlements there still remained some isolated development (excluding roads and railways) that was mostly composed of individual dwellings. Because of an almost complete lack of direct information, a surrogate figure for land provision had to be employed for this category. From the density-size rule, the actual provision was clearly well in excess of the mean figure for small settlements as a whole, and the figure eventually used, 50.1 ha/1000p, was the one recorded for the urban area of the smallest sub-category of small settlements.[6] These places were essentially hamlets, only one stage removed from isolated dwellings as such.

A substantial part of the urban area of the country consists of roads, railways and civil airfields lying outside settlements, and this transport land in the countryside was newly estimated for 1961. To do this, representative fence-to-fence widths were multiplied by the linear distances recorded for various classes or types of roads and railways.[7,8,9] For roads, the fence-to-fence widths adopted were 50 m for motorways, 25 m for trunk and class I, 15 m for class II, and 8 m for class III and unclassified roads in Rural Districts. For railways, the fence-to-fence widths adopted, which were taken to include associated railway land like stations, were 50 m for multiple track, 30 m for double track, 25 m for single track and 5 m for sidings (as single track). The national totals for railway land calculated in this way had the estimated areas within settlements subtracted from them to obtain the figures required. Following his calculations of the area of civil airfields in the United Kingdom, R.N.E. Blake also estimated the 1965 areas for England and Wales and for Scotland on a pro-rata basis.[10] These figures, which are comparatively small (e.g. only approaching 14,000 ha for England and Wales), were adjusted to 1961.

Due to the lack of directly measured data for Scotland, the land provisions used in the estimates were essentially proxy figures derived from English and Welsh material. As a consequence, the Scottish urban figures must be expected to have a lower degree of accuracy than those for England and Wales.

When the various urban categories and components just discussed were summated, figures for the total extent of urban land in 1961 were obtained (Table 10). In England and Wales the area amounted to 1,490,000 ha, or 9.9 per cent of the land surface. Rounding up the area figures for convenience, the total urban area of England and Wales could be taken as nearly 1,500,000 ha and of Scotland as 200,000 ha, or only 2.6 per cent of the land surface. This made a grand total for Britain as a whole of about 1,700,000 ha, or 7.4 per cent of the surface area in 1961. The most recent estimates (for 1971), obtained by up-dating, are 1,646,000 ha (11 per cent) for England and Wales and 225,000 ha (2.9 per cent) for Scotland, making a grand total of 1,871,000 ha (8.2 per cent) for Great Britain.

Other estimates

Broad confirmation of these figures for urban land is given by the work of other researchers. In particular, Tony Champion has made detailed investigations into urban land provisions, and the figures from his studies of early town maps (for around 1950) provide supporting evidence for the material presented here.[11] On the basis of his density calculations, he also attempted a computation of the urban area by the density method.[12] His up-dated estimate for England and Wales in 1960 was 1,556,000 ha, or very little more than that calculated above. The difference was almost entirely accounted for by his use of a larger provision of land for isolated dwellings in 1950/51 (83.6 ha/1000p).

Another approach to measurement of the urban area has been adopted by several other researchers. As part of a larger project on land quality and urban growth in England and Wales, Guy Swinnerton made a generalised assessment of the extent of urban land by a systematic point sampling procedure on Ministry of Agriculture Land Service land classification maps.[13] Allowing for some minor differences in definition, the proportion obtained of 9.8 per cent of the land surface under urban use was virtually identical with the percentage recorded in this chapter.

Using a similar point sampling technique, but working in much greater detail, R.C. Fordham produced an estimate for the whole of Britain in 1961.[14] His figure for England and Wales alone was 1,345,000 ha (9.0 per cent), or 145,000 ha less than the figure estimated here. Again, the difference was caused basically by variations in definition. In using standard Ordnance Survey maps, Fordham found difficulty in identifying urban land which was not built-up. In particular, he was unable to include urban parks (apart from playing fields), cemeteries and allotments in his measurements, while his allocation of certain other uses was also in doubt. Such omissions can easily account for the discrepancy in area which has been noted.

More recently, as we have seen in the previous chapter, Alice Coleman has been engaged on a point sampling exercise to estimate the extent of major land uses on her Second Land Utilisation Survey maps. Her urban figure for 1963 is 1,649,000 ha (10.9 per cent), which is again not particularly divergent from the present estimate, considering the possible discrepancies arising from variations in survey dates and in definitions.[15] Even more confirmatory is Margaret Anderson's urban estimate of 9.7 per cent of the land surface for 1962 (Table 7).

Finally, and perhaps most interesting of all, the Department of the Environment (DoE) has carried out a measurement of 'developed areas' in England and Wales using maps produced from a national coverage of air photographs taken in 1969, together with Ordnance Survey maps.[16] The definition of the urban area as a whole, though not of its component land uses, coincided fairly closely with the one used here, except that mineral workings were wholly included. Unfortunately, however, it was only possible to map and measure continuous areas of developed land of 5 ha and above. As a result, small developed sites and parts of the transport system were not included in the calculations, whereas conversely, some agricultural and rural land was improperly absorbed because of the generalising of boundaries.

The figure for urban land obtained from this survey was 1,485,000 ha, or 9.9 per cent of the land surface. This is 161,000 ha less than the present estimate of 1,646,000 ha for 1971; but allowing for urban growth in the intervening period, the difference is reduced to 131,000 ha. Reference to Table 10 indicates that the area of isolated dwellings, excluded to some extent from the Department of the Environment's measurements, amounted to

137,000 ha in 1961. With a further adjustment of this order, the DoE total of urban land matches very closely indeed with the 1971 estimate used here. The correspondence may, nevertheless, be more apparent than real, for the amount of 'isolated dwelling' land included in the total, and the area of rural transport land excluded, is not really known.

A general conclusion from these studies is readily drawn. The earlier 1950/51 calculation by Best reduced the normally accepted figure for the urban area by about one-third. Compared with this major correction, the various recent estimates are concerned only with obtaining a somewhat greater precision within rather narrow limits. Indeed, the main distorting element has now become inconsistencies in the detailed definition of urban land. With this variation allowed for, there seems little dispute that the urban area of England and Wales in 1961 covered approximately 10 per cent of the land surface, rising to about 11 per cent by 1971.

Regional distribution

An indication of how unevenly this urban land is spread across the country is given by the three estimates made by different researchers for the 1960s, as shown in Table 11. Because of the varying size of the Economic Planning Regions employed (Fig. 3), compari-

Table 11 Proportion of regional areas under urban land (Economic Planning Regions, Figure 3)

	Fordham 1961	Champion 1960	Champion 1970	Dept of Environment 1969
	per cent [a]			
North West	22	23	26	22
South East	13	17	19	17
West Midlands	12	12	13	12
Yorkshire/Humb.	10	11	12	10
East Midlands	9	10	11	9
South West	7	7	8	6
East Anglia	4	6	7	7
Northern	7	6	7	6
Wales	3	6	7	4

[a] Of total regional area

Figure 3 Economic Planning Regions of England and Wales, 1971

sons of the percentages within them under urban use need to be treated with care; but even so, these sets of figures show a marked similarity, although they are obtained by three different methods of calculation.

Fordham used point sampling to arrive at his results, and his difficulties in recording urban land which was not built-up probably explain why his estimates tend to be on the low side compared with the other sets of statistics, particularly in the south-east, East Anglia and Wales.[17] Champion employed a refined density computation and was able to derive figures for both 1960 and 1970.[18] These show that all regions increased their urban coverage over the decade, but that the greatest gain was in the north-west rather than in the south-east – a conclusion which will be considered further in Chapter 7. Although of roughly the same date as Champion's 1970 statistics, the data obtained from the 'developed areas survey' of the Department of the Environment are consistently lower.[19] This is only to be expected, however, for it will be recalled that the survey did not encompass developed land of under 5 ha in extent. Bearing in mind this disparity, the figures of the DoE and Champion seem to confirm each other quite closely.

One or two points come out very definitely from the distribution pattern which is seen, and Champion's map (Fig. 4) illustrates the situation cogently. The most dominant area of urban use is concentrated along the so-called axial belt, which runs diagonally across the country from the north-west, through the midlands, to the south-east. The north-west is easily the most urbanised region, with

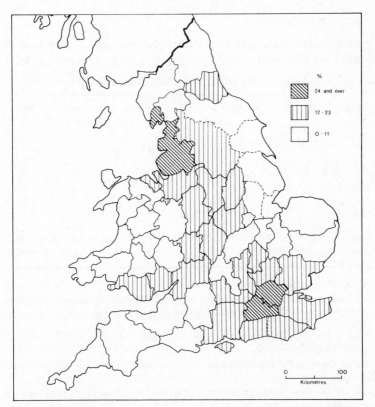

Figure 4 The distribution of urban land by counties in England and Wales, 1970 (After Champion, 1974)

around a quarter of its surface covered by urban development, or more than twice the national average. The south-east also has a high proportionate content of urban land; but the midlands, together with Yorkshire and Humberside, are nearer the national average.

Outwards from this urban spine, it is interesting to observe that the urban land-use element falls away sharply. Because of this, the more peripheral parts of Britain, such as East Anglia, the south-west, the north and Wales have a proportionate urban cover that is no more than about 7 per cent, and perhaps a good deal less in some cases. Scotland is even lower with 3 per cent. There are, therefore, large parts of Great Britain where urban encroachment over the land surface is still not very great in total area, and where urban land is, indeed, a rather minor land use in its physical extent.

Urban area composition

Up till now, the discussion has been concerned almost entirely with the total area of urban land rather than with its component land

Table 12 Composition of the urban area in England and Wales, 1961

Land use	All urban land [a]	Main urban area [b]	Large and medium towns [c]	Small settlements [d]	New towns [e]
			per cent		
Housing (NRA [f])	49	54	46	79	50
Industry	5	7	8	4	9
Open space	12	17	18	11	19
Education	3	4	5	2	9
Four main uses	69	82	77	96	87
Residual uses [g]	31	18	23	4	13
Total urban area	100	100	100	100	100

[a] Total urban area of England and Wales
[b] Including small settlements of under 10,000 population, but excluding isolated dwellings and transport land outside settlements (i.e. the aggregate area of c and d below)
[c] Towns of between 20,000 and 500,000 population – which form the most typical and extensive part of the whole urban area
[d] Small towns and villages of under 10,000 population, but excluding isolated dwellings
[e] Designated new towns of about 20,000 to 100,000 population. Proposed situation
[f] Net residential area
[g] Including transport land

uses. However, following the work already referred to of Jones and Rogers, a firmer land-use sub-division of the urban area of England and Wales in 1961 has become possible than could be done for 1950/51.[20] The findings are shown in Table 12 on a percentage basis for various categories of settlement. The DoE figures from its 'developed areas survey' in 1969 cannot be added as they are not directly comparable because of serious differences in definition.

Housing is clearly the most extensive single land use within the urban area, and nearly half of all urban land is taken up by it. More detailed examination reveals notable contrasts between the different sectors of the total urban area. In large and medium towns the proportion of residential land falls to 46 per cent, whereas in small settlements the figure is as high as 79 per cent. Because of roads and railways in the open countryside, transport land (one of the residual uses) at about 17 per cent is the second largest use of urban land as a whole, but this is not so in the separate constituent groups of towns and small settlements. In these cases, open space is the second most extensive use, ranging from 11 to 19 per cent. All other land uses are far less dominant. Even the proportion of land under manufacturing industry in the larger towns is no more than 8 to 9 per cent of the total area; and most other land-use percentages are much smaller still.

Within the overall urban area, the radical differences in land-use structure between large and medium towns on the one hand and small settlements on the other are particularly evident. The very high proportion of residential land in small settlements compared with that in larger places is complemented by much lower percentages under industry, open space, education, and especially the residual uses. This atypical structure reflects the essentially dormitory character of many small towns and villages, and the lack of industrial and service functions associated with them. Compared with older towns, the new towns show a greater proportion of land in the four main uses and less in the residual uses.

The density-size rule

More significant in the structure of settlements than the proportionate composition of urban land is the provision of land for various uses and for the total urban area itself. As we have seen, the land provision (in ha/1000p) is a measure of density which relates the number of people with the land available for their use. Because of the great diversity of human settlements within the total urban area of the country, there has been considerable scepticism about the possibility of recognising consistent patterns of structure and density. However, it can now be seen that, initially, the main problem encountered in the approach to this topic was one of insufficient data which were both reliable and comparable.

The idea that town size (expressed by population) and density might be related arose from work carried out by Best in the 1950s. Preliminary analyses by the Ministry of Housing and Local Government in 1958 of the first round of development plan submissions supported this contention, and showed quite clearly that land provision tended to decline progressively as town size increased.[21] Unfortunately, only grouped data were then available so that the investigation could not be taken further at that time. Additional work on the supposed 'hierarchy of densities' in towns and villages had to await the analysis of revised and new town map submissions made in development plans for the period around 1961 and the study of small settlements and new towns. Table 13 provides a summary of this information.

When the full range of these data was considered, the evidence for declining land provision with increasing population size of settlement was very clear. In the smallest settlement groups, for example, the provision of land for housing was four to five times greater than in the largest towns sampled. With the four main uses and total urban area the difference was less than this, but still very substantial. Figure 5 shows these relationships across the whole urban spectrum when plotted on logarithmic scales. Interestingly, the three curves do not parallel one another. The divergence between the total urban area curve and that for the four main uses over the sector relating to larger towns and cities is accounted for by the greater provision of residual uses, which cover land associated with the important service functions of larger settlements like shops, offices, transport, public buildings, statutory undertakings and so forth. With housing a similar divergence is seen to occur. In very small settlements the urban structure is dominated by residential land, and therefore the housing provision is not a great deal below that for the entire four main uses: but with increasing population size of settlement, the downward trend in residential provision is steeper.

A correlation and regression analysis of the ungrouped material was carried out, and logarithmic transformations of the variables

Table 13 The provision of land for the main urban uses in various categories of settlement in England and Wales, 1961

Urban category	Population group '000s		Housing (NRA) [a]	Industry	Open space	Education	Four main uses	Residue	Total urban area
					ha/1000p				
Large towns	Over 500 [b]	(5)	7.2	1.2	2.7	0.4	11.5	3.5	15.0
	200–500	(3)	8.9	1.5	3.2	1.3	14.9	3.7	18.6
	100–200	(16)	9.8	1.6	3.5	0.8	15.6	4.3	19.9
Medium towns	50–100	(39)	10.7	2.0	4.8	1.4	19.0	5.5	24.5
	20–50	(53)	13.3	2.3	5.4	1.4	22.4	8.1	30.5
	10–20	(51)	15.5	1.7	6.8	1.6	25.5	10.2	35.7
Small settlements	Under 10	(260)	27.4 [c]	1.2	4.0	0.7	33.3	1.3	34.6
New towns [d]	20–100	(12)	11.7	2.1	4.5	2.0	20.3	3.0	23.3

The sample number of settlements is given in brackets after each size group

a Net residential area
b Figures for about 1950 from A.G. Champion (1972)[11]
c Including commercial land
d Proposed situation

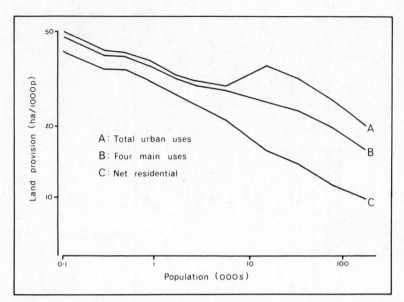

Figure 5 Density-size rule (grouped data). Declining land provision with increasing population size of settlement for the total urban area and the main urban uses as indicated by grouped data for about 1961

provided a linear relationship (Fig. 6). For each of the three density variables of housing (net residential area), the four main uses and the total urban area, a highly significant relationship with population was observed. In each case the significance was at least at the 99 per cent level. The strongest correlation was for housing, where nearly two-thirds of the variance in log residential provision was accounted for by log population. For the total urban area the relationship found was: log provision = $1.867 - 0.095$ log population.

These significant statistical relationships indicate what is called the *density-size rule*.[22] In words rather than in numerical terms, it can be stated in the following way:

> As the population size of settlement increases, the land provision (ha/1000p) declines exponentially (i.e. the density of development in persons per hectare rises at a decreasing rate).

Naturally enough, differences in size of population cannot be held to explain more than a part of the whole variation to be seen in densities. Individual small settlements in particular have a great amount of diversity in land provision, but even in this sector some

72

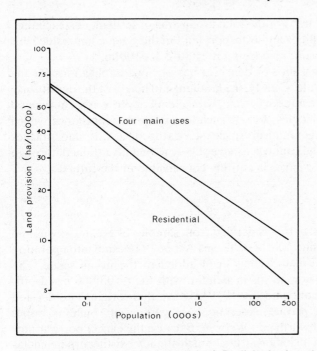

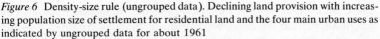

Figure 6 Density-size rule (ungrouped data). Declining land provision with increasing population size of settlement for residential land and the four main urban uses as indicated by ungrouped data for about 1961

20 per cent of the variation in structure is accounted for by population size. With larger towns and cities, there is less individual diversity in densities and about 40 per cent of the variation in land provision is related to differences in population size.

It is apparent, especially from the work of Tony Champion, that planning authorities have been proposing and achieving a reduction in densities (i.e. increased land provisions) in all size categories of town, so that settlements of down to about 10,000 population have been loosening out their land-use structure quite consistently since the 1950s.[23] Below 10,000 population there are indications that the reverse trend has operated and that small towns and villages have been tightening their densities, often by infilling with housing development on sites which were spaciously developed in previous decades and contained large gardens. Such information suggests that there is a *pivotal* provision or density (a term first coined by Colin Clark) towards which urban space standards are converging, with higher density areas losing population and lower density dis-

73

tricts gaining it.[24] For the total urban area of settlements (excluding isolated dwellings and transport land in the open countryside) this pivotal provision has been put at 30–5 ha/1000p.[25]

This convergence of densities has obvious implications for the density-size rule. Clearly, the gradient and height of the density-size rule curve will alter over time, with a tendency towards a horizontal alignment. Needless to say, such an extreme circumstance, which would signify identical space standards in towns and villages throughout the country, is never likely to be fully attained, through a much flatter curve is entirely conceivable in the future.

New towns

The density-size rule is derived from samples of existing towns and villages, but since the New Towns Act of 1946 came into operation an additional element has been added to the urban scene. The twenty-eight new towns in Britain, with their 103,000 ha of officially designated land (by 1979),[26] have their origins in older and smaller-scale private experiments in garden city building, especially at Letchworth and Welwyn. Because the earlier postwar new towns did not include nearly so much already existing urban land as their later counterparts, the aggregate area designated for all new towns in Britain by 1961 was no more than 28,300 ha, of which some 17,000 ha were proposed for development. In England and Wales the corresponding figure for development was about 14,000 ha, or only some 0.9 per cent of the urban area of the whole country at that time. In spite of this, new towns were often criticised on the grounds that they wasted land by the adoption of excessively low densities of development – 'prairie' planning as it was often called.

The facts as set out in Table 13 completely refute these long-standing assertions. Indeed, they show that the opposite situation is nearer the mark.[27] The proposed land-use structure for twelve new towns in England and Wales in 1961 demonstrates that, for their population size, they fitted very closely into the density ranking of existing towns. This is particularly true of the four main uses, whereas the residual uses are distinctly low in provision. The net result for the total urban area provision is to place it in the density hierarchy between the large towns and the medium towns. Consequently, the new towns as a whole are in no way exceptional in respect of land provision, though there is considerable variation individually.

The three Scottish new towns of the 1950s particularly helped to depress the average space standards, while most of the London region new towns were relatively more open. The most tightly developed of all was Cumbernauld in Scotland with a provision of residential land (5 ha/1000p) which was only about a third of that in places like Bracknell and Stevenage. In the 1960s, a number of further sites were designated and certain of the earlier master plans were modified and extended. Champion was able to use nine of these new land-use schedules to investigate trends in new town space standards.[28] What he found was a somewhat paradoxical situation. In line with government policy to tighten up residential densities in order to save land, the average housing provision was reduced from 11 ha/1000p to under 9 ha/1000p. In compensation, however, the open space provision was increased, so that, overall, the total urban area provision also rose by around 2 ha/1000p. In this way, the main object of the exercise was defeated by reducing residential living space while at the same time increasing the land provision for the urban area as a whole.

After about 1967, with a certain relaxation of the official high density policy, new towns were sometimes a little more liberal in their standards. Milton Keynes in particular originally advocated an average residential density of 16 ha/1000p; but new economic constraints in the 1970s again tended to result in cutbacks in space standards. Consequently, it is apparent that new towns have not been at all wasteful in their use of rural land for development. On the contrary, they have normally been more conservative in their demands than have expanding older towns. Indeed, up to the 1960s the annual scale of agricultural displacement by the new towns in England and Wales represented only about 4 per cent of the total annual turnover of all farmland to urban development.[29]

Extension of urban land

Gains to the total stock of urban land in Great Britain are known from material obtained from the agricultural census, and the information on land transfers derived from it is considered in detail in the next chapter. Unfortunately, the figures for urban growth in Scotland do not go back continuously and comparably before 1960/61. In England and Wales, on the other hand, these data provide an extended time-series back to the 1920s and further, so that estimates of the entire urban area at various dates over the whole of the twentieth century may be made (Table 14).

The figures are based on the 1961 urban area as computed in this chapter, but a useful check is provided by the extent of urban land as given in the First Land Utilisation Survey which refers to the first half of the 1930s. This figure amounts to 1,112,000 ha – a magnitude which is in close agreement with the presently estimated area of 1,023,000 ha for 1931, when account is taken of definitional irregularities and varying dates of survey in the former computation.

The figures in Table 14 demonstrate the very rapid extension of urban land that occurred in the first half of the twentieth century, and particularly in the period from 1920 to 1939. This short span of about twenty years, culminating in the sprawl of low-density suburbia, undoubtedly saw the fastest rate of urban expansion this country has ever experienced. Indeed, it contributed strongly to an actual doubling of the urban area over the period between 1901 and the early 1950s. Heavily constrained by the operation of effective planning controls since 1947, the postwar rate of urban growth has been noticeably lower, and by the end of the century, it appears probable that urban land will not take up more than about 14 per cent of the land surface.

The provision of urban land has also continued to increase throughout this century. Around 1900 it was no more than 21 ha/1000p; by 1971 it was 34 ha/1000p, or more than half as much

Table 14 Urban growth in England and Wales, 1901–2001

Year	Population millions	Urban area		Urban land provision ha/1000p
		'000 ha	per cent	
1901	32.5	674	4.5	20.7
1921	37.9	854	5.7	22.5
1931	40.0	1,005	6.7	25.1
1939	41.5	1,206	8.0	29.1
1951	43.8	1,339	8.9	30.6
1961	46.1	1,490	9.9	32.3
1971	48.8	1,646	11.0	33.7
2001 [b]	51.3	2,117	14.1	41.3

[a] Proportion of total land surface
[b] Population estimated as well as urban land

again. This radical lowering of densities and the complementary amelioration in the provision of urban living space reflects a profound change in urban structure. Very probably, the process will continue for some time yet, and certainly into the twenty-first century, until a better balance is achieved between the provisions of land in large and small settlements. The present rate of gain in land provision for the whole urban area is some 1.4 ha/1000p each decade, but this may increase considerably in the next decade or two (Table 14) leading to a further lowering of densities and marked improvement in living space.

Summary

There is now fairly general agreement that the urban area of England and Wales extended to approximately 10 per cent of the whole land surface in 1961 and to about 11 per cent by 1971. A new and detailed estimate of urban land in 1961 gives a figure of nearly 1.5 million ha for England and Wales and almost 200,000 ha for Scotland. By 1971 these figures had increased to 1.65 million ha and 225,000 ha, respectively.

Urban land is distributed very unevenly over the country. Parts of an urban spine, stretching diagonally across England from northwest to south-east, have up to a quarter of their area under urban use. Away from this belt, the proportion falls sharply to about 7 per cent or less in peripheral regions. Scotland has around 3 per cent.

Residential land takes up about half the urban area of England and Wales. Transport land and open space are the next largest users, with industry and other land uses a long way behind.

The varying provision of urban land in towns and villages according to their population size is indicated by the density-size rule. Over time, urban space standards in settlements appear to be converging towards a pivotal provision of 30–5 ha/1000p, with higher density areas losing population and lower density districts gaining it.

New towns, for their population size, fit closely into the density ranking of existing towns. As a whole, they are in no way exceptional in respect of land provision, and they are characterised by high or medium densities of development rather than by 'wasteful' low densities.

Urban land in England and Wales doubled in extent over the first half of the twentieth century, but the highest rate of gain was in the 1930s. By the year 2001, the urban area will probably occupy little more than 14 per cent of the land surface compared with only 4.5 per cent in 1901. Urban living space, or the provision of urban land per thousand population, is continuing to increase at a national level: in other words, the overall urban density is still falling.

References

1   This chapter is an extended and revised version of: Best, R.H. (1976) 'The extent and growth of urban land', *The Planner*, 62 (1), 8–11.

2   Best, R.H. (1957) 'The urban area of Great Britain – an estimate of the extent of urban land in 1950', *Town Planning Review*, 28 (3), 191–208.

3   Ministry of Housing and Local Government (1955) *Town and Country Planning Act, 1947 – First Review of Approved Development Plans*, Circular 9/55, HMSO.

4   Jones, A.R. (1974) 'An analysis of the major features of urban land use and land provision in cities and towns of England and Wales in about 1960, with special reference to development plan data', unpublished PhD thesis, University of London.

5   Best, R.H. and Rogers, A.W. (1973) *The Urban Countryside*, London, Faber & Faber.

6   ibid., Table 13.

7   Ministry of Transport (1962) *Roads in England and Wales, Report for the year 1961–62,* App. 1, HMSO.

8   Scottish Development Department (1962) *Scottish Roads Report, 1961–62*, Table 3, HMSO.

9   British Transport Commission (1961) *Annual Report and Accounts*, Vol. II, HMSO.

10   Blake, R.N.E. (1969) 'The impact of airfields on the British landscape, *Geographical Journal*, 135 (4), 508–24, and personal communication.

11   Champion, A.G. (1972) *Variation in Urban Densities between Towns of England and Wales*, Research Paper No. 1, School of Geography, University of Oxford.

12   Champion, A.G. (1974) *An Estimate of the Changing Extent and Distribution of Urban Land in England and Wales, 1950–70*, RP 10, Centre for Environmental Studies.

13   Best, R.H. and Swinnerton, G.S. (1974) *The Quality and Type of Agricultural Land Converted to Urban Use*, SSRC Final Report.

14   Fordham, R.C. (1974) *Measurement of Urban Land Use*, Occasional Paper No. 1, Department of Land Economy, University of Cambridge. See also: 'Urban land use change in the United Kingdom during the second half of the twentieth century', *Urban Studies*, 12 (1), 1975, 71–84.

15 Coleman, A.M. (1978) 'Planning and land use', *Chartered Surveyor*, 111 (5), 158–63.

16 Department of the Environment (1978) *Developed Areas 1969 – A Survey of England and Wales from Air Photography*, Planning Intelligence Directorate (3).

17 Fordham, R.C. (1974) op. cit.

18 Champion, A.G. (1975) op. cit.

19 Department of the Environment (1978) op. cit.

20 Best, R.H. and Coppock, J.T. (1962) *The Changing Use of Land in Britain*, London, Faber & Faber.

21 Ministry of Housing and Local Government (1959) *Annual Report, 1958*, Cmnd. 737, App. XXII, HMSO.

22 Best, R.H., Jones, A.R. and Rogers, A.W. (1974) 'The density-size rule', *Urban Studies*, 11 (2), 201–8. See also: Jones, A.R. (1975) 'Density-size rule, a further note', *Urban Studies*, 12, 225–8, and Craig, J. and Haskey, J. (1978) 'The relationships between the population, area, and density of urban areas', *Urban Studies*, 15 (1), 101–7.

23 Champion, A.G. (1974) op. cit.

24 Clarke, C. (1967) *Population Growth and Land Use*, London, Macmillan. See also: Craig, J. and Haskey, J. (1979) 'Pivotal density: what is it?' *Urban Studies*, 16 (2), 217–23.

25 Best, R.H. *et al.* (1974) op. cit.

26 Blake, P. (1979) 'Britain's new towns; facts and figures', *Town and Country Planning*, 47 (2–3), 132–50.

27 Best, R.H. (1964) *Land for New Towns – a Study of Land Use, Densities and Agricultural Displacement*, Town and Country Planning Association.

28 Champion, A.G. (1970) 'Recent trends in new town densities,' *Town and Country Planning*, 38 (5), 252–5.

29 Best, R.H. (1972) 'Land needs of new and old towns', in Evans, H. (ed.) *New Towns: The British Experience*, London, Charles Knight.

5
The conversion of agricultural land

Build your houses, build your houses, build your towns,
  Fell the woodland, to a gutter turn the brook,
Pave the meadows, pave the meadows, pave the downs,
  Plant your bricks and mortar where the grasses shook,
  The wind-swept grasses shook.

(F.L. Lucas: *Beleaguered Cities*)

Agriculture pushed out its frontiers into the forest and wasteland over most of the fifty to sixty centuries after the first farmers arrived in these islands. It is less than a hundred years ago since this extension finally came to an end and agriculture found itself the chief supplier of land for the newly expanding uses of urban development and forestry. With the changes brought about in the countryside following the Parliamentary enclosures and the growth of manufacturing industry in the eighteenth and nineteenth centuries, urban development gathered momentum. Back in the mid-eighteenth century, as many as 80 per cent of the population of England and Wales lived in rural areas; by 1931 the same proportion lived in urban areas and only 20 per cent in the country.

This radical progression in socio-economic structure from a predominantly agricultural to a highly urban-industrial society saw a rapid increase in population accompanying the upsurge of manufacturing industry. To accommodate these additional people, existing towns had to grow in size and new industrial towns also came into being. Yet despite all these developments, the total extent of urban expansion remained relatively restricted until the twentieth century. It is not difficult to understand why. The new houses and factories were exceedingly cramped compared with those of the present day. The 'by-law' terrace housing, built in close ranks of a hundred or more dwellings per hectare along a gridiron pattern of streets, was characteristic of the growing industrial towns. Open space was at a minimum and industrial sites were embedded in the residential districts, or were at least very close at hand. Quite apart from the cheapness of this layout, workers had normally to be able to walk to their place of employment. Later, the train, tram and horse-bus were to widen out the location of their housing areas. For much of the nineteenth century, however, most towns were compact ones of high density. They were towns whose limits were comparatively sharp and clearly defined. Dispersion of settlement was slight, and industry, housing and railways were inevitably found in a close spatial relationship to each other.

Although improving transport facilities between home and workplace allowed the outward spread of residential areas, it was not until after the First World War that any fundamental alteration in urban structure became apparent. Again, in large part, it was a change made feasible by better transport – by the extension of electric train and motor bus services and, later still, by the private car and motor vehicles in general, particularly after 1950. Also, in the early years of the present century the garden city movement was increasing its influence, and a few pioneer settlements of more open layout like Bournville and Letchworth demonstrated that better living conditions could be achieved. But it was not until the 1920s, with the adoption of housing standards advocated in the Tudor Walters Report, that more spacious development at lower overall densities became at all widespread.

These interwar years, then, saw the turning point in urban structure and design. From now on, until the Second World War, the semi-detached house, built at a density of not more than 30 per hectare, was characteristic of residential areas. The traditional terrace house, less demanding of land but often unsatisfactory in terms of living space, disappeared almost completely from public favour. In its place, the new and more spacious suburbia spread swiftly, and at times it seemed almost inexorably, into the open and frequently unkempt countryside of the 1930s.

Recording losses and gains

It was from about this period that statistical records of the transfer of farmland into urban use began to be compiled for the first time in a standardised form. But the amount of quantitative information about urban growth has remained very generalised and unsatisfactory up to the last two or three decades, and the erroneous views so frequently held and expressed about the rate of urban expansion derive in no small part from the inadequacy of statistics on this subject. It was not until as recently as the 1950s that the annual additions to the area of urban land in Britain were known with any reasonable precision. Moreover, published regional statistics for change were virtually non-existent until the 1970s. It is not altogether surprising to find, then, that urban growth in this country, or in overseas countries for that matter, is considered almost exclusively by reference to increases in population rather than by extensions in the actual area of urban land.

Probably the most reliable and certainly the most consecutive set of statistics for urban demands on land comes from the agricultural returns made by farmers in June of each year. As part of their returns, farmers are required to make a special entry in a section called the 'Change in area of holding' which indicates the area and the new or former use and occupier of those pieces of farmland which have been disposed of, or acquired, in the preceding twelve months. This information is then compiled and consolidated for England and Wales, Scotland and the United Kingdom as a whole and is published in a very summarised form in the official Agricultural Statistics.[1]

These national statistics for land-use change are net figures, comprising losses from and gains to the agricultural area (excluding common rough grazings). They are summarised and subdivided under four main headings which indicate the uses to which farmland is being transferred or, in certain cases, from which it is being gained.[2] These are:

(a) urban, industrial and recreational uses (urban development);
(b) government departments (mainly armed services);
(c) forest and woodland (Forestry Commission and private);
(d) other adjustments (corrections, reclassifications, etc.).

The first heading relates to the interchange between agricultural land and urban development. Since 1968, these 'urban, industrial and recreational uses' specifically include sports grounds, allotments, mineral workings, civil airfields, roads and reservoirs. Figures for earlier years, which were collected on a slightly different basis, have been adjusted accordingly and appropriate corrections, usually only small-scale, have been made.[3] This arrangement is very satisfactory as the figures for conversions of farmland to urban use now coincide, from the point of view of definition, almost exactly with urban land as recorded in the two previous chapters.

The second heading refers to transfers of farmland to or from certain government departments, both civil and service, though excluding the Forestry Commission. Most of the conversions are to or from service training areas and military airfields. The third heading is straightforward and covers alienations of farmland to forest and woodland, both Forestry Commission and private, while the final heading is, in practice, a residual item which relates the 'Change in area' data to the annual Agricultural Statistics. It includes corrections, unexplained differences, reclassifications and land not previously recorded. Although the same sort of information is collected in Scotland as in England and Wales, the figures are given under rather more detailed headings. Fortunately, it is possible to aggregate them into the same categories.

The Ministry of Agriculture, Fisheries and Food and the Department of Agriculture and Fisheries for Scotland have always been cautious in commenting on the accuracy of these statistics and recommend that they should be treated with some reserve as they are thought to be incomplete. This attitude that the data *understate* the losses of agricultural land is not uncommon,[4] but there is no real evidence to support this contention. Indeed, such information as does exist often tends, if anything, to favour the opposite viewpoint – that the 'Change in area' data may incline towards *over-estimating* the conversion of farmland to other uses. It is known, for instance, that there is frequently a time-lag in the recorded changes. A farmer may dispose of some land to a developer, and this land can be described as having gone over to housing or some other urban use, although in fact it may not have been developed immediately, or even for several years. On occasion, it can revert to agricultural use without development having occurred at all. In effect, the farmer records the *intended* use of the piece of land being transferred, after it has ceased to be used for agricultural purposes.

These circumstances were first brought to light by an article in the official journal of the Ministry of Agriculture which, in listing gains to agriculture from other uses between 1939 and 1945, noted that much of the recovery under a heading 'Previous use uncertain' was 'undoubtedly due to the return to agricultural use of land taken for building development some years previously, and not built on'.[5] A subsequent investigation conducted by the Ministry of Agriculture in Warwickshire between 1943 and 1956 confirmed this situation.[6] It showed that about three-quarters of the farmland 'cleared' for development in any particular year was converted from agricultural use in the following four years: the bulk of the remainder continued to be farmed indefinitely.

A useful check on the general correctness of the 'Change in area' data for agricultural/urban transfers of land is provided by the figures for change between the First and Second Land Utilisation Surveys of England and Wales as given by Alice Coleman (Table 6 and its discussion in Chapter 3). When difficulties of precise dating are taken into account, it is seen that the magnitude of the loss to urban use compares quite well with the figures from Best's calculation for change (coinciding with 'Change in area' data) over a fairly similar thirty-year period. Sample data obtained by the County Planning Officers' Society on expected losses to urban growth from 1975 to 1985, as foreseen by structure plans, also suggest that the magnitude of the county 'Change in area' figures are reasonably sound.[7] This assessment is further corroborated by A.M. Blair who, as part of a wider investigation, studied the shifts of farmland into urban use between 1960 and 1973 in Essex.[8] From his own large sample of 313 farms, he found that the annual average rate of farmland conversion to other uses (largely urban) was 0.16 per cent of the sample area, compared with an almost identical annual loss of 0.15 per cent derived from the 'Change in area' data for Essex between 1962 and 1967.

But if the 'Change in area' material can be used with reasonable confidence for indicating agricultural/urban transfers, the figures it provides for conversions to forest and woodland are more open to question. This is partly because a great deal of afforestation occurs on rough grazing land which is the most poorly documented item in the agricultural returns; and transfers from common rough grazings are not recorded at all.[9] Even more to the point, the Forestry Commission compiles its own statistics for change in area based on new plantings between censuses, and these data sometimes do not match up too well with those for similar periods of time derived from the 'Change in area' section of the agricultural returns. This is not to say that the Forestry Commission data for changes in the years between censuses are necessarily the more correct. They are not net figures, and the time-lag effect in the planting of converted land should also be remembered here: so must the fact that the estimates for changes in private woodland are far more difficult to ascertain than the carefully recorded data relating to Forestry Commission land.

The uncertainty is emphasized by the discrepancies noted between 1961 and 1971. In Great Britain, the 'Change in area' figure for agricultural/woodland transfers over this period was 230,000 ha, whereas the figure derived from Forestry Commission data was 168,000 ha.[10] On the other hand, the change in woodland area in England and Wales over the twenty years from 1951 to 1971 was set at 141,000 ha by the 'Change in area' data. This is virtually identical to the figure of 144,000 ha obtained from Forestry Commission material for these two dates. Nevertheless, it is patently obvious that, between the widely-spaced and intermittent woodland censuses, it is often difficult to reach a firm conclusion on what is the correct net scale of transfer from farmland to forest and woodland.

A particularly important advance in the determination of shifts in land use came about in the mid-1970s. From 1975, local planning authorities were asked by the Department of the Environment to provide an annual return of changes in land use within their administrative areas.[11] Altogether fifteen categories of land use were to be distinguished in this return, and transfers of land between them recorded in some detail. Inevitably though, the whole emphasis in the operation was on urban changes; that is, shifts between individual urban uses and between the rural and urban sectors or, in other words, areas which are normally covered by planning permission. In this context, therefore, forest and woodland is not distinguished as a separate category from the heading of 'agriculture and fisheries'. This new source, then, should eventually provide a complementary urban-oriented set of data on land-use changes to the present 'Change in area' statistics of the Ministry of Agriculture. But with staff shortages and other constraints in planning offices, the collection of this material did not get away to a very auspicious start, and it seems that several more years will pass before these latest statistics can settle down into a useful and reliable data source for monitoring alterations in land use.

In the meantime, the 'Change in area' statistics remain the chief source of information, although their publication has now become more irregular and no figures after 1975 for the whole of the United Kingdom are available at the time of writing (1980). Moreover, misinterpretations of this material abound. Time and again, the total reduction of farmland is ascribed almost wholly to urban growth, without any recognition that the figure encompasses the even greater demands which are often made for forestry purposes and/or the apparent but unreal changes which characterise the

Table 15 Conversions of agricultural land to urban and other uses in England and Wales, Great Britain and the United Kingdom. The figures are net, annual averages for the periods stated – usually five years. They exclude transfers from common rough grazings

Period	Annual average farmland transfers to			Other adjustments [d]
	Urban use [a]	Govt depts [b]	Woodland [c]	
		'000 ha		
England and Wales				
1922–26	9.1	0.0	0.6	7.8
1926–31	21.1	0.0	2.7	+ 6.1
1931–36	25.1	1.4	1.6	+ 3.2
1936–39	25.1	8.3	6.8	+ 4.4
1939–45	5.3	41.0	7.7	+31.1
1945–50	17.5	+14.6	7.3	+ 4.6
1950–55	15.5	+ 2.5	9.1	+ 6.8
1955–60	14.0	+ 1.2	8.0	1.5
1960–65	15.3	+ 1.0	6.6	0.9
1965–70	16.8	+ 0.6	5.5	2.5
1970–75	14.9	0.4	3.0	12.5
1974–79	10.8	+ 0.3	0.9	9.4
Great Britain				
1960–65	17.8	+ 0.6	24.5	1.2
1965–70	19.7	+ 0.5	25.0	2.9
1970–75	16.8	0.4	27.1	11.9
United Kingdom				
1961–65	17.9	+ 0.8	21.8	+ 1.6
1965–70	20.9	+ 0.6	26.6	3.9
1970–75	17.6	0.2	27.8	12.4

+ Plus figures indicate net gains to the agricultural area
[a] Urban, industrial and recreational development, including allotments and mineral workings
[b] Mainly service training areas, and excluding Forestry Commission
[c] Forestry Commission and private woodlands
[d] Corrections, reclassifications and unexplained differences

figures recorded as 'other adjustments'.

Since the end of the 1960s, this latter element of distortion has been very evident. As we saw in Chapter 2, the Ministry of Agriculture has fundamentally revised the lower size limit of holdings from which returns are required. This is now determined on a productiv-

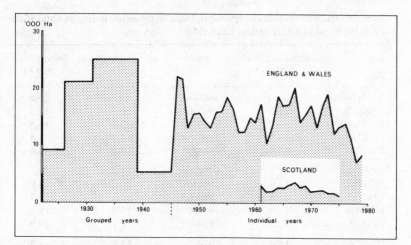

Figure 7 Transfers of agricultural land to urban use in England and Wales and in Scotland

ity rather than on an areal basis. The result has been that the last decade has seen large numbers of holdings dropped from the returns with their areas therefore appearing under the heading of 'other adjustments', which includes corrections, reclassifications and unexplained differences. Such changes are, in fact, mainly 'paper' or 'accounting' alterations only, and yet they are often included, even in official statements of land losses, as though they were real changes.

Figures for net conversions of agricultural land to urban and other uses, including woodland, are available from 1922 onwards in England and Wales. Less satisfactorily, comparable data for Scotland, and therefore for Great Britain, have only been issued since as recently as 1960. Similar statistics for Northern Ireland have even greater constraints attached to them. The available data are set out in Table 15 and, graphically, in Figure 7. Where possible, they are recorded as five-year averages from 1922 to 1979 in order to reduce variability and give a better indication of trends. Table 16 gives figures for agricultural/urban conversions in individual years, where available, since 1945; but in looking at these data the comments made earlier should be recalled on the time-lag which is often associated with development on newly transferred farmland.

As might be expected, this long period of over half a century in England and Wales has been marked by significant fluctuations in

Table 16 Annual transfers of agricultural land to urban use in England and Wales since 1945 and in Great Britain since 1960

Year	England and Wales '000 ha	Year	England and Wales '000 ha	Great Britain '000 ha
1945/46	22.0	1960/61	17.4	20.4
1946/47	21.6	1961/62	10.3	12.3
1947/48	13.0	1962/63	13.4	15.5
1948/49	15.5	1963/64	18.7	21.4
1949/50	15.6	1964/65	17.0	19.6
1950/51	14.1	1965/66	17.2	20.3
1951/52	13.0	1966/67	20.2	23.8
1952/53	15.8	1967/68	14.1	16.7
1953/54	15.9	1968/69	15.5	18.5
1954/55	18.5	1969/70	17.1	19.0
1955/56	16.4	1970/71	13.2	15.2
1956/57	12.3	1971/72	17.0	19.2
1957/58	12.4	1972/73	19.2	21.0
1958/59	14.8	1973/74	12.3	14.1
1959/60	14.0	1974/75	13.0	14.3

the rate of land conversions from agriculture. Neglecting the direct and dramatic changes resulting from the Second World War, there are three really outstanding features which call for comment: firstly, that the scale of urban growth and agricultural displacement was far greater in the 1930s than in any subsequent or previous period of comparable length; secondly, that contrary to popular belief, there has been no sustained increase in the loss of farmland to urban use in the postwar years; and thirdly, that in Britain as a whole, the annual extension of forest and woodland now often outpaces that of urban growth. These major conclusions are underlined by a more detailed consideration of land-use trends in the interwar and post-1945 periods.

Interwar losses to urban use

The chief urban demands on land have always come from house-building rather than from other urban uses like industry, open space or transport. To some considerable extent, therefore, urban growth can be explored by reference to the scale of residential development and particularly to suburban expansion since 1918. After the First World War, Britain experienced an increased demand for houses compared with the first decade of the century, and from the early 1920s suburban expansion went ahead strongly.

Surprisingly enough, even the depression of the interwar period did not check house-building greatly when the country was considered as a whole, though the impact varied substantially in different regions. London and the south-east were relatively prosperous at this time, and so it is not unexpected to find that over one-third of the houses built privately in England and Wales between 1930 and 1939 were located in the home counties.[12] During the period of economic uncertainty in the early 1930s, the building societies were firm outlets for investment and, consequently, finance for house purchase was fairly readily available. After 1932, rates of interest and costs of construction fell, while economies of scale were brought about by the entry of larger firms into the building industry, followed by the construction of a greater number of more sizeable housing estates.

The economic factors contributing to residential growth in the interwar period were bolstered by a new social outlook. Although actual house sizes did not change materially, and may even have declined for a time, the extent of house-plots increased substantially. More liberal space standards were increasingly adopted in reaction to the legacy of crowded and dreary Victorian towns, and a density of some thirty houses per hectare became fairly general as a recognised standard in much new housing development. The application of this standard meant that two-storey houses with gardens, and often semi-detached, became the rule in new construction. This led to a halving of the residential densities which had hitherto been thought acceptable for many of the population, with the result that proportionately more land was required to house a given number of people.

By the late 1920s, therefore, the urban area as a whole had begun to expand with some rapidity at about 20,000 ha per year. But the steepest upturn in this rate of growth took place in the early 1930s when the number of houses built annually rose to well over 300,000. Agriculture, largely unprotected from overseas competition, was now at a very low ebb. It was a bad time for farmers, and it was often said that the farmer's best crop was houses. Consequently, cheap building sites on open farmland, which public transport services and private motor vehicles made progressively more accessible, helped to stimulate the stampede from town to suburban living.

Space and light, a garden of one's own, grounds for recreation and leisure, an escape from the cramped and dirty towns to the true countryside – these objectives, whether adequately achieved or not, became the requirements of a growing sector of the population. Their attainment was made simpler by the fact that planning control, as it has operated since 1947, was virtually non-existent. As a result, in many areas an amorphous, unplanned sprawl of development took place which was often enormously wasteful of land. It was of little wonder, therefore, that at this period the loss of agricultural land to urban uses in England and Wales attained its all-time peak with an annual average transfer of over 25,000 ha between 1931 and 1939.[13] In marked contrast, the rate of population increase was at one of its lowest points so far this century.

The start of the Second World War in 1939 brought an abrupt end to this exodus into suburbia and, for the next few years, alienations of farmland for urban purposes were reduced by almost four-fifths. House-building was severely curtailed, though a fair amount of other constructional development still took place, such as the building of factories and industrial plants, which averaged about 5000 ha per year. Against this, the necessity to produce more of our own food led to the temporary ploughing up and cultivation of many urban sports fields and parks, while house-gardens were similarly turned over more fully to the production of vegetables and fruit.[14] These temporary operations helped to relieve the food import situation and assist in replacing a small portion of the loss of agricultural products incurred by the transfer of so much land at this time (over 40,000 ha per year) to government departments, and particularly to the fighting services. Much of this loss from agriculture to military use was only temporary, however, and the early postwar years saw a substantial return of land from wartime service training grounds and airfields to its former agricultural use.

Transfers to urban use since 1945

As might be expected, with the end of hostilities in 1945 there was a complete reversal of many wartime land-use trends (Table 15 and Fig. 7). Right up to the early 1950s, land used for military purposes was returned to agriculture at a considerable rate. Thereafter, the pace slackened until eventually the amount released dwindled to very small proportions. As for urban demands on land, they showed an immediate and marked rise after 1945 as housing, industry, recreational open space, schools and similar uses began to make up the leeway lost during the war. But this surge of constructional activity, which more than trebled the annual scale of wartime acquisitions, was short-lived, and in any case it did not attain the immediate prewar rate. For two years only, until 1947, the loss of farmland in England and Wales for intended urban use was at over 20,000 ha a year. After this, the gathering financial crisis of the early postwar period applied a violent brake, and until the mid-1950s the annual conversion was usually well below 16,000 ha. Housing, which normally accounts for 50 per cent or more of all annual urban land requirements, rose to a peak of over 200,000 completions in 1948 and then fell back for the next three years.

At this point, the country was entering a new and significant phase in its land-use history. The war had seen the publication of a number of reports concerned with land planning for postwar Britain, and in the late 1940s legislation was enacted to give substance to many of the recommendations which were made. In 1946, the New Towns Act was rapidly followed by the designation and building of the first round of new towns. The Agriculture Act of 1947 gave recognition to the importance of agriculture and afforded the industry support and stability. But arguably most important of all, the Town and Country Planning Act of 1947 laid the foundations for effective land planning and, among many other things, instituted development plans and development control by local planning authorities.

As Peter Hall has pointed out, one of the principal policies pursued since that time by government and planners alike has been the attempt at urban containment.[15] The concept was one of the main planks in the recommendations made by the wartime committee on land utilisation in rural areas (the Scott Committee), the report of which was published in 1942.[16] There were, in fact, virtually two Scott Reports – a majority one and a minority one – and they reflected the fundamental cleavage of opinion which had come about, even by that date, between preservationist and expansionist attitudes towards the use of rural land.

The majority report presented the conventional attitude of the time. It considered it essential that the area of farmland, and particularly the better quality land, should be maintained and preserved from urban development wherever possible, and that the outward spread of towns should be strictly regulated. Farming the countryside was thought to be the best means of maintaining its desirable characteristics – a concept which is seriously questioned today. On the other hand, S.R. Dennison in his minority report arrived at almost exactly the opposite conclusion on several matters. With the wisdom of hindsight, it is now evident that he often saw more clearly and accurately ahead than did any of his colleagues, which was no small achievement at that time in history when food supplies were gravely endangered by enemy action.

> In planning the use of any land [he said], full weight should in every case be given to all considerations relevant to the national interest, and there should not be, as my colleagues suggest, a prior right given to agriculture over other interests. There are, indeed, many more pressing social needs than that of preservation of land for agriculture.

In the event, it was probably understandable that Dennison's proposals should be disregarded and that the preservationist recommendations of the majority of the committee should come to form the basis for government policy and action in the postwar years. Certainly, as we entered the 1950s, the pressure to tighten urban densities in order to 'save' land began to increase at the expense of standards for urban living space. Urban containment had become the order of the day. The policy was expressed very forcibly by Harold Macmillan in 1952 in his Foreword to *The Density of Residential Areas*.[17] 'It is essential', he said, 'that the amount of land taken (for development) should be kept as small as possible . . . It is important to save every acre that can be saved.' Just why it was so important to save farmland by reducing urban living space when agricultural productivity was escalating rapidly was never adequately explained.

Nevertheless, ten years later in 1962 this policy was still being promoted. In a bulletin significantly entitled *Residential Areas – Higher Densities*, the housing minister at that time, Sir Keith Joseph, contended that 'we need to allocate more land for housing and we need higher densities, especially in the pressure areas. We need not one or the other, but both – more land and higher densities.'[18] The dilemma of needing to build more houses but wanting to save land was becoming increasingly pronounced, and the high density policy persisted. From the late 1950s, this policy was given an additional impetus by the ill-fated architectural predilection for residential high-rise blocks, even though it was well-known that progressively smaller land savings were made for the overall urban area as residential densities were increased. Eventually, by the end of the 1960s, this Corbusier-inspired dream of skyscraper housing estates turned sour, with increasing protests on social, psychological and economic grounds.[19,20] But in spite of this change of heart, the general approach to land saving did not alter and was continued right through the 1970s to the 1980s.[21] The emphasis still remained on tighter residential development with little garden space, though building at above three storeys was avoided for the most part.

Returning to 1952 and the beginnings of official high density policy, it seems likely that concern for land saving was being stimulated because the economy was by then going ahead more strongly and urban land requirements and housing completions were showing a marked upturn. In 1953 the Development Charge was lifted, and by 1954 with further political pressures and economic incentives under the Macmillan regime at the Ministry of Housing and Local Government, the number of houses constructed reached a high-point of over 300,000. This impressive total was very short-lived, and indeed was not exceeded again until ten years later in 1964. Concurrently, urban land requirements peaked at a new high level of over 18,000 ha in 1954/55, but then fell back sharply to under 13,000 ha for two years.

This period was also marked by another significant event. For some years, private housing completions had shown a steady increase and, in 1958, they exceeded those of public authority housing for the first time since the war. This growing prominence of the private sector in housing construction saw an even closer relationship come about between urban land demands and economic trends. The country was now embarked upon a particularly severe period of economic oscillation with booms and recessions following each other in quick succession. To a large extent, urban land acquisitions and agricultural land losses followed suit. For example, the relaxation of economic restrictions in 1960 was accompanied by a jump in urban land requirements to over 17,000 ha in the following year. But this rise was dramatically halted by Selwyn Lloyd's 'little budget' in the summer of 1961 with a drop in agricultural land conversions to intended urban use of only between 10,000 and 11,000 ha in 1961/62.

In general, however, the 1960s was the decade of affluence, when urban demands on land were rather high for the most part, with an annual average of over 17,000 ha in the seven years from 1963 to

1970. In 1966/67, conversions even topped 20,000 ha, but the impending enactment of the Land Commission Bill may have helped to encourage this high rate of transfer, as the following year saw the figure slump to little more than 14,000 ha. In contrast, the first half of the 1970s showed a worsening of economic problems along with escalating prices in the land and housing markets. There was a short recovery in 1972/73 when farmland conversions to intended urban use rose to over 19,000 ha, but the rest of the period experienced only a relatively small turnover of land.

Since 1975, the year of the Community Land Act, the continuing and deepening recession in the economy has resulted in a steep decline in land transfers. In 1975/76 the loss was 14,000 ha, but for the two years 1977/79 it averaged less than 8000 ha annually – the lowest level for any year since the end of the war. In 1979, the government brought in legislation to allow district councils to take over many planning powers from the county councils. The net effect in the long run may be to loosen and reduce some of the locational constraints on land-use change which the upper tier of local government might formerly have wished to impose because of its less localised viewpoint.

Clearly then, for two or three decades there appears to have been a fairly close association between economic trends and conversions or, more exactly, intended conversions of farmland to urban use. Nevertheless, a glance at Figure 7 will confirm that the fluctuations in land transfers which have occurred have been confined mainly to between 12,000 and 19,000 ha a year in England and Wales. The average annual rate of transfer over the thirty years from 1945 to 1975 was 15,700 ha. This is well under two-thirds of the rate attained in the 1930s. But what is perhaps of even greater significance is that, contrary to popular belief, the years since 1945 have seen no sustained increase in the loss of farmland to urban uses. Indeed, in the last decade for which there is comprehensive information, from 1965 to 1975, the average transfer was 15,900 ha per year compared with the higher figure of 16,500 ha from 1945 to 1955. Therefore, the common supposition that since the end of the war, and especially in the last decade or so, urban land demands have consistently increased is now seen to be very far removed from the truth.

In Scotland, over the fifteen years since 1960 when figures first became available on a comparable basis to those in England and Wales, agricultural displacement by urban growth has been at the rate of about 2400 ha per year on average. Over the same period from 1960 to 1975, the figure for England and Wales has been an average of 15,700 ha, making a total for Great Britain of 18,100 ha per year. The comparable figure for the United Kingdom is 18,800 ha per year.

From this discussion, it will be apparent that certain factors have stimulated urban growth and farmland losses, while other influences have operated to constrain them. Most of the factors already referred to have been short-term, producing a fairly quick response in altered land requirements; but population change, which has not been mentioned so far, may result in both fairly immediate and also much longer-term demands on land for housing and other urban facilities.

Taking then, first of all, the more persistent factors contributing to urban growth in the period since 1945, there was the rising birth rate up to the early 1960s, accompanied by a growing total population and a smaller household size. Increases in household formation have been particularly important right up to the present time, and all these population movements have led to greater accommodation and other demands which are themselves reflected in additional requirements for urban land. In the late 1940s and the early 1950s, the provision of new housing and associated development, and the related take-up of land, was dominated by public sector requirements – by local authority building and the construction of the new towns – though economic recessions often restricted growth. But by the 1960s, rising affluence was stimulating private housing and other urban-industrial development to a marked degree, while the redevelopment of the central areas of cities from this time onwards led to a dispersal of population to new estates on the outskirts.

Working against this outward thrust of urban extension were a number of continuing constraints. Planning control, instituted and operated under the 1947 Act (and later legislation) helped very effectively to contain sprawl and resulted in a far more compact, planned growth than would otherwise have been attained. The policy of tightening up densities of housing, especially after 1952, was also aimed at reducing urban spread and saving agricultural land. This was assisted by the fact that farming was now in good heart and more resilient to urban pressures than in the 1930s, while agricultural and rural preservationist groups also brought growing pressure to bear. Rising land and property prices in an inflationary economy became particularly curbing in the 1970s and helped to reduce urban demands on land; as did the increased difficulty of getting mortgages and the steep fall in the birth rate up to the end of the 1970s. In general, therefore, the unfavourable economic climate after the easier years of the 1960s had a marked effect on damping down the pressures for urban extension.

Conversions to forest and woodland

The recorded transfer of agricultural land to urban use in Great Britain is now distinctly less than the area reported as being lost to forestry and woodland each year. From 1961 to 1975, the average annual conversion from farmland to forestry was between 24,000 and 26,000 ha, the estimate from Forestry Commission data being rather more than that from the 'Change in area' material. Even taking the lower figure, this compares with only some 18,000 ha a year that was transferred from agriculture to urban use over much the same period.

By far the largest gains to the forest area were in Scotland where, according to the Forestry Commission, they amounted to over 30,000 ha per year between 1972 and 1975, which was a great increase on the 1960s. Meanwhile, the gain in England and Wales was steadily reduced from about 10,000 ha per year to only 6000 ha, or considerably less than this according to 'Change in area' data. Afforestation and woodland extension seem to have been particularly forceful in England and Wales during much of the 1950s, but the more recent steep fall in the rate of growth has been attributed to the increasing difficulties of land acquisition because of the inflating cost of land and the disincentive provided by legislation on capital taxation.[22]

Despite the inadequate statistics, therefore, there is really no doubt that the most extensive acquirer of agricultural land in the 1970s was the forest and woodland sector, with urban development only in second place. This was a complete reversal of the situation in the interwar years when urban growth far outpaced the land demands made by other uses. Nevertheless, it should be recognised that losses of agricultural land cannot be assessed on the basis of area alone: the farmland taken for forestry is often of the poorest quality, while urban uses inevitably absorb a higher proportion of better and more productive farmland.

Summary

Probably the most reliable and certainly the most consecutive set of statistics for urban growth at the expense of agricultural land comes from the 'Change in area' section of the agricultural returns made by farmers in June of each year. Conversions of farmland to certain other uses are also covered.

These statistics suggest that care should be taken not to exaggerate the growing extent of urban land since the Second World War. The scale of agricultural displacement by intended urban use in England and Wales was far greater in the 1930s, at 25,000 ha a year, than in any subsequent or previous period of comparable length. The thirty years between 1945 and 1975 saw an average annual rate of conversion of 15,700 ha which was well under two-thirds of the 1930s' figure.

In this same period since 1945 there was no sustained increase in the transfer of farmland to urban use. However, considerable fluctuations occurred from year to year mainly within the range of 12,000 to 19,000 ha, but after 1975 there was a steep decline. These variations were often closely associated with oscillations in the national economy.

Turning to the most recent period for which complete data exist, the conversion of agricultral land to intended urban growth between 1960 and 1975 averaged about 15,700 ha a year in England and Wales and 2400 ha in Scotland. This makes a total for Great Britain of approximately 18,100 ha per year.

Forestry, rather than urban development, has been the chief acquirer of agricultural land in Great Britain as a whole in most of the period since 1960. In the years from 1961 to 1975, the average annual turnover of farmland to this use was between 24,000 and 26,000 ha, most of the increase being in Scotland.

References

1   Ministry of Agriculture, Fisheries and Food, Department of Agriculture and Fisheries for Scotland and Ministry of Agriculture, Northern Ireland (annual or periodic) *Agricultural Statistics – United Kingdom*, HMSO. Statistics for England and Wales and for Scotland are given in separate publications.
2   Ministry of Agriculture, Fisheries and Food, Department of Agriculture and Fisheries for Scotland (1968) *A Century of Agricultural Statistics, Great Britain 1866–1966*, HMSO.

3   Best, R.H. (1968) 'Extent of urban growth and agricultural displacement in post-war Britain', *Urban Studies*, 5 (1), 1–23.

4   Department of Education and Science (1966) *Report of the Land Use Study Group*, HMSO.

5   Anon. (1949) 'Losses and gains of agricultural land in England and Wales', *Agriculture*, 56, 233–6.

6   Ministry of Agriculture, Fisheries and Food (1958) *Warwickshire – A Study of the Loss of Agricultural Land for Urban Development*, ALS Technical Report No. 4.

7   Agriculture EDC (1977) *Agriculture into the 1980s: Land Use*, National Economic Development Office, Appendix A.

8   Blair, A.M. (1978) 'Spatial effects of urban influences on agriculture in Essex, 1960–1974', unpublished Ph.D. thesis, University of London. See also: Blair, A.M. (1980) 'Compulsory purchase: a neglected factor in the agricultural land loss debate', *Area*, 12 (3), 183–9.

9   Centre for Agricultural Strategy (1976) *Land for Agriculture*, Report No. 1, University of Reading, Appendix 1, by R.B. Tranter.

10 Forestry Commission: personal communication.

11 Department of the Environment (1974) *Statistics of Land Use Change*, Circular 71/74, HMSO.

12 Johnson, J.H. (1967) *Urban Geography: An Introductory Analysis*, Oxford, Pergamon.

13 Best, R.H. (1968) op. cit.

14 Best, R.H. and Ward, J.T. (1956) *The Garden Controversy*, Wye College.

15 Hall, P. (1974) 'The containment of urban England', *Geographical Journal*, 140 (3), 386–417. See also the two-volume book of this same title (London, Allen & Unwin, 1973) by Hall *et al*.

16 Ministry of Works and Planning (1942) *Report of the Committee on Land Utilisation in Rural Areas* (Scott Report), Cmnd, 6378, HMSO.

17 Ministry of Housing and Local Government (1952) *The Density of Residential Areas*, HMSO.

18 Ministry of Housing and Local Government (1962) *Residential Areas – Higher Densities*, Planning Bulletin No. 2, HMSO.

19 Stone, P.A. (1965) 'Some economic aspects of town development', *Town and Country Planning Summer School, Report of Proceedings*, Town Planning Institute, 123–37.

20 Best, R.H. (1966) 'Against high density', *New Society*, 8 (217), 787–9.

21 Department of the Environment (1980) *Development Control – Policy and Practice*, Circular 22/80, HMSO.

22 Centre for Agricultural Strategy (1976) op. cit.

6
Forecasts and food supplies

The same line of reasoning that leads to the expectation that the city will diffuse itself until it has taken up considerable areas and many of the characteristics, the greenness, the fresh air, of what is now country, leads us to suppose also that the country will take to itself many of the qualities of the city. The old antithesis will indeed cease, the boundary lines will altogether disappear; it will become, indeed, merely a question of more or less populous. There will be horticulture and agriculture going on within the 'urban regions', and 'urbanity' without them.

(H.G. Wells: *Anticipations*)

Not many men or women are gifted, like H.G. Wells, with a controlled yet wonderfully perceptive imagination which can transcend the confines of the age in which they live. Most attempts at inventing the future, whether by novelists or scientists, are in reality very constrained by existing conditions.[1] Today, therefore, the science fiction of future events is heavily dominated by the prospects of overpopulation, food shortages, nuclear hazards, energy constraints and computerised controls – all pressing problems that we can see around us in various parts of the world at the present time. To leap ahead in the mind and construct a reasonably correct outline of the future which is not necessarily a purely straight-line development of present trends demands a conceptual ability that is not given to the majority of mankind.

We are talking now of futures which imply human action or involvement. In contrast, the prediction of events in the natural, non-biological environment can be far more precise and reliable. There is little chance that the time of sunrise or of high tide on a specified day many years hence will not be exactly as forecast; but even in the physical world events do not always conform to a predictable pattern. It is, for instance, difficult enough to forecast the weather in the British Isles just a day ahead, never mind a week or a month; and at the moment, earthquakes and volcanic eruptions are virtually unpredictable.

99

In the sphere of human activity, with all its inherent uncertainties, the situation is still worse. E.F. Schumacher has made the point very persuasively.[2] The future, he says, can never really be forecast, though it can be explored. 'In practice all prediction is simply extrapolation, modified by known "plans".' Computer assistance can allow a more sophisticated treatment and perhaps a better grasp of the complexities of a changing world, so long as the model-building does not lend a spurious sense of accuracy and reality to the whole operation.[3] In the final analysis, it is arguable that well-considered prognostications by the informed and complex human mind, unaided by electronic devices, can do just as well, or even significantly better. But whatever the approach, forecasting in the social sciences is a hazardous business, and many wrongful predictions of economic and population trends have made us only too well aware of this in the last few decades. It has been the same with land use, where the inexactitude and variability of projections over even fairly short periods of time have been remarkable.

It is now known, for example, that the actual growth of urban land at the expense of agriculture in England and Wales over the twenty years from 1951 to 1971 was a little more than 300,000 ha. At the very beginning of the 1950s, Stamp estimated that the likely transfer (between his maximum and minimum estimates) could be as much as 600,000 ha.[4] On the other hand, the Ministry of Housing and Local Government, working on the basis of development plan material, put the urban requirement at no more than 200,000 ha,[5] though this figure was subsequently raised slightly by The Economist Intelligence Unit.[6] Clearly, the range of error has been substantial in past calculations. Nevertheless, it is both useful and desirable to look forward and assess what the structure of land use may be at a not too distant date if recent trends, with reasonable modifications of them, were to be continued.

Towards 2000

In Chapter 4, the extent of the urban area of England and Wales by 2001 has been forecast at 14 per cent of the surface, compared with 11 per cent in 1971, an increase of about 1 per cent a decade. In fact, this projection may well be rather generous, considering the economic constraints which have been experienced across much of the 1970s. Yet even if the average annual turnover were increased to 20,000 ha per year (and note that this total has been reached in only one year since 1947), the proportion of urban land at the turn of the century would still only be raised to 15 per cent.

The urban extension to 14 per cent suggested here for England and Wales is largely supported by a forecast for the United Kingdom made by the Economic Development Committee for Agriculture, though this is for the more limited period up to 1985.[7] The report contends that

> there is expected to be a limited growth in total population over this period (1975–1985), due mainly to the continual fall in fertility rates. If present economic conditions persist, then growth rates in GNP and in per capita real disposable income may be slower than they have been over the past decade. Certain areas have shown a tendency to increase, rather than decrease, urban densities. On the other hand, the adult working population is expected to increase significantly; the trend for smaller households is likely to continue; and parts of the inner areas of many large conurbations are still obsolescent and congested and in need of redevelopment at lower densities. In view of the above factors, it is considered appropriate to put the average rate of transfer of UK farmland to urban development over the next ten years at rather less than 20,000 ha per annum.

The same report also considers the likely turnover of farmland to forest in the United Kingdom between 1975 and 1985. Because of economic constraints, it will probably be lower than the rate over the first half of the 1970s, and the figure is put at a maximum of 33,000 ha a year. About 80 per cent of this new planting is likely to take place in Scotland. Looking further ahead, the Forestry Commission has made some proposals for planting programmes between 1978 and the year 2000 in Great Britain.[8] The area of potentially plantable land in Scotland amounts to 1.7 million ha and in England and Wales to 1.3 million ha. At present this land is used for hill sheep farming, the management of red deer and grouse, crofting and common grazing, nature conservation and amenity and recreation. Consequently, many limitations apply to the transfer of such areas to forestry. Taking into account these difficulties in acquiring land, it is forecast that the increase in forest and woodland (both public and private) from 1978 to the end of the century could be 455,000 ha; that is an annual average gain of 20,700 ha per year, or a noticeably lower rate than that achieved in the 1960s and 1970s.

A later and most comprehensive report on the United Kingdom

forest industry by the Centre for Agricultural Strategy at Reading University gives a four-fold range of planting targets up to the year 2030.[9] It is the second highest of these options (Programme A) which, for the total productive forest area of Great Britain by 2000, comes closest to the forecast made here (Table 17). Interestingly, it is also calculated that an additional 1.1 million ha of forest, out of the 3 million ha potentially available, could be planted without adversely affecting the space requirements for water gathering, amenity, conservation and improved farming activities. This is well over twice the figure of 455,000 ha suggested above as being the probable expansion of the forest and woodland area to the end of this century. Although gradually increasing in their intensity, there-fore, the conflicts between afforestation and other uses of land do not seem likely to reach critical proportions until well into next century.

With these estimates of rates of change in urban development and afforestation, it is possible to construct forecasts of the national land-use structure of England and Wales and Great Britain in 2001. In Table 17, they are compared with the position in 1971. These forecasts, however, are little more than a projection of trends, and although any short-term economic fluctuations are unlikely to affect them to a marked extent, longer-term and more fundamental shifts in economic, technological or social situations – like a change in density policy – could produce a rather different outcome. The basis of the urban projection has been the annual average rate of extension over the fifteen years up to 1975 (Table 16) although, interestingly, this figure for England and Wales (15,700 ha) is exactly the same as the average for the whole period from 1945 to 1975. For the woodland figures, Forestry Commission estimates have partly formed the basis of the calculation. These are again related to present trends, and they indicate a smaller rate of exten-sion than the Forestry Commission would, ideally, like to attain.

From these forecasts, it seems probable that agricultural cover-age will continue to fall sharply, by some 4 to 5 per cent, to below three-quarters of the land surface by the end of the century. This decline is broadly what is expected in official quarters. In a paper on 'Agriculture in 2000 A.D.' referring to the United Kingdom, the Ministry of Agriculture, Fisheries and Food says that

> farming can be expected to continue to make rapid improve-ments in its efficiency, and total output may be substantially greater by the end of the century than today from a land area

Table 17 Estimated land-use structure for England and Wales and for Great Britain in 2001 compared with 1971

Year	Agriculture	Woodland	Urban land	Other land	Total land area
			'000 ha		
England and Wales					
1971	11,515	1,115	1,646	750	15,026
2001	10,980	1,230	2,120	700	15,030
Great Britain					
1971	17,741	1,853	1,871	1,279	22,744
2001	16,540	2,540	2,410	1,250	22,740
			per cent		
England and Wales					
1971	76.6	7.4	11.0	5.0	100.0
2001	73.0	8.2	14.1	4.7	100.0
Great Britain					
1971	78.0	8.2	8.2	5.6	100.0
2001	72.7	11.2	10.6	5.5	100.0

The estimates for 2001 are rounded to the nearest 10,000 ha

about 4 per cent to 7 per cent smaller, reductions being offset by much greater yields and stocking densities.[10]

On the other hand, the 3 per cent increase postulated in the woodland coverage of Britain maintains the amount of rural land as a whole at well above 8 ha in every 10. Even so, for the first time the extent of the British urban area will probably have topped the 10 per cent mark by a considerable margin, though this is hardly a prospect which suggests that a swamping of the countryside by urban growth is going to be a very immediate problem in many areas in the near future.

Further ahead

Certain conjectures about the further expansion of urban land after the end of this century warrant some brief attention. Projected forward at the post-1945 rate of growth, the urban area would take up approximately one-quarter of England and Wales by the close of the twenty-first century.[11] Still further ahead, if growth were to continue, a particularly important threshold might occur around 2300, by which time all land could be used up for urban purposes that is not now specially protected in some way for amenity or agricultural reasons (e.g. as green belts, national parks, high-grade farmland, etc.). Such areas account for just under two-thirds of the land surface, and any substantial incursion into them for urban use would mark a serious threat to the remaining reserves of open countryside. Long before that time, of course, anything resembling the present rural landscape would have disappeared entirely, particularly in lowland areas.

Eventually, the complete demise of the countryside would come about when urban development extended to a full coverage of the whole land surface. This would occur in another 800 years or so in England and Wales at recent rates of urban growth. Yet, if anything in forecasting is reasonably certain, it is that present trends are *not* likely to continue across long periods of time into the future. Many unforeseen and deranging factors will inevitably intrude to modify and distort accustomed processes. So, for planners in the next century, it is quite conceivable that their problems may take on a very different complexion from those that we see today. Perhaps it may even happen that they will not be concerned with urban overgrowth at all, but will be involved instead with the equally intractable predicament of a declining population and an overextended and underused stock of urban land.

In looking so far ahead, it is salutory to recall the projections on population and land provision made almost three hundred years ago by Gregory King when he attempted to foresee the distant future.[12] In 1696 he wrote:

> That in probability the next doubling of the people of England will be in about 600 years to come, or by the year of our Lord 2300. At which time it will have 11 million of people; but that the next doubling after that, will not be (in all probability) in less than 12 or 1300 years more, or by the year of our Lord 3500 or 3600. At which time the Kingdom will have 22 million of souls, or 4 times its present number in case the world should last so long. Now the Kingdom containing but 39 million of acres, it will then have less than 2 acres to each head, and consequently will not then be capable of any further increase.

Unfortunately for King's prognostications, a reference to Table 1

104

will confirm that, only about 150 years later, there were already some 18 million people in England and Wales and each of them, even then, had no more than an average of two acres of land. Although the year 2000 has not yet been reached, the amount available is now well under one acre apiece, and the density on the total land surface seems likely to tighten still more, rather than be incapable of further increase. Who, then, can really say what the year 3500 will bring – if the world should last so long?

Gardens and farms

In considering urban growth it is too often assumed that building on farmland involves a complete loss of food output from the land that is taken for development. Yet, demonstrably, this is not so. Most homes in Britain have gardens and, even though their average size may be small, they can, and frequently do, produce a domestic supply of vegetables and fruit. The stimulus to a widening interest in gardening came particularly from the unparalleled spread of suburbia in the 1930s. There were then over 600,000 ha of houses with gardens, and the outward spread of semi-detached house-building at a density of about thirty to the hectare ensured to each occupier a plot of open ground to be treated as he or she wished – for relaxation, recreation, and for more prosaic activities.

Prior to the Second World War, we have no precise knowledge of how gardens were used or what they produced, but with the outbreak of hostilities in 1939 the rationing of food and its lack of variety put a premium on garden and allotment produce. By 1944, 66 per cent of houses in England and Wales had gardens and 45 per cent were growing vegetables and fruit.[13] Indeed, in reply to a question in parliament in the same year, it was officially stated that the production from gardens, allotments, and similar plots of land represented 10 per cent of home-produced food.

After the war, the early economic crises promoted an increasingly conservationist attitude towards building on agricultural land, and by the 1950s 'the great garden controversy' as it was called became an important element in the arguments used in support of moderate housing densities and against the growing trend to tighten space standards in residential development.[14] At that period, a not inconsiderable proportion of the urban area was still producing food crops, and the output obtained from that land formed an important part of the total supply of vegetables available for consumption.

One of the main features of the garden controversy was the debate as to whether the gardens of housing estates produced as much food as the farmland they replaced, bearing in mind the fact that the house and garage of the typical suburban home covered only about one-fifth of the whole area of the plot. A variety of answers could be given to this question according to the sort of comparison which was made; but it could at least be said that if the typical housing estate of the early 1950s, with around 14 per cent of its area cultivated, was compared with 'better-than-average' farmland (the type of land often taken for development) then the value of output to the nation was found to be roughly the same in both cases, when allowance was made for the saving in distributive costs which resulted from growing food domestically instead of on the farm. (In the 1950s, the domestic output of vegetables and soft fruit, valued at retail prices, was some £300 per cultivated acre, or £42 per house-plot acre, whereas the output from better-than-average farmland, valued at farm-gate prices, was approximately £45 per acre.)

It was against this background of garden and farm output that the effects of differences in housing density on garden use and productivity were also appraised. The Ministries of Agriculture and Fisheries and of Housing and Local Government combined in a survey of local authority housing estates in the five county boroughs of Bristol, Doncaster, Hull, Southampton and York. The conclusion reached was that, where food crops were grown, there was a strong tendency (statistically significant in Bristol and Southampton) for the proportion of the plot cultivated to rise as housing density fell (land provision increased). In Bristol, where the tendency was most clearly marked, the increase in cultivation appeared to be greatest over the range from thirty to twenty houses to the hectare. It was impossible to make a reliable estimate of the level of food output at various densities of housing, but in the circumstances which have been outlined it was evident that the argument that building at higher densities resulted in a considerable saving of food could not be substantiated. Conversely, residential development at more open densities, while allowing for the provision of gardens of a reasonable size, would mean that the loss of output from the farmland absorbed was likely to be offset, or more than offset, by the production of fresh food at low cost by the consumers themselves.

Farmers have sometimes taken exception to these comparisons of garden and farm productivity, as though their agricultural virility were being questioned. But they have no need to feel disturbed.

Gardening is a hobby rather than a commercial enterprise; and it thereby involves, on small plots of land, very labour-intensive production which farmers could not and would not want to match when growing less intensive crops like cereals or sugar beet commercially. Equally, the contentions about garden output only have weight so long as the urban area of the country forms a relatively small proportion of the total surface area. Any suggestion that complete urbanisation of our land surface could maximise national food production is absurd. Not only would the range of cropping be severely and disastrously restricted, but it would imply a return towards a laborious, subsistence type of peasant economy. While this might commend itself to some more extreme environmentalists, the associated fall in standards of living and changes in social structure which would be entailed would hardly be acceptable to the majority of people when other options were available.

Unfortunately, no further general studies of garden use and productivity have been made since the original investigations of the 1940s and 1950s, though in 1964 a study of the gardening market in Britain produced some interesting additional information.[15] It was found that eight out of ten British households now had a garden, but three-quarters of these were less than a quarter of an acre (0.1 ha) in size while only one in twenty-five was over half an acre (0.2 ha). Indeed, more than half of all gardens, including the space taken up by the house and any garage or outbuildings, were of less than one-sixteenth of an acre (0.025 ha), or a plot measuring some 50ft × 50ft (15m × 15m). Nearly half the gardens (48 per cent) had vegetable plots, compared with a much higher proportion of 68 per cent in England and Wales alone during the wartime period in 1944. The number of vegetable plots increased over the size-range from very small to medium-sized (0.25 acre, or 0.1 ha) gardens, where they were found in two out of three of the sample. As in the 1944 study, the north of England had a particularly low proportion of cultivated vegetable plots, though allotments may have countered this deficiency to some extent.

Since the early 1960s it seems likely that garden use has changed a good deal, although there is no statistical evidence on the subject. The growth in affluence over the first half of this period was reflected in the substantial increase in car ownership and leisure pursuits which took place, and which tempted people to spend more of their greater amount of free time away from their gardens. Food crop cultivation probably declined as more easily kept lawns and flower beds extended. No doubt the process was assisted by the continuing pressure from government policy and escalating house prices to increasingly restrict the plot sizes in new residential development. There have, however, been countervailing trends. The spreading use of freezers for storing home-produced vegetables and fruit, and the stimulus to grow more domestic cheap food at a time of rapidly rising prices have also to be taken into account. Whatever the net effects, there is no question that gardening in one form or another is still at, or very near, the top of the list of outdoor leisure activities – a circumstance that the boom in garden centres over the last decade or so demonstrates only too well.[16] Clearly, private gardens – sometimes called the outside room – are an exceedingly important part of our national heritage, whether they are used for food growing, flower cultivation, children's play, clothes drying or just for relaxation and sitting in. In new housing development, we should beware of reducing their area to a size that is going to adversely restrict some of the many and varied activities which take place in them.

Although gardens provide an additional supply of vegetables and fruit for human consumption, an even more significant increment to food supplies during this present century has come from farms themselves as an outcome of replacing the agricultural horse by the tractor. Just as the tractor needs to be fuelled with oil, so the horse has to be fed with home-produced or imported feed. Unlike the tractor, this means that horses make considerable demands on land for their energy inputs, the average farm horse requiring something like 1.5 ha to support it.

In 1925, there were 773,000 horses used for agricultural purposes in England and Wales, but by 1965 the number had dropped to no more than 19,000 – a decline of 754,000.[17] If all these displaced farm horses had been fed from domestic sources, the saving in land by substituting tractors would have amounted to the formidable total of 1,131,000 ha. Yet the actual loss of farmland to urban use over these same four decades was only about 660,000 ha. Consequently, between 1925 and 1965, and even allowing for imported feedstuffs for horses, the area of agricultural land absorbed by urban growth was more than compensated for simply by the return of farmland to the production of food mainly for human beings as a result of the displacement of the farm horse by the tractor.

There is, of course, also a large and growing number of non-farm horses used for recreational and other purposes, like police and army work. Altogether, it has been estimated that the number of farm and non-farm horses in the United Kingdom in 1977 was around 500,000 and that they made use of no less than 525,000 ha of land.[18] On present trends, not much of this area is likely to find its way back into the production of food for human consumption.

Land budgets

Although of interest in the contribution it has made to our total food consumption, the additional produce provided by gardens and the displacement of farm horses is somewhat peripheral to the longer-term prospects of feeding ourselves in this country. In the first part of this chapter, we have already been looking ahead by estimating possible shifts in the overall structure of land use; and the results of these types of calculation have given rise to further investigations which have sought to examine the question of whether home-produced food supplies will be adequate over the next decade or two.

Perhaps the most fundamental point to grasp in this connection is that a loss of agricultural land does not necessarily involve a reduction in the total output of the agricultural area: indeed, the opposite normally applies. Any diminution in food supplies that might have resulted from the transfer of farmland over the last few decades has been made up many times over by the increase in productivity on the land remaining in agricultural use. For instance, between 1966/67 and 1971/72 there was a 0.5 per cent loss of farmland in the United Kingdom, but the fall in output associated with this land was offset by a far greater 15 per cent increase in agricultural gross output, net of inputs (less feed, seed and livestock), over the same period on the remaining agricultural area. Yields of individual agricultural products, taken by themselves, have also escalated remarkably since the end of the war (Table 18) in the same way that the net output of agriculture has.[19] These trends reflect the transformation of farming to a modern industry from what was basically a traditional activity before 1939.

Important as these increases in output and yields are in determining future levels of food supply, they take no account of equally significant items like population growth and rises in real incomes which push up the demand for food. More complex and comprehensive studies of whether home food supplies will be sufficient by the

Table 18 Increase in average yields of certain important agricultural products from the 1940s to the 1970s

	1946–48	*1967–69*	*1976–78*
Wheat (tonnes per ha)	2.3	3.9	4.7
Barley (tonnes per ha)	2.2	3.6	4.0
Potatoes (tonnes per ha)	17.2	24.9	27.3
Milk (litres per cow)	2,402	3,673	4,447
Eggs (per bird)	114	211	240
Tomatoes (tonnes per ha)	–	96.6	136.1

Source: National Farmers' Union (1979) *He Cares*, compiled from UK Agricultural Statistics

end of the present century have therefore been attempted. They make use of land budgets in which the future demand for agricultural land is assessed on the basis of a range of assumptions relating to population growth, changes in real income, the income elasticity of demand for food products and the level of national self-sufficiency. The results derived from these estimates are then integrated and compared with the agricultural production potential likely to be achieved after transfers of farmland to other uses and trends in the productivity of land have been taken into account. The initial concept and methodology of land budget studies, covering both the demand and supply aspects, were prescribed by Gerald Wibberley and Ruth Gasson in the 1960s.[20] Subsequent work has been built on this foundation and, in particular, Edwards and Wibberley produced at Wye College an agricultural land budget for the United Kingdom from 1965 to 2000.[21]

It is clear, in retrospect, that the Wye College budget tended to overestimate the magnitude of the variables adopted, and those used in the 'low demand assumption' now seem to be more appropriate, although even some of these (e.g. population at 67 million in 2000) still appear far too high in the light of subsequent forecasts. If, as appears likely, the demand for increased home production of food is low because of a slow growth in both population and real income per head; if there is only around a 10 per cent loss in potential agricultural production through urban extension and afforestation; and if there is a slow increase in self-sufficiency to 65 per cent of total national needs by the year 2000; then a low exponential yield increase of 1.0 per cent per annum or a linear growth of 2.5 per cent would meet the low demand assumption.[22]

The conclusion reached, therefore, is basically reassuring. From all the calculations made, it appears that

> it is possible for home agriculture to feed a growing population and maintain or possibly increase self-sufficiency levels and at the same time release land for urban growth, forestry and recreation at a rate which allows adequately for their likely future development.[23]

Some years later, this study was in effect repeated by the Centre for Agricultural Strategy (CAS) at Reading University using more up-to-date parameters for the various factors involved, though methodologically it paralleled the earlier work.[24] Given an expected population of 61 millions, a low increase in output per unit area of 1.5 per cent per year (linear), an anticipated growth in real disposable incomes of 2 to 3 per cent a year, and a transfer of land to non-agricultural uses approaching 10 per cent of the existing agricultural area, it should, according to the report, 'just be possible to maintain the existing ratio of domestic production to total requirements'. This was not a very encouraging statement and, in other words, the adequacy of home food supplies by 2000 was supposed to be on a knife-edge with little room for manoeuvre. Consequently, a real danger existed of land scarcity in the near future.

In this 'most likely' estimate of the CAS the population projection for 2000 was again much higher than would now be acceptable while the increase in output may have been set at a rather low level. Indeed, several commentators considered that the case was considerably overdrawn.[25,26,27] The most substantial assessment of this work was by two independent investigators, Wise and Fell, from the Agricultural Research Council who, in a detailed article, carefully analysed and compared the Reading and the earlier Wye College studies.[28] Significantly, they concluded that 'contrary to the impression conveyed in the CAS report, their estimates are more "optimistic" than those of Edwards and Wibberley', and 'both studies, in fact, lead to the same overall result, namely that expected increases in agricultural productivity should maintain, and even modestly increase, the degree of United Kingdom self-sufficiency in primary agricultural products.'

In terms of land use, the findings were even more forthright. On the basis of these land budget calculations, they declared that 'there appears to be little justification for the considerable publicity given to the suggestion that losses of agricultural land to the urban sector constitute a main threat to the United Kingdom food supply'.

Self-sufficiency

Wise and Fell pressed home this analysis still more. In their discussion, they pointed out that neither of the land budget studies envisaged a situation in 2000 in which complete self-sufficiency in temperate food supplies was being aimed at (an extremely dubious economic objective in any case). Yet even had they done so, the reduction, or even prevention, of further loss of farmland to urban growth would not have reduced the necessary growth in agricultural productivity by more than a very small amount. Marked changes in other sectors of the budgets would be needed to bring about such a result, and fundamental alterations in the structure of British agriculture and in the eating habits of the population might become inevitable.[29],[30] Moreover, Margaret Anderson rightly contends that a move towards complete self-sufficiency in food might well lead to a stimulation rather than a diminution of urban growth.[31] She comments that most of the scenarios proposed to bring about this objective of self-supply entail a large increase, perhaps by more than 50 per cent, in the number of people directly employed in agriculture. Clearly, these people would have to be found homes on or reasonably close to their workplaces, and consequently a massive and widespread rural building programme would be required. This would conflict directly with present policies to contain village and small town expansion and to protect all reasonably good farmland from development.

The complicating social and economic factors – and they are many – which complete self-sufficiency in temperate foods would imply, mean that the attainment of this objective would be difficult, though certainly not impossible, if the country were prepared to forgo many cherished aspects of its present standard of living. Anderson has summarised the position by indicating that the possible ways of attaining far greater self-sufficiency than at present are threefold: to change the pattern of agricultural output; to reorganise farms and farming methods; and to attempt to reduce the population.[32] Needless to say, substantial difficulties would be experienced in trying to put any of these solutions into effect.

All the same, one additional aid towards greater home production of food which may come about in the next few decades is the partial replacement of traditional agricultural products by alternative and synthetic foods, especially industrially-produced meat and dairy produce. In his work on food substitutes, Michael Boddington calculated in 1973 that, even by the year 2000, about 3 million to 3.5 million hectares of land in this country could be released from agriculture through the introduction of protein substitutes.[33] This process would not only release poorer quality pasture land, but might also allow better land under fodder crops to be turned to alternative uses.[34] Food substitutes, however, are not mentioned as a serious possibility in the land budget studies which have been discussed, and therefore their potential effects are not allowed for in the calculations made.

A final aspect of the food supply position which has also been neglected in existing land budget studies is that the United Kingdom is now an integral part of the European Economic Community. This is particularly pertinent when it is appreciated that the EEC as a whole could, without dispute, be easily self-sufficient in temperate foods. Not only is this so, but the 1970s have also demonstrated most forcibly that the main and continuing problems of EEC agriculture (and of UK agriculture in certain products) are not any shortage of land or production, but the converse dilemma of a persistent surplus of several basic products and the abandonment of marginal farmland not needed any longer for agricultural purposes[35]: in other words, not too little food but too much. How the food supply prospects for the people of the United Kingdom can, in these circumstances, be considered as gravely threatened is, to say the least, not very apparent.[36]

Summary

Forecasts of future changes in land use between 1971 and 2001 suggest that the agricultural coverage of Great Britain will fall by some 5 per cent to below three-quarters of the land surface. Conversely, forest and woodland will probably extend over another 3 per cent of the surface and urban land by well over another 2 per cent.

In England and Wales alone, the extent of the urban area by 2001 is likely to be about 14 per cent of the surface compared with 11 per cent in 1971. Looking further ahead, urban uses would occupy approximately one-quarter of the land surface by the end of the twenty-first century, if urban growth continued at recent rates – a most unlikely occurrence. On the same basis, the whole land surface of England and Wales would be fully covered by urban development in another 800 years or so.

Building on farmland does not involve a complete loss of food output. Eighty per cent of British homes have gardens, and although these are normally quite small, some 14 per cent of the whole house-plot was used for the cultivation of vegetables and fruit in the 1950s. At that time, in financial terms, the gardens of housing estates produced approximately as much food as the farmland they replaced, and there was a tendency for the proportion of the plot cultivated to rise as housing density fell (land provision increased). Another source of additional food supplies has come from the replacement of the farm horse by the tractor. In the forty years prior to 1965, the loss of agricultural land to urban growth was more than compensated for by the decline in the land needed for the feeding of farm horses.

Land budgets for the United Kingdom, compiled for up to the year 2000, indicate that forecasted transfers of farmland to woodland and urban growth will not affect the ability of agriculture to feed a growing population and to maintain, or even increase, the level of self-sufficiency in temperate foods. Complete self-sufficiency in temperate foods (a doubtful economic goal anyway) would be possible, but only if the country were prepared to forgo many accustomed aspects of the present standard of living. However, land budget calculations have neglected the potential contribution of alternative and synthetic foods and the integration of the United Kingdom into a largely self-sufficient EEC agricultural structure.

References

1 Gabor, D. (1963) *Inventing the Future*, London, Secker & Warburg.
2 Schumacher, E.F. (1973) *Small is Beautiful*, London, Blond & Briggs.
3 Kennedy, B. (1979) 'A naughty world', *Transactions of the Institute of British Geographers*, 4 (4), 550–8.
4 Stamp, L.D. (1950) 'Planning and agriculture', *Journal of the Town Planning Institute*, 36 (4), 141–52.
5 Anon. (1954) 'Estimating the spread of towns into the country', *Manchester Guardian*, 30 August.
6 The Economist Intelligence Unit (1957) 'Land use and farming – a pointer to the next twenty years', *Agricultural Review*, 2 (8), 60–3.

7   Agriculture EDC (1977) *Agriculture into the 1980s: Land Use*, National Economic Development Office.

8   Forestry Commission (1977) *The Wood Production Outlook in Britain: a Review*. See also: Institute of Terrestrial Ecology (1979) *Upland Land Use in England and Wales*, Countryside Commission.

9   Centre for Agricultural Strategy (1980) *Strategy for the UK Forest Industry*, Report No. 6, University of Reading.

10 Ministry of Agriculture, Fisheries and Food (1979) 'Agriculture in 2000 A.D.', in Royal Commission on Environmental Pollution (1979) *Seventh Report: Agriculture and Pollution*, Cmnd. 7644, App. 6, HMSO.

11 Best, R.H. (1972) 'March of the concrete jungle', *Geographical Magazine*, 45 (1), 47–51.

12 Barnett, G.E. (1936) *Two Tracts by Gregory King*, Baltimore, Johns Hopkins University Press.

13 The Social Survey (1945) *Domestic Food Production*, Central Office of Information.

14 Best, R.H. and Ward, J.T. (1956) *The Garden Controversy*, Wye College.

15 Contimart Ltd (1964) *Gardening Survey, Part 1: The Gardening Market in Britain*.

16 *Countryside Commission (1979) Leisure and the Countryside*, CCP 124. See also: Patmore, J.A. (1970) *Land and Leisure*, Newton Abbot, David & Charles.

17 Ministry of Agriculture, Fisheries and Food, Department of Agriculture and Fisheries for Scotland (1968) *A Century of Agricultural Statistics, Great Britain 1866–1966*, HMSO.

18 Riley, P.J. and Warren, D.S. (1979) 'Horses, farming and fuel', *New Ecologist*, 9 (2), 46–50.

19 Coppock, J.T. (1972) 'Farming for an urban nation', in Chisholm, M. (ed.) *Resources for Britain's Future*, Harmondsworth, Pelican, 36–49.

20 Gasson, R. (1966) 'The challenge to British farming, 1960 to 1970', *Westminster Bank Review*, 32–41.

21 Edwards, A.M. and Wibberley, G.P. (1971) *An Agricultural Land Budget for Britain 1965–2000*, Wye College. See also: Wibberley, G.P. (1959) *Agriculture and Urban Growth*, London, Michael Joseph.

22 Davidson, J. and Wibberley, G.P. (1977) *Planning and the Rural Environment*, Oxford, Pergamon.

23 Edwards, A.M. and Wibberley, G.P. (1971) op. cit.

24 Centre for Agricultural Strategy (1976) *Land for Agriculture*, Report No. 1, University of Reading.

25 Peters, G.H. (1977) Review of *Land for Agricultural* in *Town and Country Planning*, 45 (12), 553–4.

26 A.G. Champion (1977) Review of *Land for Agriculture* in *Journal of Agricultural Economics*, 28 (3), 320–2.

27   Whitby, M.C. and Willis, K.G. (1978) *Rural Resource Development: An Economic Approach* (2nd edn), London, Methuen.

28   Wise, W.S. and Fell, E. (1978) 'UK agricultural productivity and the land budget', *Journal of Agricultural Economics*, 29 (1), 1–7.

29   Mellanby, K. (1975) *Can Britain Feed Itself?* London, Merlin Press.

30   Blaxter, K. (1975) 'Can Britain feed herself?', *New Scientist*, 65, 941.

31   Anderson, M.A. (1975) 'Land planning implications of increased food supplies', *The Planner*, 61 (10), 381–3.

32   ibid.

33   Boddington, M. (1973) 'A food factory', *Built Environment*, 2 (8), 443–5.

34   Calder, N. (1967) *The Environment Game*, London, Secker & Warburg.

35   Organisation for Economic Co-operation and Development (1976) *Land Use Policies and Agriculture*, Paris.

36   Best, R.H. (1977) 'Agricultural land loss – myth or reality?' *The Planner*, 63 (1), 15–16. See also: Ritson, C. (1980) *Self-Sufficiency and Food Security*, Centre for Agricultural Strategy, Paper No. 8, University of Reading.

7
Regional urban growth and agricultural displacement[1]

Greater London, bounded by sea to south and east, had eaten further into Northern Province and Western Province: the new northern limit was a line running from Lowestoft to Birmingham; to the west the boundary dropped from Birmingham to Bournemouth. Intending migrants from the Provinces to Greater London had, it was said, no need to move; they merely had to wait.

(Anthony Burgess: *The Wanting Seed*)

It is all too often assumed that the conversion of agricultural land to other uses, and particularly to urban use, occurs at a broadly similar rate across most of the country, or at least over relatively large parts of it. If any concession is made to regional differentiation, it is usually to allow that urban growth and agricultural displacement are particularly rapid in the midlands and the south-east (or so it is suspected), with afforestation focused on Highland Britain. More precisely, new urban development is thought to be concentrated along a belt of country stretching from Lancashire in the north-west, diagonally through the midlands, to the London conurbation and the south-east coast. This tract has been variously described as the axial belt, coffin, hour-glass and dumb-bell, the last two appellations indicating rather more exactly its supposed shape and form.[2] Nowadays, following the terminology used for describing urban regions in the United States, it has become more fashionable to designate this area as Megalopolis England.

A detailed study by Peter Hall and his associates concluded that this tract could be meaningfully defined in terms of sixty-three Metropolitan Economic Labour Areas, stretching 432 km from the Sussex to the Lancashire coasts in the form of the extended dumb-bell already mentioned.[3] Although, in total, the megalopolitan region occupied only 35 per cent of the land area of England and Wales, it contained nearly 70 per cent of the population and over 70

117

per cent of the employment. Overall, less than 18 per cent of the megalopolitan area was taken up by urban uses in the early 1960s, but the north-western part in Lancashire and Cheshire was the most heavily urbanised with 22 per cent, while the area around London came next with a little over 20 per cent. The other sectors had between 12 and 19 per cent of their land surface developed for urban purposes.

In line with the Peter Hall project, nearly all the studies which have contributed towards this idea of a fairly broad, but basically linear, growth area across England have been based on investigations of population changes, the number and hierarchy of cities and towns, employment statistics, the increase of industrial sites of various types, new transport facilities, and newly planned urban developments.[4] The areal extent of this urban growth each year and its changing magnitude over time had been impossible or very hazardous to assess because of the complete lack of any exact regional statistics on land-use changes. By the 1970s, however, the situation altered radically. New data on urban growth and agricultural displacement by counties became available, so that regional increments of development in various parts of the country, and the varying rates of change, could now be examined in some detail.

Regional land-use charges, 1955–60

Prior to the 1970s, studies of regional shifts in land use had to rely on the county Agricultural Statistics as their source of data. Paradoxically, as we have seen in Chapter 2, the comparability of these statistics over a number of years was often vitiated by their increasing completeness and accuracy. This was because of the progressive inclusion of farmland previously escaping enumeration, allied with certain alterations in definition and the return of land to agricultural use from the fighting services. With these restrictions in mind, the analysis of regional change in England and Wales had eventually to be confined to the five-year period from 1955 to 1960. An additional difficulty in the analysis was that transfers of farmland to forestry and other uses could not be separated statistically from those to urban development. However, because afforestation was concentrated in the north and west of the country, it was possible to achieve some rough differentiation from areas in which urban growth was predominant.

From the investigation (Fig. 8) it was found that the average rate

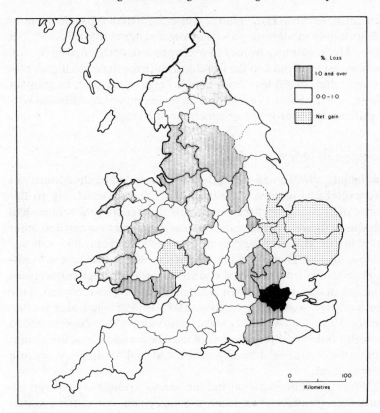

Figure 8 Transfers of farmland to all other uses in England and Wales by counties, 1955–60

of land transfers from agriculture to all other uses in England and Wales amounted to 0.7 per cent of the total area of the country between 1955 and 1960.[5] Compared with this figure, much of England showed only a low rate of agricultural land losses (not exceeding 0.5 per cent) with net gains of farmland actually occurring in a group of counties in East Anglia and around the Wash – the most productive agricultural region of the country. Indeed, the whole eastern side of England from Kent up to the north of Yorkshire experienced very little change from its essentially agricultural character over the years in question. Similarly, the west, south-west and parts of southern England showed only a slow, or very slow, net rate of change from agriculture to other uses.

In all, as many as twenty-five of the old administrative counties

119

fell into the 'low rate' group, while a further thirteen counties showed only moderate rates of change, ranging from 0.5 to 1 per cent. The remaining twenty-two counties, concentrated in Wales, north-west England and the London area, experienced a higher rate of agricultural land loss amounting to over 1 per cent. In many of these, afforestation as well as urban development contributed very significantly towards the greater rate of change.

Location of urban growth

In the late 1960s a new set of data was provided by the Ministry of Agriculture to replace the earlier restricted material. Up to this time, the 'Change in area' section of the agricultural returns had produced figures for the conversion of farmland to urban and other uses, but the data were aggregated and published only on a national basis with no regional breakdown. After 1968, however, the Ministry made available a set of county statistics for agricultural displacement and urban growth in England and Wales recorded in the form of five-year averages from 1945 to 1965 and also for the period 1962–67.[6] At a later stage, figures for 1965–70 were added as well.[7] Individual years were not used because of some misgivings about the degree of accuracy of the material for single years at a county level.

Within each five-year period the *annual average* area of agricultural land transferred to urban use was given, but as the counties varied considerably in size, the losses for different counties were not comparable. Hence, it was necessary to convert the hectares into percentages of the total county areas. These percentages, which related to the average proportion of the county areas converted from agricultural to urban use *each year* over the stated period, were all far less than unity and were rounded to two places of decimals. For the most part, changes in county boundaries over the periods under examination did not cause any statistical difficulties, apart from the creation of the Greater London Council area in 1965. Previous to this year, farmland losses within the original London Administrative County were divided between the adjoining counties of Middlesex, Surrey and Kent, except for the 1962–67 period when the new boundaries associated with the GLC area were employed throughout.

The definition of 'urban development' used in the context of this investigation coincided closely with the definition as discussed in

Chapter 2, and the figures covered transfers to residential areas, buildings of all types, industry, schools, recreational and other open space (including allotments), roads and railways, and even reservoirs, though they excluded alienations of farmland to mineral workings (except in 1965–70). Often, there was probably a time-lag in the recorded conversions, with development being delayed, especially if the land in question was held for speculative purposes (see Chapter 5).

The regional shifts of land out of agriculture and into urban use are summarized in the five maps in Figure 9, covering the five-year periods between 1945 and 1970. Only three conversion rates are distinguished on these maps so as to indicate the regional variations over time more distinctly. The first class-interval, for an annual transfer rate of 0.0–0.1 per cent, represents a small rate of change which is nearly always below, and frequently well below, the national average. The second class-interval, 0.1–0.2 per cent, usually reflects a moderate conversion of land which is often fairly close to, or rather above, the national average. The third interval, 0.2–0.3 per cent or more, indicates a relatively high rate of urban growth and agricultural loss which is about double, or more than double, the national average.

To begin with, it will be useful to consider the five maps as a composite whole (see also Fig. 14). If this is done, the concept of a broad and homogeneous belt of fairly substantial urban growth and agricultural displacement extending diagonally across the country from north-west England to the south-east coast is seen to be of somewhat doubtful validity. Instead, it would be more correct to distinguish two widespread areas of fairly rapid urban growth, the two ends of the previously mentioned dumb-bell, separated from each other by a rather narrow band of country, running south-west from the Wash to Wiltshire, and showing below-average rates of change. Of these two growth areas, which consisted of counties with above-average conversion rates from 1945 to 1965, the more southerly coincided very largely with the Greater London conurbation and its surrounding counties. This area is the London Region which, as its name implies, is focused on the metropolis itself.[8] Not unexpectedly, the rate of conversion from agricultural to urban use declined outward in a fairly regular gradient from the home counties towards East Anglia, the midlands, south-west England and the south coast.

In contrast to this region, which is ordered around a single major

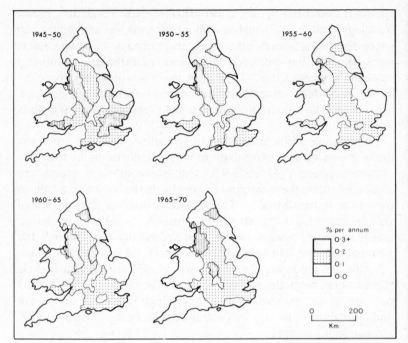

Figure 9 Regional transfers of agricultural land to urban use in England and Wales, 1945–70. Note that in 1945–50 Middlesex had an exceptionally high conversion rate of 0.5 per cent

nucleus, the area of substantial urban growth and agricultural displacement in the north and west of the country comprised a group of several northern and midland conurbations. In particular, there was a strip of counties connecting the Lancashire, Merseyside and West Midlands conurbations where new development and agricultural land losses were most marked (over 0.2 per cent). This strip adjoined a group of more easterly counties, from the West Riding, through Nottinghamshire, to Leicestershire, with lesser rates of urban growth. A physical separation of these two components was effected by the Pennines and the Peak District which formed a green heart to the urban agglomeration. The whole area has been called the Central Urban Region by R.H. Osborne following the terminology originally used by K.C. Edwards and E.M. Rawstron.[9] This is a convenient, collective name and will also be adopted here.

As well as these two main areas of urban growth, there were also two other smaller and somewhat detached centres. In the northeast, the county of Durham, which included part of the Tyneside and Teesside conurbations, provided an outlier from the Central Urban Region. At the other end of this tract, there was a rather tenuous connection through Worcestershire and Gloucestershire with the South Wales conurbation where fairly rapid change was also in progress.

If the London Region and the Central Urban Region and its outliers were abstracted, there remained large parts of the country which were experiencing below-average rates of agricultural/urban conversion. Although these areas contained some cities and sizeable towns, they could be regarded as the predominantly rural regions of England and Wales. Indeed, there were within these regions extensive areas of relative remoteness where urban growth was extremely small. To bring the situation into its true perspective, it should be noted that as many as thirty-two counties had agricultural/urban conversion rates below the national average (0.1 per cent), and twenty-one at or below 0.05 per cent, the average for Wales. Such areas were particularly prevalent along the eastern side of England, in the south-west and in Wales.

Regional trends

The generalised features in the pattern of urban growth can be discerned in varying degrees on each of the five maps in Figure 9. When the maps are considered in sequence, however, significant and quite dramatic regional trends immediately become apparent. It will be noticed that, over the twenty years from 1945, the rate of agricultural/urban conversion in the Central Urban Region as a whole was similar to, or greater than, that in the London Region (Table 19). Although this fact can be seen from the actual conversion rates alone, it is confirmed more definitely by the translation of the original data into index numbers. This adjustment removes the distortion introduced by variations in the national rates of transfer when making comparisons in the sequence of quinquennial time periods.

But what is perhaps still more unexpected is that the differential between the overall urban growth rates of the two regions increased rapidly after the end of the 1950s. This divergence, which gathered momentum in the 1960s, resulted in a marked and growing shift of emphasis in the conversion of agricultural land to urban use towards the northern and western parts of England and Wales and away from the south-east. The widening gap between the conversion

Table 19 Rates of agricultural/urban conversion of land in the major regions of England and Wales, 1945–65. Actual conversion rates, and an index to remove distortions for comparative purposes, are recorded

Area	Five-year average			
	1945–50	*1950–55*	*1955–60*	*1960–65*
Conversion rate (per cent)				
Central Urban Region	0.20	0.18	0.15	0.20
London Region	0.19	0.18	0.14	0.12
Rural regions	0.06	0.04	0.03	0.05
England and Wales	0.12	0.10	0.08	0.10
Conversion index				
Central Urban Region	172	183	183	196
London Region	163	176	169	125
Rural regions	49	39	42	50
England and Wales	100	100	100	100

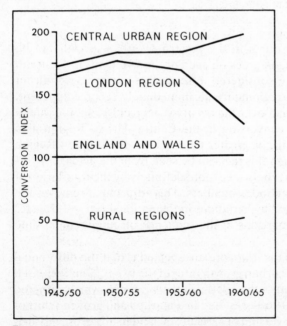

Figure 10 Trends in urban growth and agricultural displacement in the London Region, Central Urban Region and the predominantly Rural Regions of England and Wales, 1945–65, as indicated by an agricultural–urban conversion index

rates for the two regions is shown graphically in Figure 10.

As so often happens, such broad generalisations about large regions of the country are in danger of masking certain smaller-scale, but equally revealing, variations. Indeed, the slowing-down of transfers of agricultural land to urban use in the London Region, and the apparent saturation of development being approached in some parts of the conurbation, can perhaps best be appreciated by reference to the trends in individual counties or small county group-ings. With this point in mind, it will be observed that, in the years from 1945 to 1950, the regional configuration of urban develop-ment was not, in fact, so very different from the conventional views on the subject. The distinction between the London Region and the Central Urban Region growth areas was fairly well defined, but, although the latter region had a slightly greater agricultural/urban conversion rate and index, it was in the London Region that the heaviest concentration of land-use change was to be found, in the counties to the north and west of the metropolis. More especially, the north–south strip of home counties from Hertfordshire, through Middlesex, and into Surrey had an annual rate of transfer which was close to, or well over, 0.3 per cent. Indeed, the first two of these counties at the heart of the London Region had the highest conver-sion rate of all areas in England and Wales at this time.

Away from this central core around London itself, urban growth in the region was widespread, though noticeably less intense. Mod-erate rates of conversion, of between 0.1 and 0.2 per cent, extended into East Anglia and even to the Wash in one direction, and to the south coast in another. On the other hand, the Central Urban Region showed moderate or high rates of urban expansion over a very considerable area. In particular, a north–south line of counties from Lancashire to Warwickshire, together with the outliers of Glamorgan and Durham, had high agricultural/urban conversion rates of between 0.2 and 0.3 per cent a year. Nevertheless, in no single sector did the scale of land conversion attain the level to be seen in the inner portions of the London Region.

This general pattern of urban growth and agricultural displace-ment was already beginning to alter somewhat by the years 1950–55. Hertfordshire, where several new towns were being built, dominated the picture with a rise in its conversion rate to 0.4 per cent. But in contrast, Middlesex and Surrey, which had previously been so outstanding, now had a marked slackening in their rates of land transfer. Moreover, it is of significance that the rates of urban expansion in the northern parts of the region towards the Wash and East Anglia had also diminished, and the clear-cut gap with relatively little land-use change, located between the London Region and the Central Urban Region, became more definite.

The next quinquennium, from 1955 to 1960, is generally regarded as the period when economic affluence was becoming more established after the stringent years immediately following the end of the war. However, the actual rate of agricultural/urban conversion in this period declined very noticeably over the whole country and its constituent regions in line with strong government monetary action to combat the inflationary economy (Chapter 5). Especially noteworthy was that the high scale of transfers towards the centre of the London Region fell away markedly once more, and that, apart from Middlesex, the entire constellation of counties surrounding the metropolis showed a shift of land into urban use which was of only moderate proportions – 0.1 to 0.2 per cent a year. This rate was continued across Northamptonshire and into the Central Urban Region, where the West Midlands conurbation showed a similar decline in conversion rates. Only Lancashire and Cheshire retained a substantial transfer of 0.2 to 0.3 per cent, and they were joined at this level by Monmouthshire. England and Wales, as a whole, now presented a comparatively unvaried aspect with the urban growth areas all having only a moderate magnitude of agricultural/urban conversion, apart from the few counties which have been specifically mentioned.

These years in the second half of the 1950s saw the crucial changeover in emphasis of regional land conversions, and between 1960 and 1965 a very different situation emerged. As previously noted, the land conversion index of the Central Urban Region increased, whereas the index for the London Region sharply diminished. But the changes in individual counties were occasionally even more pronounced, a few of those in the north-west increasing their conversion rates markedly. Under these altering circumstances, it is not surprising to discover that, by the first half of the 1960s, the two counties with the highest agricultural/urban conversion rates in the country, Cheshire and Lancashire, were both located in the north-western part of the Central Urban Region, a complete contrast with the situation in 1945–50. Even so, taking the long view, the increase in their rates above the level of the early postwar years was not nearly so startling as the decline to be seen in the two corresponding London Region counties. Over this period

Hertfordshire and Middlesex, as well as Surrey and many adjacent counties, showed substantial reductions in their conversion rates, sometimes by as much as one-half to two-thirds. Hence, the Central Urban Region started to become particularly prominent in its scale of urban expansion and agricultural displacement while the London Region continued to fade. These trends generally persisted to 1970, though the 'rural' constriction between the two regions showed signs of disappearing.

Urban growth patterns, 1962–67

The last completely comparable set of figures (Table 20) and the larger-scale map (Fig. 11) for the overlapping period from 1962 to 1967 confirm the general trend of urban growth patterns. A map of population change over almost the same period (Fig. 12) is also included for comparative purposes and will be discussed later. The more detailed representation of counties used for recording the rates of land conversion helps to emphasise still further the consid-erable distinction between the north and the south of the country during the mid-1960s. A virtual saturation of development was being approached in the inner parts of the London Region with a number of adjacent counties hovering around the 0.1 per cent (or national average) level of change. The section of the conurbation extending from Hertfordshire to Surrey, which had the highest transfer rates in the early postwar period, was now almost com-pletely altered in this respect and had been replaced by a 'depres-sion' in the centre of the region. This reflected the even lower rates of urban growth being experienced towards the regional core com-pared with the outer metropolitan areas and was, of course, a situation which paralleled population trends.

In marked contrast, Cheshire and Lancashire in the Central Urban Region maintained a high annual rate of agricultural land transfers to urban use (0.29 per cent) which was above that of even the early postwar period (0.26 per cent). Moreover, after a tempor-ary lapse in 1955–60, Durham, certain of the midland counties, and parts of South Wales were now also showing considerable conver-sion rates. Consequently, the Central Urban Region and its outliers were continuing to experience a distinctly greater rate of agricul-tural/urban conversion than the London Region. It is hardly neces-sary to add that this conclusion, and those previously reached concerning the trends occurring in these two regions, ran directly

Table 20 Transfers of agricultural land to urban development in England and Wales by counties, 1962–67

County	Five-year average 1962–67		County	Five-year average 1962–67	
	ha	per cent		ha	per cent
Bedford [a]	136	0.11	Somerset	323	0.08
Berkshire [a]	206	0.11	Stafford [b]	705	0.24
Buckingham [a]	222	0.11	Suffolk (E and W)	287	0.07
Cambridge and Isle of Ely	78	0.04	Surrey [a,c]	230	0.14
			Sussex, East [a]	189	0.09
Cheshire [b]	753	0.29	Sussex, West [a]	138	0.08
Cornwall	234	0.07	Warwick [b]	542	0.22
Cumberland	133	0.03	Westmorland	52	0.02
Derby [b]	286	0.11	Wiltshire	242	0.07
Devon	442	0.06	Worcester [b]	255	0.14
Dorset	165	0.07	Yorks., E. Riding	237	0.08
Durham [b]	683	0.26	Yorks., N. Riding	370	0.07
Essex [a,c]	546	0.15	Yorks., W. Riding [b]	1,261	0.17
Gloucester [b]	485	0.16			
Hampshire and Isle of Wight [a]	631	0.15	*England*	14,683	0.11
Hereford	58	0.03	Anglesey	142	0.20
Hertford [a]	305	0.19	Brecon	20	0.01
Huntingdon and Peterborough	152	0.12	Caernarvon	54	0.04
			Cardigan	31	0.02
Kent [a,c]	411	0.11	Carmarthen	38	0.02
Lancashire [b]	1,409	0.29	Denbigh	101	0.06
Leicester [b]	386	0.18	Flint [b]	112	0.17
Lincoln (Holland)	44	0.04	Glamorgan [b]	468	0.22
Lincoln (Kesteven)	87	0.05	Merioneth	33	0.02
Lincoln (Lindsey)	235	0.06	Monmouth [b]	297	0.21
Greater London [a,c]	113	0.07	Montgomery	28	0.01
Norfolk	296	0.06	Pembroke	65	0.04
Northampton	229	0.10	Radnor	8	0.01
Northumberland	276	0.05			
Nottingham [b]	434	0.20	*Wales*	1,398	0.07
Oxford	155	0.08			
Rutland	31	0.08			
Shropshire	224	0.06	*England and Wales*	16,081	0.11

The hectares recorded are the annual averages for the five-year period from 1962–67. The percentage figures are these losses expressed as a proportion of the total county area

[a] London Region counties
[b] Central Urban Region counties
[c] The figures relate to the areas of Greater London and the adjacent counties as designated in 1965

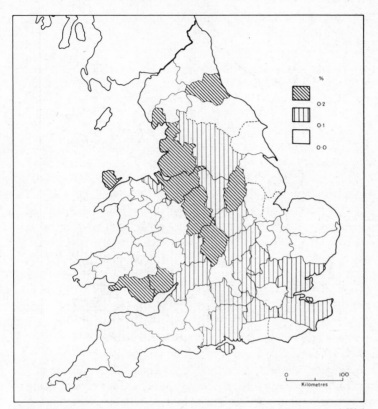

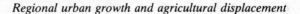

Figure 11 Transfers of agricultural land to urban use in England and Wales by counties, 1962–67

counter to conventionally held concepts.

Whatever the difference between the trends in the London Region and the Central Urban Region, it is also instructive to make some comparisons with those other parts of the country which had experienced a much slower process of urban growth in the postwar period. As seen previously, the conversion rates in most of these predominantly rural regions were well below the average for England and Wales. This situation was further stressed by the land conversion index which had been at, or below, 50 (England and Wales 100) over the whole postwar period up to the late 1960s for the combined rural sectors outside the two main urban growth regions. A selection of individual counties made from these largely rural regions (e.g. Westmorland, Lincoln, Devon and Cardigan) all

129

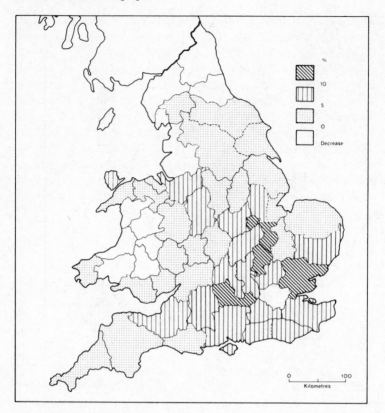

Figure 12 Population changes in England and Wales by counties, 1961–66. The data are derived from the reports of the 1961 Census and the 1966 Sample Census

showed fairly standard features of land-use change over the years from 1945 to 1967. In this time, there was only a relatively slow, and frequently a very slow, rate of agricultural/urban conversion with a certain amount of variability at a rather low level. As a result, the contrast in rates of urban development between the largely rural and the more generally urban parts of England and Wales was well emphasised, just as the difference between the London Region and the Central Urban Region had been in the decade or so up to 1970.

This distinction between the central core of urbanising regions and the peripheral distribution of more rural regions is brought out in Figure 11. In many ways it reflects the marked differentiation recognised by Paul Cloke in his detailed study of spatial patterns of rurality in 1961 and 1971.[10] However, he points to what he considers to be two significant departures from these findings in his own work. Firstly, the rural 'gap' between the London Region and the Central Urban Region is shown to be closing quickly, and secondly, there was a significant spread of urbanisation from the London conurbation towards Wiltshire and East Anglia by 1971. In fact, these trends are, on the whole, confirmed by Tony Champion from the further data on regional land conversions for the period from 1965 to 1970.[11]

In Scotland, the corresponding figures for land conversions from 1962 to 1967 also show a considerable range of difference between counties and regions (Fig. 13). Predictably, rapid urban growth was

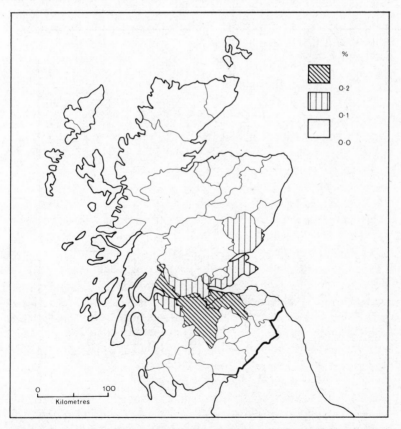

Figure 13 Transfers of agricultural land to urban use in Scotland by counties, 1962–67

closely confined to the central lowlands, with West Lothian, Midlothian and Dunbarton all having a high conversion rate of over 0.3 per cent a year of the total county area.[12] Altogether, only eleven counties, or less than one-fifth of the land area of country, had agricultural/urban transfer rates higher than the Scottish annual average of 0.035 per cent. The remaining four-fifths of the country had very small, and often negligible, rates of urban growth and agricultural displacement.

Champion subsequently analysed in greater detail certain of the regional aspects of urban growth in England and Wales.[13] In particular, he was able for the first time to present a sound picture of proportionate urban coverage by counties as it existed in about 1950 and 1970 (Fig. 4), while also giving a broader indication of

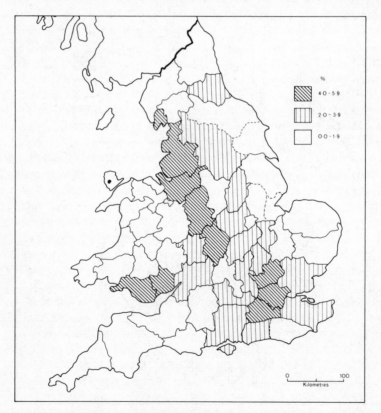

Figure 14 Transfers of agricultural land to urban use in England and Wales by counties, 1950–70 (After Champion, 1974)

urban growth over the whole twenty years from 1950 to 1970, again based on 'Change in area' data (Fig. 14). The features already discussed are once more apparent at this generalised level, and Champion also points out that a comparison of the cartographic information demonstrates how urban expansion over time is tending to reinforce existing patterns of urban coverage, especially along the 'axial belt'.

Urban growth and population change

It remains to seek an explanation for the different trends in the rates of conversion of agricultural land into urban use which have been outlined in the two main urban growth areas of England and Wales. Initially, in the early postwar years, natural growth of population allied with the 'drift to the south' seem to have borne at least some relation to land-use changes, with a noticeable concentration of population increase and urban extension in the London Region. Even then, however, certain northern counties with a low rate of population growth showed a substantial annual extension of urban land.

Figures 11 and 12 record the spatial pattern of change in urban land and population, respectively, at a more recent date, over roughly the same period in the 1960s. A comparison of the two maps does not suggest that any clear relationship between population increase and the regional scale of urban growth was maintained. On the contrary, the two patterns which are revealed are contradictory to a large extent. At this time, population was still increasing most rapidly in the London Region, whereas the conversion of agricultural land to urban development, as already shown, was greatest in the Central Urban Region. Indeed, two counties with very high agricultural/urban transfer rates, Lancashire and Durham, actually had absolute decreases in population.

Although these discrepancies between changes in population and urban growth patterns seem confusing at first sight, in reality they are not too difficult to explain. Most importantly, it must be recognised that natural growth of population and inter-county migration are by no means the sole generators of areal gains in urban land. It is easy to neglect the fact that, when shifting their location, the majority of households move only short distances. Therefore, while towns and conurbations can expand physically by gaining population on their peripheries, much of this increase may result from people moving out from nearer the urban central area to the urban fringes. As such movements often do not involve inter-county exchanges, urban extension can easily occur without any corresponding shifts in population being apparent at a county or regional level.

This migration over short distances is particularly relevant to the present discussion when people are moving from high density central areas in older cities and towns to lower density estates built on rural land in the outskirts. In this process, an additional area of land compared with the original site is obviously required to accommodate the same population. The magnitude of this increase in land requirements can be gauged by contrasting the figures of residential land provision in county boroughs, which included a high proportion of northern industrial towns, and in large town map areas, which were sizeable settlements with a considerable element of twentieth-century suburban housing. These 1961 land provisions of 9.4 ha/1000p and 13.0 ha/1000p, respectively, point to the much greater openness achieved in towns with a higher proportion of more recent development.[14]

Migration of this type was often associated with urban redevelopment of central areas in the 1960s, and another aspect of such movements is that household formation is normally accelerated.[15] This has also been an important contributory factor to the general increase in land needs. But, although over half of all urban demands on land arise from new residential development, it must not be forgotten that a more adequate provision of land for other urban uses, such as open space, schools and factories, also helps to swell the requirements for land. For many urban land uses, northern towns have had a distinctly poorer provision of space in general than towns in other parts of the country, so that inevitably there was a tendency for new development to make good the deficiency.[16] Taken together, these factors can account for much of the greater rate of urban growth experienced in the north of the country.

To sum up, then, it may be said that the high rate of urban growth and agricultural displacement in several northern and western counties reflected the increasing adoption of more adequate and reasonable standards of urban living space which had already been more widely achieved in the south. Indeed, in this latter part of the country, a contrary trend contributed to the situation seen there. In certain parts of south-east England, densities of development were low, and even exceptionally low, by British standards, and there has been every indication of a tightening-up of space provisions over many years within the existing urban area.[17] For example, the more numerous open spaces in lower density districts and the sites of older houses with extensive grounds have often been developed to accommodate more houses and many more people at higher density without adding to the existing stock of urban land or using up any farmland in the process. A study by Tony Champion has given considerable substance to this trend.[18] He shows how, between 1950 and 1970, all the south-eastern counties except Greater London had a reduction in urban land provision (a tightening of densities) of up to 10 ha/1000p, with Buckinghamshire, Hertfordshire and Essex being most severely affected. In marked contrast, Wales and the north of England recorded an increase in urban provision of over twice the national average of 3 ha/1000p.

In this connection, it is interesting to recall the evidence adduced by Clark, Best and others (Chapter 4) for postulating that space provisions in predominantly residential areas are converging towards a 'pivotal' density, with higher density areas losing population and lower density areas gaining it. For England and Wales, it has been suggested that such a pivotal density in towns may be 30–5 ha/1000p for all urban uses, including open space, industry, schools, shops, offices, public buildings and transport, as well as housing.[19] The differential rates of regional urban growth which have just been discussed lend further, if indirect, support to this general contention.

Finally, one very important methodological conclusion arises from the study of this altering regional configuration of urban extension and agricultural displacement. Because of the lack of data on land-use changes, it has become commonplace to use figures for past and projected trends in population, derived from census information, as indicators of alterations in land use. Such substitute material is now seen to be of very dubious value in this context and, on occasion, may give a completely distorted impression of the areal changes which are actually occurring.

At least three different factors contribute materially to the extension of urban land, though they are closely interrelated in practice. Firstly, there is growth in the national economy with the additional demands on land for new factory sites, transport facilities, and so on, which such a process involves. Secondly, there is a combination of natural population growth and in-migration which, over time, expresses itself through the demand for additional housing, schools, recreational provision, commercial requirements, statutory undertakings and the like; and thirdly, there is the increase in urban space standards for the existing population and the associated need for extra increments of land which stem from the increasing affluence of society. Therefore, no direct and simple relationship necessarily exists between growth in population and the extension of urban land, although many planning studies made since the war would imply that it does.

Summary

The Ministry of Agriculture, Fisheries and Food provided a set of regional statistics for the conversion of agricultural land to urban use in England and Wales for five-year periods from 1945 to 1970. These data indicated that the existence of a broad zone of fairly substantial urban growth and agricultural displacement, coinciding with the so-called 'axial belt' or 'dumb-bell' stretching diagonally across England, was of somewhat doubtful validity until the 1970s. It was more correct to distinguish two widespread areas of relatively rapid urban growth separated from each other by a rather narrow band of only weakly urbanising country. One of these divisions, termed the Central Urban Region, was composed of counties chiefly in the north-west of England and the West Midlands. The other division could be largely equated with the London Region. The remaining, predominantly rural, parts of England and Wales showed relatively small rates of urban growth and agricultural displacement.

Since 1945, regional conversion rates of agricultural land into urban use have altered significantly. Until the end of the 1950s, the Central Urban Region had, overall, only a slightly greater conversion rate or index than the London Region, but subsequently the gap widened sharply. Nevertheless, in the period 1945–50 the counties with the highest rates of transfer were at the core of the London Region. After this, however, the home counties showed a progressive decline in their conversion rates until the 1970s. This fading-away of the rate of change in the London Region meant that the most prominent area for urban growth shifted to the Central Urban Region and particularly to the north-western counties which increased their agricultural/urban conversion rates to above even the relatively high levels attained in 1945–50. This situation, which is completely contrary to established concepts, also underlines the point that radical improvements in urban space standards for the existing population, as in the northern counties, can contribute very substantially to urban demands on agricultural land.

No direct and simple relationship necessarily exists between population growth and the extension of urban land. At least three interrelated factors contribute materially to urban demands on land and, therefore, to the corresponding scale of agricultural displacement. These are: (a) growth in the national economy and the additional land needs for factory sites, transport, etc.; (b) natural population growth and in-migration, giving rise to land requirements for new housing, schools, playing fields and so forth; and (c) the increase in urban space standards, and the concomitant extra increments of land which stem from increasing affluence. Hence, statistics for population growth alone, especially when summarised at a county level, are very inadequate (and often completely inaccurate) substitutes for measures of the areal extension of urban land.

References

1 This chapter is based on a considerably modified version of: Best, R.H. and Champion, A.G. (1970) 'Regional conversions of agricultural land to urban use in England and Wales, 1945–67', *Transactions of the Institute of British Geographers*, 49, 15–32.

2 Smailes, A.E. (1961) 'The urbanisation of Britain', in *Problems of Applied Geography*, Warsaw, Polish Academy of Sciences, 131–40. See also: Best, R.H. (1965), 'Recent changes and future prospects of land use in England and Wales', *Geographical Journal*, 131 (1), 1–12.

3 Hall, P. *et al.* (1973), *The Containment of Urban England*, London, Allen & Unwin. See also: Clawson, M. and Hall, P. (1973) *Planning and Urban Growth: An Anglo-American Comparison*, Baltimore, Johns Hopkins University Press.

4 Willatts, E.C. (1962) 'Post-war development: the location of major projects in England and Wales', *Chartered Surveyor*, 94 (7), 356–63.

5 Best, R.H. (1965) op. cit.

6 Best, R.H. and Champion, A.G. (1970), op. cit.

7 Champion, A.G. (1972a) 'A comparative analysis of evolving land use patterns in selected areas of England and Wales and their relationship to regional variations in urban expansion rates since 1945', unpublished Ph.D. thesis, University of Oxford.

8 Coppock, J.T. and Prince, H.C. (eds) (1964) *Greater London*, London, Faber & Faber.

9 Osborne, R.H. (1964) 'Population', in Watson, J.W. and Sissons, J.B. (eds) *The British Isles – A Systematic Geography*, London, Nelson, 331–57.

10 Cloke, P.J. (1979) *Key Settlements in Rural Areas*, London, Methuen.
11 Champion, A.G. (1972a) op. cit.
12 Champion, A.G. (1969) 'The changing land requirements of planned urban development with particular reference to the land use structure and land provision adopted by British new towns since 1960', unpublished M. Phil. thesis, University of London.
13 Champion, A.G. (1974) *An Estimate of the Changing Extent and Distribution of Urban Land in England and Wales, 1950–70*, Centre for Environmental Studies, RP 10.
14 Jones, A.R. (1974) 'An analysis of the major features of urban land use and land provision in cities and towns of England and Wales in about 1960, with special reference to development plan data', unpublished Ph.D. thesis, University of London.
15 Cullingworth, J.B. (1960), *Housing Needs and Planning Policy*, London, Routledge & Kegan Paul.
16 Champion, A.G. (1972b) *Variations in Urban Densities between Towns of England and Wales*, RP 1, School of Geography, University of Oxford.
17 Bruce, M.W. (1967) 'An analysis of changes in urban land use in England and Wales since 1950 from development plan statistics for town map areas', unpublished M. Phil. thesis, University of London.
18 Champion, A.G. (1974) op. cit.
19 Best, R.H. (1968) 'Competition for land between rural and urban uses', in *Land Use and Resources: Studies in Applied Geography*, Institute of British Geographers, Special Publication No. 1, 89–100.

8
Land quality and rural land use

What would the world be, once bereft
Of wet and of wildness? Let them be left,
O let them be left, wildness and wet;
Long live the weeds and the wilderness yet

(Gerard Manley Hopkins: *Inversnaid*)

It is often contended that urban growth absorbs too great an amount of good quality farmland. Back in 1942, the Scott Committee on land utilisation in rural areas was in no doubt about it. Their report stated quite unequivocally that 'much of the population expansion has been on to the best or at least good agricultural land'.[2] Ten years later, Harold Macmillan – then the housing minister – was dispensing the same theme. 'Many thousands of acres', he wrote, 'are being taken for development every year; and much of this is good agricultural land.'[3]

Yet, in fact, there was no real evidence to confirm this conventional wisdom. Very little was known at the time about the spatial aspects of urban growth, and there were no detailed maps classifying land quality or land capability for the whole country. All that existed in published form were two 10 miles to the inch sheets covering the entire surface of Britain. They had been produced by Dudley Stamp on the basis of his First Land Utilisation Survey conducted in the 1930s.[4] Consequently, although they proved of inestimable general value, their small scale and increasingly dated information very much restricted their use.

To rectify this deficiency, the Land Service of the Ministry of Agriculture, Fisheries and Food has published, since the end of the 1960s, a set of land classification maps on the one-inch scale which covers the whole of England and Wales in 113 sheets.[5] For the first time, therefore, there now exists a comprehensive set of material which can be employed not only to assess land quality in this country

139

at national and regional levels in a readily understandable way, but which gives some indication of the quality of land being converted to urban uses. The Departments of Agriculture for Scotland and Northern Ireland have used slightly different classifications in dealing with transfers of farmland in their own countries. The Soil Survey of Great Britain has also been using a more detailed land-use capability classification in its work; but the emphasis of its categorisation is towards poorer land areas, and relatively few maps (1:25,000 scale) have been produced so far.[6]

Agricultural land quality grades

The agricultural area on the Land Service maps of the Ministry of Agriculture is classified into five grades according to land quality. Because of the difficulties in taking account of socio-economic factors in such a classification, the land grades are based only on physical criteria like height, slope, climate, soil and drainage, and the extent to which these factors impose constraints on agricultural use and the range of crops produced.[7] A very brief summary of the classification scheme is as follows:

Grade 1   Land with very minor or no physical limitations to agricultural use.

Grade 2   Land with some minor limitations, particularly in soil texture, depth or drainage.

Grade 3   Land with moderate limitations due to soil, relief or climate.

Grade 4   Land with severe limitations due to adverse soil, relief or climate.

Grade 5   Land of little agricultural value with severe limitations due to adverse soil, relief or climate.

Two other categories of land are also defined on the maps:

(a) The main areas of primarily urban, built-up land (in red), including sites for which planning permission had been granted at the time of survey but excluding small settlements and isolated dwellings.

(b) Other primarily non-agricultural land (in orange) which includes mainly woodland, but also some sports fields, airfields, military land and mineral workings.

In spite of the detail recorded on the maps the problem of scale still poses difficulties. Reasonable accuracy in classification is only guaranteed for blocks of land more than about 80 ha in extent, and therefore the maps are of greater value at the structure plan level than for use in the location of small sites for building and development. A related deficiency is that nearly half of all the agricultural area is taken up by Grade 3, or medium quality, land. Clearly, the category is so broad that it encompasses land with wide differences in basic fertility and this can be confusing to those using the maps. The Ministry of Agriculture is now subdividing this grade into three new divisions which will eventually be shown on the printed maps.[8] This will allow a more realistic grouping of categories. In particular, it will become possible to include the better quality Grade 3 land with the good land areas of Grades 1 and 2, where it more truly belongs. Indeed, in a very critical assessment of the Land Service's classification, Michael Boddington even goes as far as to contend that 'there is little to distinguish Grades 1, 2 and 3 in terms of their output potential. The main distinction between these grades is simply in the range of crops that each may support.'[9]

The proportionate composition of the total agricultural area and the total land area of England and Wales by the five land quality grades is set out in Table 21.[10,11] The corresponding national figures from the Soil Survey's land-use capability classification (as quoted by Burnham) are added for comparison. In Table 22, additional data compiled by the Departments of Agriculture for Scotland and Northern Ireland are matched and compared with the land quality grades used for England and Wales, so giving an overall picture for the United Kingdom (Fig. 15).[12]

From the figures for England and Wales, the small amount of undoubted first-class (Grade 1) agricultural land in the country is at once apparent – no more than around 3 per cent of the total. But this consists of extremely fertile areas with virtually no constraints for farming use. If Grade 2 land, with just a few physical limitations, is added to the Grade 1 category, then about 17 per cent can be classified as really good land. With the better portions of Grade 3 land also included, the augmented total of good, or reasonably good, agricultural land probably rises to about one-third of the whole agricultural area. We should, therefore, be a little wary when undue emphasis is placed on what is often said to be the 'very small' area of good land that is available for farming purposes.

Nevertheless, it is the over-wide category of medium quality land which takes up the lion's share of the agricultural area. As we have

Table 21 Land quality in England and Wales by grades, as derived from the Land Service Classification (MAFF) and the Land-Use Capability Classification (Soil Survey)

Grade	LSC		LUCC	
	per cent [a]	per cent [b]	Class	per cent
1	2.3	2.8	1	3.5
2	11.9	14.6	2	13.3
3	39.6	48.9	3	50.4
4	16.0	19.8	4	18.9
5	11.3	13.9	5–7 (total)	(13.8)
Urban	8.5	–	5	7.3
Other	10.4	–	6	5.8
			7	0.7
Total	100.0	100.0		100.0

Sources: MAFF (1977a)[10]; Burnham (1979)[6]

LSC Land Service Classification (MAFF)
LUCC Land-Use Capability Classification (Soil Survey)
[a] Proportion of total land area
[b] Proportion of agricultural land area

seen, this Grade 3 category in reality ranges from quite good to rather poor land, and in total its proportionate coverage is no less than 49 per cent, or very nearly one-half, of all farmland. Poor land (Grades 4 and 5) also covers an extensive area, and together these two grades make up slightly more than a third (34 per cent) of all farmland. In practice, this means that there is a considerable part of the countryside with severe restraints on agricultural use, where farming is frequently very difficult and productivity low.

In Scotland the situation is a great deal more extreme than this. Taken together, land in Grades 4 and 5 covers a predominant proportion of the surface – 84 per cent; and of this area Grade 5 land by itself comprises nearly three-quarters of all agricultural land, or of what is considered to be agricultural land in the official statistics. This land quality situation is a reflection of the immense part of Scotland which is covered by poor rough grazings, deer forest and so forth. At the other end of the spectrum, good land in Scotland (Grades 1 and 2) is very limited indeed, and extends to less than 3 per cent of the country.

Although Scotland may differ radically from the rest of Britain in terms of land quality, in England and Wales alone the various grades of agricultural land are also distributed very unevenly across the whole surface (Fig. 16). This comes out clearly in Table 23, where land quality grades are recorded by Economic Planning Regions. From these data, it is at once apparent that a great deal of the farmland in the Highland Zone is of poor quality. In Wales, 80 per cent of the agricultural land is in Grades 4 and 5, which is approaching the figure in Scotland, while in the Northern Region the figure is over 59 per cent. Much of this poor land, and especially the Grade 5 category, is, in many ways, probably more suited for forest and recreational uses than for agriculture.

By way of contrast, the Lowland Zone is dominated by land of better quality (Grades 1 to 3). Nearly 40 per cent of the agricultural area of East Anglia, for instance, is good quality land (Grades 1 and 2), and in the East Midlands the corresponding figure is about 27 per cent. On the other hand, it should be recognised that even in

Table 22 Agricultural land quality in England and Wales, Scotland and the United Kingdom by grades, 1976

Grade [a]	England and Wales	Scotland	United Kingdom
	'000 ha		
1	330	20	350
2	1,691	155	1,882
3	5,638	880	6,975
4	2,298	660	3,489
5	1,623	4,765	6,450
Total	11,580	6,480	19,146
	per cent		
1	2.8	0.3	1.8
2	14.6	2.4	9.8
3	48.9	13.6	36.5
4	19.8	10.2	18.2
5	13.9	73.5	33.7
Total	100.0	100.0	100.0

Source: Agriculture EDC (1977)[12]

[a] Land Service (MAFF) grades for England and Wales with Scottish and Northern Ireland equivalents

Land Use and Living Space

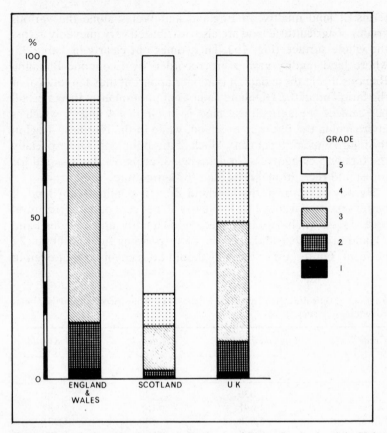

Figure 15 Agricultural land quality in England and Wales, Scotland and the United Kingdom by grades, 1976

these predominantly fertile regions there is still a considerable proportion of poor land. The lowest amount is in East Anglia, but even here the figure is almost 9 per cent. Elsewhere, it is often distinctly more: the south-east has 16 per cent. Consequently, throughout Lowland Britain there is a considerable area of land, unattractive for farming, which might prove entirely adequate for the extension of non-agricultural uses like urban development, recreation and nature conservation.

As the land quality grades on the Land Service maps are allocated solely to agricultural land, they cannot be used directly to indicate the quality profiles of land associated with other major uses such as urban development and woodland. However, Guy Swinnerton

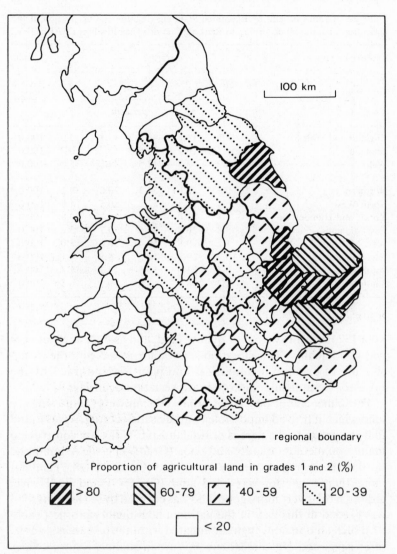

Figure 16 Distribution of good agricultural land (Grades 1 and 2) in England and Wales by counties and regions

attempted to obtain an indication of this relationship by extrapolating the quality gradings on to the ground covered by other land uses.[13] In this way, and by the use of point sampling, he was able to demonstrate that rather more than half of the forest and woodland

Table 23 Grades of land by Economic Planning Regions as a proportion of the agricultural land area, according to the Land Service Classification (MAFF)

Country or region	Grade					Total
	1	*2*	*3*	*4*	*5*	
	per cent					
England and Wales	2.8	14.6	48.9	19.8	13.9	100.0
England	3.3	16.7	54.0	15.7	10.3	100.0
Wales	0.2	2.3	17.5	44.2	35.8	100.0
Northern	0.0	2.6	38.3	20.0	39.1	100.0
North-West	5.4	11.5	47.7	20.5	14.9	100.0
Yorks. and Humberside	1.3	22.0	39.6	16.3	20.8	100.0
East Midlands	5.8	20.8	60.5	9.7	3.2	100.0
West Midlands	1.2	19.8	59.4	16.6	3.0	100.0
East Anglia	10.3	29.3	51.5	8.8	0.1	100.0
South-East	3.1	21.0	59.8	14.7	1.4	100.0
South-West	1.7	8.1	64.0	19.7	6.5	100.0

Source: MAFF (1977a, b)[10,11]

area (52 per cent) was poor quality land, and as little as 8 per cent was good quality. This situation is not unexpected with the extensive use of exposed upland areas and poor lowland tracts by the Forestry Commission and other afforestation agencies.

The same cannot be said of urban uses, however. Allowing for land which it proved impossible to grade satisfactorily, it was found that the present urban areas of England and Wales are constructed mainly on medium quality and poor (Grade 4) land. Around one third of the aggregate area was poor land (Grades 4 and 5) and not more than a quarter was good land (Grades 1 and 2). Hence, although relatively more good land was covered by settlements than was graded in this way in the national land quality profile (Table 21), such land in no way predominated within urban areas, as is so often suggested. Needless to say, this urban quality profile provides only an 'average' indication of the national situation in settlement coverage: individual towns can be found which occupy either good or poor land over most of their developed areas.

Extension of large towns

An examination in more detail by Best and Swinnerton of the

Table 24 The quality of agricultural land converted to urban use between 1931 and 1971 in a sample of 34 county boroughs

Agricultural land	Land quality grade		
	Good	Medium	Poor
		per cent	
Existing quality			
1931	10	44	46
1951	9	40	51
Converted to urban use			
1931–51	13	53	34
1951–71	12	52	36

possible relationship between land quality and recent urban growth was carried out by analysing a large sample of populous cities and towns in England and Wales – an urban sector in which considerable expansion has occurred.[14] All these urban areas were former county boroughs for which adequate land-use and land quality information existed. Almost inevitably, the data constraints meant that the sample of thirty-four out of a total of eighty-three such towns was not truly representative geographically. Nevertheless, these large urban concentrations gave at least some general indications of the processes and patterns of land quality displacement brought about by urban spread over the forty-year period from 1931 to 1971. To ensure comparability, 1951 administrative boundaries were used throughout the study. Interestingly, in 1951, almost 40 per cent of the aggregate administrative area of the sample county boroughs was in agricultural rather than urban use. It was this land which was primarily 'at risk' by the spreading outwards of the towns.

The land quality composition of this agricultural sector of the sample county boroughs and the quality structure of the land transferred to urban use is given in Table 24. It might be imagined that, with the operation of statutory planning control in the period from 1951 to 1971, there would have been a greater attention paid to land quality in the land conversion process than previously. Yet, surprisingly, the evidence does not support this contention at all strongly. The figures show that the take-up of good and medium quality land by urban expansion was only marginally smaller between 1951 and 1971 than over the two earlier decades.

The explanation seems to be that, in reality, the land quality factor has not figured very emphatically as a reason for restricting development, in spite of persistent government encouragement and pressure towards this particular end. From a questionnaire sent to planning authorities it appeared that, on average, land quality came only fifth in the list of factors which were considered to act as a restraint on development. Quite realistically, more importance was usually attached to the availability of land, urban layout, topography and visual amenity, in that order. Support for these conclusions is provided by a similar, but more recent survey, conducted among members of the County Planning Officers' Society.[15] Most planning authorities claimed that high quality land is regarded as a physical constraint on development, but only a quarter assessed the limitation as being very important. Another 27 per cent saw the constraint as of rather lesser significance, though still of high or considerable importance. The remaining 48 per cent were either indeterminate, did not reply, or considered that the constraints should not be operated strongly.

Despite this rather low priority accorded to land quality in planning decisions on the extension of urban land, Table 24 does not give cause to think that a very disproportionate amount of good quality land was, in practice, being absorbed by the thirty-four sample towns as they extended in area. This outcome, however, was partly related to their comparative concentration in the north and west of the country where poor land is more dominant in the overall pattern of land quality. Even so, it is apparent from the data that no more than 12 per cent of the land taken for development between 1951 and 1971 was of good quality while 88 per cent was of medium and poor quality. Nevertheless, it might be argued with some justification that still less good land could have been taken if greater weighting in the choice of new building sites had been given to the land quality constraint. A move in this direction has been taken by certain planning authorities, such as Kent and Hertfordshire, which have indicated in the structure plans for their counties a number of areas of special agricultural significance where there will be a particular presumption against non-agricultural uses.

An additional study of the twenty-three new towns in England and Wales, which have all been built since 1946 or are in the process of construction, corroborates the general picture that has just been outlined. In this case, 87 per cent of their aggregate designated area is medium or poor land while only 13 per cent is good quality. The situation in Scotland for all land being converted to urban use seems to be very different, however. Here, the good quality land (the equivalent of Grades 1 and 2) is very much more restricted in area than in England and Wales and, in location, a high proportion of it surrounds major urban areas. Consequently, figures from the Department of Agriculture and Fisheries for Scotland indicate that, while less than 3 per cent of its farmland is in this category of good land, some 26 per cent of the area transferred to urban development from 1973 to 1975 was taken from these grades.[16]

Amenity land in the countryside

We have seen that the common assumption is that urban areas tend to be located on good land. Conversely, it is also supposed that the tracts of country most often visited for recreational and holiday pursuits are areas of poor land. After all, sea-coast, mountains, hills, moors and forests would hardly suggest otherwise from their visual appearance. In England and Wales, three main types of statutory amenity area in the countryside may be distinguished: National Parks and Areas of Outstanding Natural Beauty (AONBs) designated under the National Parks and Access to the Countryside Act, 1949, and Country Parks implemented by the Countryside Act, 1968.[17] Although there were 130 Country Parks in 1977, individually they are comparatively small in size, and the intention has been to situate them fairly close to large concentrations of population. Their aggregate area amounts to only about 18,000 ha. In contrast, the land taken up by National Parks and AONBs is far more extensive. The ten National Parks are located wholly within or on the margins of the Highland Zone and cover 9 per cent of England and Wales; the thirty-three AONBs, which have a greater predominance in the Lowland Zone, take up even more of the land surface – 9.6 per cent (Fig. 17).

Until recently, virtually nothing was known of the land use and land quality of the two major amenity categories. In 1980, however, Margaret Anderson published a paper which not only gave detailed information on these topics, but also provided similar comparative figures for the entire Highland and Lowland Zones of England and Wales.[18] Her data, set out here in Tables 25 and 26, were derived from point sampling. The appropriate 95 per cent confidence limits have been omitted, but nevertheless the results bear a very close resemblance to the official figures for England and Wales obtained

149

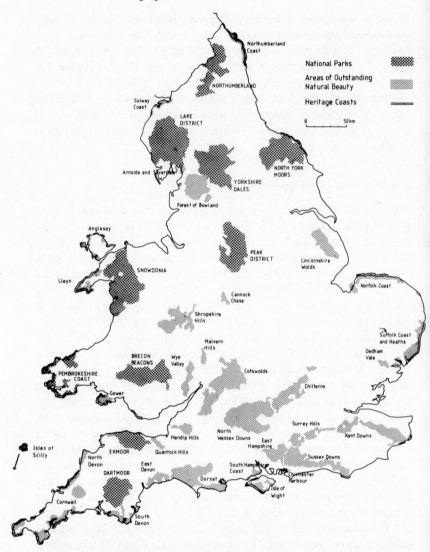

Figure 17 National Parks and Areas of Outstanding Natural Beauty in England and Wales (Source: M. A Anderson)

from a complete enumeration. This can be seen by comparing the land quality data in Table 26 with those in Table 21, and by reference back to the discussion of the land-use figures in Table 7.

From Anderson's analysis, it is apparent that the major components of the land-use structure do not differ so widely between the

Table 25 Land use in National Parks, AONBs and the Highland and Lowland Zones of England and Wales

Area	Agriculture	Woodland	Urban land	Other land	Inland water
			per cent		
National Parks	87.7	8.4	1.3	2.1	0.5
Highland Zone	82.5	7.1	7.3	2.9	0.2
England and Wales	79.1	6.9	9.7	4.2	0.1
Lowland Zone	77.7	6.4	10.8	5.0	0.1
AONBs	77.1	11.3	3.6	7.9	0.1

Source: Anderson (1980)[18]

Table 26 Agricultural land quality in National Parks, AONBs and the Highland and Lowland Zones of England and Wales

Area	Agricultural land quality grade [a]					
	1	*2*	*3*	*4*	*5*	*Unidentified* [b]
National Parks	0.0	0.3	10.4	24.5	53.1	11.7
Highland Zone	0.4	4.9	27.4	25.4	26.1	15.8
England and Wales	2.1	12.2	38.2	16.3	11.8	19.4
Lowland Zone	3.8	17.1	48.4	8.7	1.0	21.0
AONBs	1.6	9.9	42.2	16.3	8.4	21.6

Source: Anderson (1980)[18]

[a] Rural transport land and isolated dwellings (urban land) are not differentiated within each agricultural land quality grade on the Land Service maps and have been included within the grade in which they occur

[b] Major urban areas and non-agricultural land, e.g. woodland

Highland and Lowland Zones of England and Wales as might at first be assumed. With land quality, however, the disparities are far more pronounced (Fig. 18). Fairly detailed data for individual regions in England and Wales have been recorded and commented on in the first part of this chapter (see Table 23): the present analysis in giving more generalised figures for the entire Highland and Lowland Zones simply confirms the remarks made earlier. It is seen, for instance, that poor land and extensive agricultural systems dominate over half the total farmed area of the Highland Zone, whereas little more than 5 per cent of the land is in good grades.

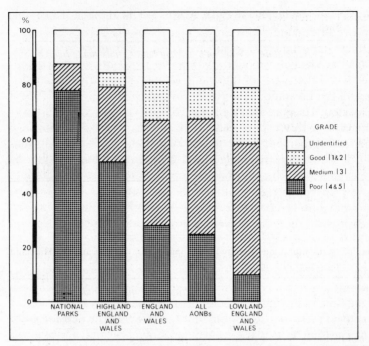

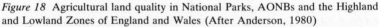

Figure 18 Agricultural land quality in National Parks, AONBs and the Highland and Lowland Zones of England and Wales (After Anderson, 1980)

Conversely, well over a fifth of all farmland in the Lowland Zone is of good quality, with a large amount of cropland, while less than 10 per cent is poor land.

None of this is unanticipated; but examination of the two main types of amenity area gives some less expected results, particularly as in the literature on the subject it is often contended that AONBs are broadly similar in character to National Parks, while at the same time allowing that they include less wild land and more improved farmland.[19] National Parks have the highest proportion of agricultural land of all the areas defined, and they clearly show an even more extreme environment than the average for the Highland Zone. Much of their land is only nominally in farming use; a large part of it is in reality very extensive rough grazing, reflecting the poor quality of 77 per cent of the land. AONBs on the other hand, although individually quite varied and different from each other, have a more lowland bias and closely resemble the average pattern for England and Wales as a whole. They have 10 per cent less of their surface in agricultural use than the National Parks, but well over half of their aggregate area is of good or medium quality, or 'improved farmland', with only a quarter in the poorer grades.

Other important contrasts are also apparent. On average, AONBs are heavily wooded (with an 11 per cent coverage) compared with other parts of the country, and particularly in comparison with the Lowland Zone (6 per cent) in which so many of them are located. They are also well in excess of even the National Parks (8 per cent) in this respect. But, as might be expected, AONBs have a far smaller percentage of urban land than either the Lowland Zone or the average for England and Wales; and the National Parks have even less – little over one per cent. AONBs are outstanding, too, in their percentage of other, miscellaneous land. In large part, this is due to the coastal location of sixteen of them, where heaths, beaches, cliffs, dunes and marshes contribute strongly to this category of use, or non-use.

The generally undulating landscape of AONBs, with farms and forest frequently combined with bays and beaches, probably has a stronger appeal to the majority of people than the bleaker and more rugged upland grazings and moors of the National Parks. But this attractive landscape is certainly not immutable. The possibility of change, arising particularly from developments in agricultural technology and practice, is far more likely here than on the barren tracts of land which provide the core of so many of our National Parks. Grade 3 land takes up a major part of the land surface of AONBs (42 per cent), and it is on this quality of farmland that upgrading and intensification of production can often be achieved most easily and effectively. It is just the sort of land most susceptible to hedge and copse removal and the ploughing of pasture, resulting in significant changes being imprinted on the existing landscape.[20]

Even in the National Parks with their more constraining physical environments, the improvement and enclosure of poorer land (particularly Grade 4) has been the cause of considerable concern and conflict.[21] In AONBs the amount of poor land is much smaller, and so potential conflict in this sector is usually less significant. It should be recognised, nevertheless, that in both of these amenity areas poor quality land can be very important for nature conservation. Of the 565 key sites in England and Wales graded 1 and 2 by the Nature Conservancy Council in 1977, 105 were in National Parks and took up some 87,000 ha; 143, or a quarter of the priority sites, were in AONBs and extended to a further 69,500 ha.[22]

It is interesting to note in this context that AONBs were originally conceived as 'Conservation Areas' in 1947, and the hope was expressed that the general conservation of landscape over considerable tracts would assist in the protection of the special areas scheduled as nature reserves.[23] The factor which often militates against this happening is the presence of intensively farmed land close to wildlife conservation areas. It has been argued persuasively by ecologists that the two do not and cannot mix, and that the only way to ensure that viable tracts of countryside are maintained for nature conservation is by allocating and managing sufficiently large areas of amenity land away from intensive agricultural systems with their heavy use of fertilisers and pesticides.[24]

One of the most successful examples of such an arrangement is in a sector of the Heritage Coast between Eastbourne and Seaford in the Sussex Downs AONB. Here, in close juxtaposition and nearly all in public ownership, a sizeable tract of land has been set aside primarily for recreation and wildlife conservation purposes. It comprises the Seven Sisters Country Park, Friston Forest, Lullington Heath National Nature Reserve, Seaford Head Local Nature Reserve, and National Trust and local authority holdings managed as public open space towards Beachy Head. The size, position and management of this substantial area ensure that it is well detached and protected from the more adverse impacts on the environment of modern farming techniques.

Planning and development control

Modern agricultural and forestry practices, particularly in Lowland Britain, are bringing about profound changes in the countryside that are radically altering the rural scene to which we have become accustomed over many generations.[25] It is not sufficiently appreciated how small an influence planning control can have under existing legislation to restrain unwanted changes in *rural* land uses in country areas.[26] Apart from some limited controls over farm buildings, neither agriculture nor forestry is subject to any significant planning constraints. In fact, it is only with proposed urban development that it is possible for planning authorities to apply really stringent controls over what is, or is not, done. This applies equally to the ordinary countryside and to the more sensitive amenity areas like National Parks and AONBs which are supposed to be specially protected.

Apart from some limited investigations on green belts, little work has been carried out to ascertain whether, or to what extent, planning control has been more effectively operated in designated amenity areas than in the open countryside. Two studies, however, are of relevance in this respect. The first by Blacksell, Gilg and their students at Exeter University examined the planning applications made over a six-year period between January 1967 and December 1972 in the former St Thomas Rural District of south-east Devon.[27] The area was largely agricultural, and contained part of an AONB which extended over nearly half of the total land surface. The planning applications considered over the period totalled 2990 and ranged in scale from housing estates to porch extensions on individual houses. Throughout, just over half the applications were for new buildings, compared with conversions or modifications of existing buildings, and about 40 per cent were for residential development.

One part of the study examined the relationship between the permission or refusal of planning applications and the quality of agricultural land as defined on the Land Service maps discussed earlier in this chapter. Interestingly, it was found that there appeared to be little difference in the success rate for applications between the different grades of farmland; the main disparity occurred instead between agricultural land as a whole and urban or other land where permission was at least three times more likely to be obtained. When residential applications alone were considered, the ratio of permissions to refusals was about 0.6:1 to 0.9:1 on farmland compared with 2 or 3:1 on urban and other land.

A further part of this same project examined how development control had been implemented within the sector of the study area which comprised the East Devon AONB.[28] Paradoxically in this supposedly protected area, 69 per cent of all applications were approved compared with only 47 per cent in the remainder of the study area. For residential applications alone, the corresponding figures for approvals were 56 per cent and 54 per cent respectively. The conclusion reached was that it was usually easier, and often much easier, to receive permission to develop within the AONB than outside it – a situation that apparently negated one of the main objectives in designating such an amenity area. An additional anomaly was that, in all the four major villages in the AONB, only one of which was officially regarded as a key settlement, a residential planning application was more likely to be approved than refused, the chances being two or three to one.

Table 27 Planning applications in 1975/76 for various parts of East Sussex, including the Sussex Downs AONB

County division	Area [a] per cent	Planning applications			
		Total [a] per cent	Residential		
			Total [b] per cent	permitted number	refused number
Low Weald	28.9	15.8	69.4	181	170
Sussex Downs AONB	13.3	2.0	76.9	23	27
Coastal urban belt [c]	8.9	57.5	56.5	793	248
Remainder of county	48.9	24.7	72.9	306	269

Source: Anderson (1981)[29]

[a] Proportion of county total
[b] Proportion of all applications in each division
[c] And Lewes

To generalise about the apparent ineffectiveness of an AONB designation from this single example could be specious and unwise, especially as a somewhat different conclusion was reached by Anderson in her study of planning decisions in another AONB in a different part of the country.[29] Her investigation took in the whole county of East Sussex for the year 1975/76, as well as contrasting the Sussex Downs AONB with other divisions of the county, particularly the Low Weald and Coastal Urban Belt (Table 27). In all county divisions more applications were permitted than were refused, but in predominantly country areas the overall ratio was 1.4:1 whereas in the urbanised coastal belt it was noticeably higher at 3.2:1.

Residential uses comprised the bulk of the 3200 planning applications analysed, and in the rural areas they amounted to 70 per cent or more of the total. Detailed study of residential applications in the AONB and Low Weald, however, revealed some interesting variations. For example, in the AONB nearly all applications for new building were for one dwelling or small groups of houses (none for single caravans), whereas in the Low Weald 10 per cent were for multiple housing estates with a further number for mobile home parks and caravans.

Differences also occurred in the land-use changes for the two areas. The highest proportion of residential applications in the AONB was for dwellings sited on gardens and other vacant urban land, followed fairly closely by alterations and conversions of existing buildings. In the Low Weald there were more than twice as many applications for building on gardens and vacant land as there were for conversions and alterations. Somewhat surprisingly, proposals for development on farm or horticultural land were the fewest in number and amounted to only around 20 per cent in both areas. The ratio of permissions to refusals on farmland was very low, being no more than 0.25:1 in the AONB but somewhat higher, 0.4:1, in the Low Weald. All these statistics indicated a strong tendency towards the consolidation of existing settlements in rural East Sussex rather than any dispersal of new housing into the countryside (cf. Chapter 7).

This trend is in line with the policy of the county in restricting residential development outside villages, but the pattern of *applications* does not, in itself, have any direct effect on the countryside. It is a decision to allow development actually to take place that ultimately affects the appearance and activity of rural areas. A study of residential permissions granted in the AONB showed that they were all given in accordance with structure plan policies and, even in the Low Weald, only 5 per cent of the approvals could be faulted as aberrant. This result indicates a close adherence by local planners to the county structure plan in which no real difference of approach is made between the designated AONB and the undesignated open countryside of the Low Weald.

It was particularly noticeable that the number of applications within the Sussex Downs AONB was relatively small, but that there were many outside it and very close to its borders. This was especially true along the southern edge where Brighton has little space in which to expand. Consequently it seems clear that, in the 1970s, the presence of the AONB constituted a real constraint on development and urban spread (Fig. 19), and that the relatively small impact that the existence of an AONB had apparently had in East Devon in no way described the situation in East Sussex. If and when, in the 1980s, the planning powers of the County are weakened in favour of the Districts, it may however prove less possible to hold the southern boundary of the AONB against the expansionist pressures of Brighton.

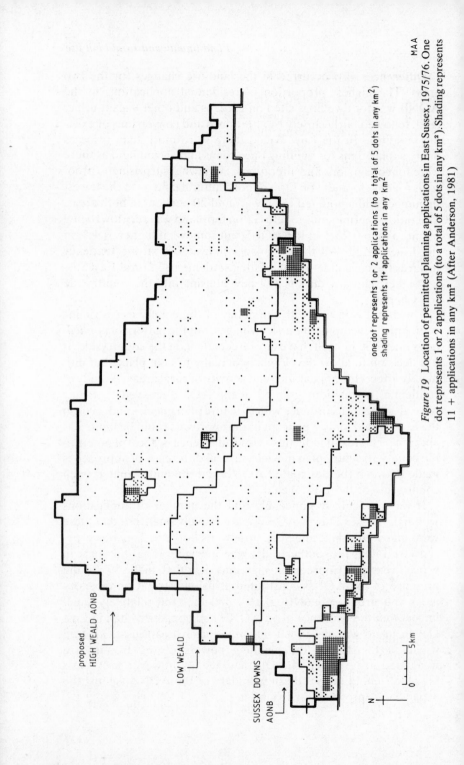

Figure 19 Location of permitted planning applications in East Sussex, 1975/76. One dot represents 1 or 2 applications (to a total of 5 dots in any km²). Shading represents 11+ applications in any km² (After Anderson, 1981)

Summary

Since the end of the 1960s the Land Service of the Ministry of Agriculture, Fisheries and Food has produced a set of one-inch land classification maps covering the whole of England and Wales. The agricultural area is divided into five main grades according to land quality. These grades are determined by constraints on agricultural use and the range of crops produced which are imposed by physical factors in the environment. Comparable figures are also available for Scotland and the United Kingdom.

In England and Wales, good quality agricultural land covers approximately 17 per cent of the farmed surface, but medium quality land takes up the lion's share with very nearly one-half. Poor land, however, also occupies an extensive area of slightly more than a third of all farmland, while in Scotland the proportion is as much as 84 per cent. Hence, over a considerable part of the surface of Britain, and particularly in the Highland Zone, farming is often difficult and productivity low. On the other hand, nearly 40 per cent of the agricultural area in East Anglia, our most productive agricultural region, is of good quality.

In aggregate, the present urban areas of England and Wales are built mainly on medium or poor quality land. An examination of 34 large towns showed that their take-up of good and medium quality land by urban expansion was only marginally smaller between 1951 and 1971, when statutory planning control existed, than over the two earlier decades between 1931 and 1951. Additional evidence from planning authorities also makes it evident that the land quality factor has not figured very strongly as a reason for restraining development.

National Parks and Areas of Outstanding Natural Beauty (AONBs) altogether cover 18 per cent or more of the land surface of England and Wales. These two main types of amenity area are often thought to be broadly similar in character, but this is not strictly true. National Parks, which are concentrated in the Highland Zone, have a much more extreme form of environment, which is reflected in a dominance of rough and poor grazings and generally poor quality land (77 per cent). In contrast, AONBs are located predominantly in the Lowland Zone and have well over half of their surface composed of good or medium quality 'improved' farmland. On average, they are also heavily wooded (11 per cent coverage) compared with other parts of the country. Their land quality profile, in contrast to that of the National Parks, closely resembles the average pattern for England and Wales as a whole.

Planning control has little or no influence over change in rural land uses, as opposed to urban development. Two studies of countryside areas, each containing an AONB, gave somewhat different indications of the effectiveness of such an amenity designation where planning decisions were concerned. In East Devon, the AONB appeared to have little impact, whereas in East Sussex the contrary situation applied. Nevertheless, a stringent and consistent use of planning control according to structure plan policies, as carried out in East Sussex, can have a marked effect in diminishing urban impact on ordinary tracts of countryside as well as on statutorily designated amenity areas.

References

1　This chapter has been written in conjunction with Margaret Anderson.
2　Ministry of Works and Planning (1942) *Report of the Committee on Land Utilisation in Rural Areas* (Scott Report), Cmnd. 6378, HMSO.
3　Ministry of Housing and Local Government (1952) *The Density of Residential Areas*, HMSO.
4　Stamp, L.D. (1948) *The Land of Britain: Its Use and Misuse* (3rd edn, 1962), London, Longman.
5　Dennis, A. (1976) 'Agricultural land classification in England and Wales', *The Planner*, 62 (2), 40–2.
6　Burnham, C.P. (1979) 'A new inventory of the land resources of England and Wales', *Area*, 11 (4), 349–52.
7　Ministry of Agriculture, Fisheries and Food (1966) *Agricultural Land Classification*, Technical Report No. 11, Agricultural Land Service.
8　Ministry of Agriculture, Fisheries and Food (1976) *Agricultural Land Classification of England and Wales: the Definition and Identification of Sub-Grades within Grade 3*, Technical Report No. 11/1.
9　Boddington, M.A.B. (1978) *The Classification of Agricultural Land in England and Wales: A Critique*, Ipsden, Rural Planning Services.
10　Ministry of Agriculture, Fisheries and Food (1977a) *Agricultural Land Classification of England and Wales*, Agricultural Land Service.
11　Ministry of Agriculture, Fisheries and Food (1977b) *Agricultural Land Classification of England and Wales: the Distribution of Each Grade of Land*, Draft Technical Report No. 11/2 (unpublished).
12　Agriculture EDC (1977) *Agriculture into the 1980s: Land Use*, National Economic Development Office. See also: Symons, L. (ed.) (1963) *Land Use in Northern Ireland*, London, University of London Press.

13 Swinnerton, G.S. (1974) 'Land classification and environmental planning', in Ministry of Agriculture, Fisheries and Food, *Land Capability Classification*, Technical Bulletin No. 30, HMSO, 109–24.
14 Best, R.H. (1974) 'Building on farmland', *New Society*, 30 (630), 287–8. See also: Best, R.H. and Swinnerton, G.S. (1974) *The Quality and Type of Agricultural Land Converted to Urban Use*, SSRC Final Report.
15 Agriculture EDC (1977) op. cit.
16 ibid.
17 Gilg, A.W. (1978) *Countryside Planning: the First Three Decades 1945—76*, Newton Abbot, David & Charles.
18 Anderson, M.A. (1980) 'The land pattern of Areas of Outstanding Natural Beauty in England and Wales', *Landscape Planning*, 7, 1–22.
19 Patmore, J.A. (1970) *Land and Leisure*, Newton Abbot, David & Charles.
20 Westmacott, R. and Worthington, T. (1974) *New Agricultural Landscapes: A Discussion Paper*, Countryside Commission.
21 Department of the Environment, Ministry of Agriculture, Fisheries and Food (1977) *A Study of Exmoor; Report by Lord Porchester*, HMSO.
22 Anderson, M.A. (1980) 'Areas of Outstanding Natural Beauty in England and Wales: the concept in practice with special reference to land uses and the policies of local planning authorities particularly in East Sussex', unpublished Ph.D. thesis, University of London. See also: Ratcliffe, D.A. (ed.) (1977) *A Nature Conservation Review*, Cambridge, CUP.
23 Ministry of Town and Country Planning (1947) *Report of the National Parks Committee (England and Wales)*, Cmnd. 7121, HMSO.
24 Green, B.H. (1975) 'The future of the British countryside', *Landscape Planning*, 2, 179–95. See also: Nature Conservancy Council (1977) *Nature Conservation and Agriculture*.
25 Shoard, M. (1980) *The Theft of the Countryside*, London, Temple Smith.
26 Davidson, J. and Wibberley, G.P. (1977) *Planning and the Rural Environment*, Oxford, Pergamon. See also: Newby, H. (1979) *Green and Pleasant Land? Social Change in Rural England*, London, Hutchinson.
27 Gilg, A.W. (1975) 'Development control and agricultural land quality', *Town and Country Planning*, 43 (9), 387–9.
28 Blacksell, M. and Gilg, A.W. (1977) 'Planning control in an Area of Outstanding Natural Beauty', *Social and Economic Administration*, 11 (3), 206–15.
29 Anderson, M.A. (1981) 'Planning policies and development control in the Sussex Downs AONB', *Town Planning Review* 52 (1), 5–25.

9
Comparative land use: Britain, Europe and North America[1]

Very often a solution turns on devising some means of quantifying phenomena or states that have hitherto been assessed in terms of 'rather more', 'rather less', or 'a lot of', or – sturdiest workhorse of scientific literature – 'marked' . . . Quantification as such has no merit except insofar as it helps to solve problems. To quantify is not to be a scientist, but goodness, it does help.

(P.B. Medawar: *Advice to a Young Scientist*)

With the growth of an urban-industrial society in Britain, we have seen in previous chapters how the insistent alteration in the traditional land-use structure has become a matter of increasing concern and even alarm. Particularly during the 1930s and in the decades after the Second World War, the rapid progress of urbanisation and the accompanying spread of towns into the countryside generated a strong preservationist reaction among many individuals and pressure groups. More recently, conflicts between rural land uses themselves have added another dimension to this changing pattern. The debate continues at the present day, though now it is often set in the context of the success or otherwise of the land-use planning process.[2]

All these arguments and discussions are very inward-looking towards the British experience alone. This does not arise solely in response to supposed British insularity; it also unfortunately reflects the lack of information about what is happening to the land-use structure of other countries. Indeed, even the overall pattern of existing land use in many so-called 'developed' nations of the western world is not known with any certainty and accuracy. Therefore, it is not really surprising that it is difficult to see the British position in any true perspective. If this could be done, it might well fundamentally alter several ingrained attitudes towards land-use structure and change here at home.

World land use

To begin with, however, it is probably expedient to consider the widest possible canvas – the land-use pattern of the whole world. According to Dudley Stamp, the face of the earth covers 51 thousand million hectares (51,000,000,000 ha), but of this immense total only something over a quarter is land.[3] The rest is water. It is obvious enough that, at present, a major part of this land area is either impossible or very difficult for man to use, basically because of restraints imposed by the physical environment. There-fore, these 'negative' areas are largely uninhabited at the moment, and in many cases are likely to remain so. We can see the reason for this if we look at the world pattern of land use or non-use (Table 28).

First of all, then, a full 40 per cent of the world's land surface is arid or desert, if Antarctica and other cold deserts are included along with the hot deserts. Approximately another 30 per cent is under forest and woodland, and these regions can quite often be mountainous as well. Consequently, deserts and forests occupy up to 70 per cent of the total surface, and it is only on the remaining 30 per cent or so that it is possible to farm reasonably well, though even here poor soils, relative aridity, remoteness, steep slopes, and so on, may restrict agricultural activity.[4] As a result, crop-growing may be

Table 28   World land use, 1977. Note that the figures exclude Antarctica

Land use	Area '000 ha	Proportion per cent
Total area (excl. Antarctica)	13,390,160	–
Land area (excl. inland water)	13,073,605	100
Cropland	1,462,017	11
Permanent pasture	3,057,986	24
Forest and woodland	4,077,002	31
Other land [a]	4,476,600	34

Source: FAO (1979)[4]

[a]   Urban, wilderness, desert, etc.

extremely difficult, and livestock farming may be the only reasonable possibility. It is also within this more habitable sector, and often in association with the better farmed land, that human settlements have developed. Hence, it is in these areas that most of the world's population lives and where most towns have grown up.

In Chapter 2 it has been stressed that forest and woodland is a biological rather than a functional category, and in the world as a whole much forest land is not really *used* by man. The largest actual land use is probably grazing by livestock which takes place on over a fifth of the world's surface. Even so, a vast part of this area is poorly productive range land, giving very little food output per hectare. The more intensely farmed regions of the earth, on which crops are grown, extend to approximately a tenth of the whole surface, and this gives about 0.4 ha per person to supply most of his or her food needs – not very much.

Finally, although forests and farms take up so substantial an area, urban development must not be neglected as a land use, in spite of the present area it occupies being so small in total extent. Probably little more than 1 per cent of the world's surface is now covered by cities, towns and villages, and the actual figure certainly bears no resemblance at all to the ludicrously exaggerated proportion of 15 per cent or so (much larger than the percentage in England and Wales alone) which has been quoted in some publications.[5] But even leaving urban areas apart, it must already be patently obvious that the land-use structure of Britain differs radically from that of the world as a whole and perhaps, therefore, from many other individual countries as well. To what extent this supposition is true must now be examined.

Recent comparative studies

The collection of land-use information has followed a remarkably similar sequence in most countries where any serious attempt has been made to delineate the land-use structure. The first data to be acquired in any systematic way have normally been statistics for agriculture, and particularly for cropland – the most productive part of this major land use. By now a reasonably sophisticated and detailed set of agricultural statistics exist for each country of North America and Europe, and particularly for those of the European Economic Community (EEC). Forest and woodland data have also been compiled for a long period in several countries, although the regularity and comprehensiveness of the collection has not really compared favourably with that of the agricultural figures. Even so, the rural sector of the land surface is well-documented in most western nations.

This is certainly not true of urban land. Where they exist at all, statistics for this major use have not been available in any comprehensive form until very recently. In fact, most countries, including those of the EEC, still have either very incomplete urban statistics or figures that are often rather dubious in their magnitudes. Marion Clawson's remarks about America are equally applicable to Europe: 'Although urban use of land is perhaps the most important major use of land in the United States today . . . in any overall and quantitative sense we know least about it.'[6] Urban land, therefore, is the undoubted poor relation where land-use information is concerned, even though the expansion of urban areas at the expense of the countryside, and particularly of farmland, is generally considered to be one of the most pressing and significant processes of land-use change which are occurring in many developed countries at the present time.

Individual western countries have often collected and compiled their own rural land-use data for extended periods of years. However, the recording and investigation of comparative land use in European countries, including those of the EEC, is a very recent event which does not date back to before the 1960s. Since that time, four main studies have been carried out covering all major land uses.

The first was made by Dudley Stamp under the auspices of the Food and Agricultural Organisation (FAO) of the United Nations and it was simply a collection of land-use data, usually referring to about 1960 or 1961, for some twenty European nations.[7] Correspondents in each country were asked to supply information by filling in a special questionnaire compiled on the basis of an agreed classification of land; but problems of omission and definition in the data were very apparent and virtually no analysis was undertaken. It was decided by the FAO to repeat and extend Stamp's initial survey with the collection of material for 1965 on the same comparative basis. The work was done by Corver and Kippers[8] using an unchanged questionnaire, and it was hoped that in this way it would be possible to define land-use changes and trends over the period from 1960 to 1965. In the event, comparability often proved difficult, with a considerable lack of information on the non-agricultural uses of land.

The first real attempt to produce a reasonably comparable, international analysis of land-use structure and change was made by Best and Mandale in their study of England and Wales, the United States, the Netherlands and West Germany.[9] It was originally intended to cover several other European countries as well but, again, the major problem encountered was that of obtaining adequate data for consistently defined land uses. Even in the four countries eventually studied statistical comparability was far from easily achieved, and it was the urban statistics which proved to be the weakest link in the chain. Nevertheless, a statement of the existing land-use structure in about 1960 was finally possible, together with some more realistic indications of land-use change between 1960 and 1965 (particularly of urban growth) than had previously been attained.

The most recently published report in this field was by the Organisation for Economic Co-operation and Development (OECD), and this differed from the previous studies in that it was more concerned with land-use policies than with descriptive and analytical material about land-use structure in OECD countries.[10] Nevertheless, the limitations of existing statistics were discussed briefly, and it was emphasised that comparisons between countries are hazardous because the categories of land use adopted are not always alike and definitions vary widely. It was recognised that errors or omissions in material were often simply due to the lack of survey facilities, and particular problems in this respect arose over the extent of abandoned farmland, information on little used agricultural land like mountain pasture and communal land, and the scarcity or absence of statistics for urban and non-agro-forestry uses. Some figures for trends in land use, and especially for urban extension, were recorded, and a final table attempted to give an overall picture of land use in OECD countries in the 1970s. Unfortunately, even a fairly cursory examination of these data showed some major gaps, deficiencies and inaccuracies.

Because of the unsatisfactory nature of these previous studies, it seemed very necessary to make a new effort to investigate European and North American land use. The work was carried out by Robin Best, Dorothy Wilkinson and John Hansen, and the objectives were as follows:

(a) to set out and, as far as possible, to harmonise the relevant data from a diverse range of statistics on land use for EEC and North American countries so as to present a comparative statement of land-use structure in the various countries at a recent date;

(b) to undertake a preliminary examination of the similarities and differences in land use between the eleven countries and, in conjunction with this, to make an initial assessment of some of the statistical problems associated with available data;

(c) to outline, within the statistical constraints, the main trends and changes in land use which have been taking place in the recent past;

(d) to review the resemblances and contrasts between the land-use situation in the United Kingdom and that in the other, and particularly the EEC, countries.

The most recent date which could usefully be selected for the compilation of overall patterns of land use was 1971. The first year of a decade often coincides with a population census year, so this was an additional attraction. Significant alterations in land-use structure do not happen with great speed at a national level, and a ten-year interval is normally sufficient for defining notable changes. Hence, 1961 was chosen as the previous inventory date so that a worthwhile depiction and assessment of trends could be allowed across a full decade. In this context, it should be noted that Denmark, Ireland and the United Kingdom did not become full members of the EEC until 1973.

Some of the countries investigated had no official or surveyed figure for the extent of urban land, and the required area was estimated by applying representative land provision figures to the census populations for 1971 and/or 1961. This was done for Belgium, Luxembourg and Ireland and, in part, for Denmark, France and Canada. Uncertainties about the extent of urban land use only serve to underline further the potential inaccuracies which may surround figures for other land uses as well. We have seen how research on British land-use statistics over many years revealed serious discrepancies in apparently sophisticated data which sometimes compromised the conclusions drawn from them. Similar investigations of data in other countries are in their infancy, and therefore many of the statistics presented and used here must inevitably be viewed with some caution. Certain possible inconsistencies will be pointed out, but no doubt many still remain.

Perhaps the most important single factor militating against reasonable comparability of data between countries is variation in the definition of land uses. The classification adopted here divides the total land area into the four major land-use categories of agriculture (sub-divided into cropland and pasture), forest and woodland, urban land, and other miscellaneous land. Such a large-grain classification helps to accommodate and resolve some of the problems encountered, but it cannot eliminate them entirely.

One of the main obstacles to the harmonisation of land-use data is that there is no clear consensus on what constitutes rural land and what constitutes urban land. Often it is only land covered with buildings which is separated out as the focal urban category, leaving aside a number of essentially urban items like railways, roads, airfields, sports grounds, parks, cemeteries and so on, especially when they occur in countryside areas. To surmount these irregularities, the procedure has been adopted whenever possible of defining the urban area as all built-up land, including transport land, with its associated open spaces. Cropland covers all types of farm and horticultural crops, including tree crops, temporary grass and fallow land, while pasture land comprises both permanent grass and rough grazings. Several EEC countries only distinguish cropland and permanent grass as agricultural land, though this may sometimes be of very poor quality: rough land, which may be grazed to some extent, is usually assigned to the 'other land' category.

Land-use structure in 1971

The structure of land use for 1971 in the entire EEC and in each of the nine member countries is recorded in Table 29 and Figure 20.[11] Corresponding figures for North America[12,13] and Sweden[14] are also given. From the point of view of territorial area, four countries dominate the EEC – France, Italy, West Germany and the United Kingdom, in that order. The other five constituent members are each far less sizeable in extent. But whether large or small, there seems at first sight to be little apparent consistency in the pattern of land use between the nine member states. This variation in land-use composition and the lack of any immediately clear-cut structural relationships has led to the listing of the nine countries in alphabetical order rather than in any possible hierarchy based on land-use structure.

However, a more careful examination of the data soon reveals

Table 29 The major uses of land in the constituent countries of the EEC and North America in about 1971, by area (A) and percentage (B)

(A)	Popula-tion	Total land area	Agri-culture	Crop-land [a]	Pas-ture [a]	Wood-land	Urban land	Other land
	millions				'000 ha			
Belgium	9.67	3,014	1,526	744	782	614	441	433
Denmark	4.96	4,237	2,942	2,653	289	480	388	427
France	51.25	52,249	31,953	18,584	13,369	14,816	2,577	2,903
W. Germany	59.19	24,288	13,160	7,743	5,417	7,175	2,858	1,095
Ireland	2.98	6,889	4,826	1,517	3,309	273	103	1,687
Italy	54.01	29,404	19,464	14,236	5,228	6,180	1,220	2,540
Luxembourg	0.34	258	134	64	70	83	17	24
Netherlands	13.19	3,372	2,179	859	1,320	297	505	391
UK	55.61	24,093	18,831	7,227	11,604	1,908	1,918	1,436
EEC	251.20	147,804	95,015	53,627	41,388	31,826	10,027	10,936
USA	203.21	915,859	515,373	190,939	324,434	212,379	27,901	160,206
Canada	21.57	922,027	69,500	38,635	30,865	493,151	5,048	354,328
Sweden	8.21	41,162	3,735	3,003	732	22,427	1,352	13,648

(B)	Total land area	Agri-culture	Crop-land [a]	Pas-ture [a]	Wood-land	Urban land	Other land
				per cent			
Belgium	100.0	50.6	24.7	25.9	20.4	14.6	14.4
Denmark	100.0	69.4	62.6	6.8	11.3	9.2	10.1
France	100.0	61.2	35.6	25.6	28.3	4.9	5.6
W. Germany	100.0	54.2	31.9	22.3	29.5	11.8	4.5
Ireland	100.0	70.0	22.0	48.0	4.0	1.5	24.5
Italy	100.0	66.2	48.4	17.8	21.0	4.2	8.6
Luxembourg	100.0	51.9	24.8	27.1	32.2	6.6	9.3
Netherlands	100.0	64.6	25.5	39.1	8.8	15.0	11.6
UK	100.0	78.2	30.0	48.2	7.9	8.0	5.9
EEC	100.0	64.2	36.2	28.0	21.6	6.8	7.4
USA	100.0	56.3	20.8	35.5	23.2	3.0	17.5
Canada	100.0	7.5	4.2	3.3	53.5	0.6	38.4
Sweden	100.0	9.1	7.3	1.8	54.5	3.3	33.1

Sources: Best (1979);[1] Hansen (forthcoming);[12] NCBS, Sweden (1980)[14]

Some slight discrepancies between the two sets of data are due to rounding of figures. Swedish figures are for about 1975

[a] Subdivisions of 'Agriculture'

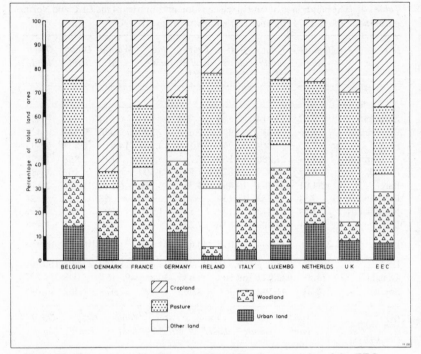

Figure 20 The pattern of land use in 1971 of member countries of the EEC

several significant features. To start with, rural land uses predominate to a marked degree, even though the countries being investigated are often highly urbanised in character. In the EEC as a whole, agriculture took up some 64 per cent of the land surface in 1971, while forest and woodland occupied about 22 per cent, making a total of 86 per cent in these two major uses alone. Much of the 7 per cent of other miscellaneous land was also specifically rural, leaving only around 7 per cent in actual urban use.

Agriculture is invariably the largest use of land in the EEC member states, taking up well over half the total land area in most cases. The proportionate range is from under 51 per cent in Belgium to 70 per cent in Ireland, and to as much as 78 per cent in the United Kingdom. The last figure is exceptional, but is explained partly by the great extent of very poor grazing and almost unutilised tracts in the United Kingdom which in other countries would be placed in the category of 'other land'. Well over 5 per cent could probably be transferred in this way, leaving the agricultural component still very high, though more comparable with Ireland and Denmark.

This irregularity is pinpointed in another way. Table 30 lists the nine EEC countries by the percentage contribution their agricultural land and agricultural output made to the total for the whole Community in 1974.[15] Three countries (France, Italy and West Germany) out of the 'big four' in terms of agricultural land area each provided over 20 per cent of the agricultural output of the EEC (in Community units of account at 1974 prices), whereas the other member – the United Kingdom – made a much smaller contribution of less than 12 per cent. Undoubtedly, the exceptionally high proportion of poor, extensively grazed or even basically unutilised land within the United Kingdom's official agricultural total helps to explain this anomalous situation, but other factors play their role as well. Beresford, for example, points out that the below-average gross product per hectare of the United Kingdom is, in part, related to the structure of holdings.[16] These are fairly large compared with the rest of Europe, and are less intensively farmed. Output per hectare, therefore, tends to be lower, on average, though this must be viewed against the advantages of higher returns to labour and to capital invested.

At the other end of the agricultural spectrum from poor pasture, the proportion of the total land area under crops, the most intensive agricultural use, shows a striking similarity in several countries. In

Table 30 Proportionate contribution of member states to the total agricultural area and agricultural output of the EEC in 1974

	Agricultural area, 1974 per cent	Agricultural output, 1974 [a] per cent
France	34.8	27.6
UK	20.0	11.7
Italy	18.7	20.8
W. Germany	14.3	21.7
Ireland	5.2	2.0
Denmark	3.1	4.3
Netherlands	2.2	7.8
Belgium	1.6	4.0
Luxembourg	0.1	0.1
EEC	100.0	100.0

[a] Measured in EEC units of account at 1974 prices

Belgium, Luxembourg and the Netherlands it is close to 25 per cent: in the United Kingdom, West Germany and France it is not a great deal higher at about 30 to 35 per cent. Only Italy and Denmark have substantially more. Other rural uses, on the contrary, show a remarkable diversity. Pasture varies from as little as 7 per cent in Denmark to 48 per cent in Ireland and the United Kingdom; while forest and woodland ranges from barely 4 per cent in Ireland to as much as 32 per cent in Luxembourg. Though not quite so extensively forested as the latter country, Belgium, Italy, France and West Germany also have a large amount of woodland which extends to between 20 and 30 per cent of their surface areas. Conversely, there is a very low coverage of woodland in the Netherlands, Ireland and the United Kingdom, and this is offset by a high proportion of pasture land, much of it of poor quality.

Considered on a world-wide basis EEC countries, for the most part, are highly urbanised, even though their extent of urban land is always far less than that of agriculture and normally of woodland as well. Admittedly, the EEC member states generally have a percentage of urban land which is higher than in many other urban-industrial societies, but these other countries also frequently have much larger surface areas encompassing extensive tracts of land that are unsuitable for human settlement. Thus, despite a greater population than the EEC, the United States has an urban area which takes up 3 per cent of the land surface, in comparison with nearly 7 per cent in the whole EEC. Canada has still less land proportionately in urban use than the United States with no more than about 1 per cent.

Having said all this, it is still very clear that no EEC country can even remotely be described as largely covered with bricks and concrete. Table 29 gives the actual position. The country with the greatest extent of urban land is the Netherlands, with up to 15 per cent of its land surface under this use, closely followed by Belgium. West Germany has nearly 12 per cent, or a figure which is not too dissimilar from the proportion in England and Wales (11 per cent), although the United Kingdom as a whole, at 8 per cent, is appreciably lower. At the opposite end of the scale, Ireland has less than 2 per cent of urban land, while Italy and France have around 4 to 5 per cent, all being more equivalent to the United States and Sweden in this respect. Significantly, 12 per cent of the Swedish urban area is composed of second homes.

Urban provisions of land also make interesting reading. It is perhaps not unexpected that Italy should have the smallest urban provision (or highest density) with only about 23 ha/1000p, but the United Kingdom also has a low figure of little more than 34 ha/1000p – a provision which is even less than in the Netherlands. West Germany and France have a noticeably greater urban space allocation at 48–50 ha/1000p, but more extreme in its relative openness is the Danish provision of 78 ha/1000p. Nevertheless, this Danish figure is in no way unusual when compared with North America where development is at much lower densities than in the EEC. This is especially true of housing – the largest urban use. In total, the provision of urban land in the United States (in 1970) amounted to as much as 137 ha/1000p (or 86 ha/1000p if transportation land were excluded) compared with 40 ha/1000p for the whole EEC. The provision in Canada was still more substantial, though inflated by the high proportion of land for transport uses.

When rural rather than urban uses are considered, the structure of land use in the United States is more akin to that of the EEC than to Canada, despite a similarity in total land mass of the two North American countries. Although the agricultural area of the United States is falling, it still amounts to 56 per cent of the surface, with 21 per cent under cropland – a situation not too different from certain EEC countries. The 23 per cent of forest is even nearer to the EEC average. In contrast, Canada farms only 7.5 per cent of its total area and has a massive 53 per cent under forest and 38 per cent in other uses or non-uses. This pattern of land use is far closer to that of Sweden with its 9 per cent in agriculture, 54 per cent forest, and 33 per cent of other land. A structure like this is simply a reflection of a relatively small and locationally concentrated population living on an extensive land area which spreads well into northern latitudes and which, as a result, is characterised by vast stretches of tundra, timber, bog and bare rock.

Changes in land use, 1961–71

The accurate assessment of changes in land use is dependent upon a sound and stable statistical inventory of existing stocks of land under the major land uses. Confusion arising from definitional and other inconsistencies in these data can seriously affect the correct interpretation of shifts in the land-use pattern. Moreover, it is ironical that a better and more complete enumeration attained for a land use across the years may actually compromise the reliability of figures for changes in the extent of that use.

More statistical camouflage comes about, in certain circumstances, by the otherwise very necessary adoption of net figures, subsuming both losses and gains, in the recording of land conversions for any particular use or uses. This is because net figures for change can sometimes conceal marked trends in different directions, perhaps in different parts of the same country, which appear to reduce the overall scale of land transfers actually taking place. Gross flows between various uses are indicated very precisely in the Netherlands, for instance, where the complicated interaction and interchange are clearly seen. Total transfers there affect some 13,000 ha annually, whereas the net balance concerns only some 8000 ha.[17] Of course, considerable reclamation of land from internal waters is important, and exceptional, in this context.

But of far more significance, in many ways, is the question of the extent to which recorded shifts in land use are actual changes on the ground as opposed to 'accounting' losses and gains of a purely statistical nature with no real substance to them. Such doubts arise for a number of reasons, but most particularly from the kind of statistical trouble discussed in previous chapters, which has been encountered when trying to assess the true magnitude of changes in land use in the United Kingdom. Here, as in most other EEC countries, the transfers of land out of agriculture between 1961 and 1971 were not only into urban and woodland uses, but also – and even more extensively – into the category of 'other land'. It has now become clear that many of these conversions were of a residual character and were not real alterations in use at all: they merely represented 'corrections, reclassifications and unexplained differences'. Since 1968, over 79,000 unproductive holdings have been dropped from the agricultural census returns and these account for up to 500,000 ha of land in Britain alone, excluding Northern Ireland.[18] Some reclassification of farmland to woodland, buildings, etc. has also occurred. Consequently, the greater part of the so-called 'loss' of farmland to non-urban and non-woodland uses (550,000 ha) can be accounted for in this way, and is, in reality, a loss on paper only.

This type of problem may well be repeated in other countries; but it must also be remembered that, unlike the United Kingdom, several member states of the EEC do indeed have an actual transfer of agricultural land to the 'other land' category by the abandonment of farmland at the extensive margin of cultivation. From the present statistics, it is impossible to determine how important a matter this may be in terms of area. Another potentially serious aspect of data compilation for land transfers in the EEC is that France is so relatively large a country in physical size that its transfers of land, by area, may often be far greater than in any other member country. Because of this weighting, French conversions, and any statistical irregularities in them, can influence the overall figures for the entire EEC to a substantial extent.

Bearing in mind these statistical qualifications, Table 31 and Figure 21 give an indication of how land-use patterns in the EEC altered between 1961 and 1971. Corresponding information for North America is also recorded. As with the existing land-use structure, the most immediately noteworthy feature is the considerable variation between the different countries; only this time it is in the rate and composition of the shifts in land use. Nevertheless, a closer study of the figures, especially as expressed in the diagram (Fig. 21), reveals certain definite regularities.

To begin with, nearly all the countries show a loss from the agricultural area which is of fairly substantial proportions. In as many as six of the EEC member states the decline is apparently of the order of 4 per cent or more of the total land area, though an unknown part of this loss may be explained by statistical irregularities. In the United States, the loss is approaching 3 per cent. Only in Ireland is a net gain of agricultural land recorded, with a large area of formerly unused territory being brought into cultivation. By far the greater part of the agricultural loss in EEC countries is from the cropland sector, whereas most of them show some increase in pasture land. Apart from Ireland, the United Kingdom is the main exception to this continental pattern in that its loss of cropland is very small indeed compared with the large decline in pasture land. Both the United States and Canada are even more different as they show a gain in cropland but a loss in pasture.

This transfer of farmland is to several different uses – urban development, forest and woodland and other miscellaneous land. Yet the only major use in which there is a consistent net gain of land in all of the eleven countries is urban development. Even so, the increase is very variable, ranging from 1.5 per cent of the land surface in West Germany down to only 0.2 per cent in Ireland and still less in Canada (Table 32). Several countries, including the United Kingdom, hover around the average gain of 0.8 per cent for the whole EEC. When urban growth is expressed as a proportion of the urban area alone rather than of the total land surface, Italy is

Table 31 Changes in land use and population in the constituent countries of the EEC and North America between 1961 and 1971, expressed in absolute terms (A) and percentages (B)

(A)	Popula-tion	Total land area	Agri-culture	Crop-land [a]	Pas-ture [a]	Wood-and	Urban land	Other land
	millions	'000 ha						
Belgium	+0.49	0	−145	−157	+12	+13	+24	+108
Denmark	+0.35	+3	−198	−145	−53	+18	+27	+156
France	+5.05	−225	−2,106	−2,342	+236	+3,203	+254	−1,576
W. Germany	+5.18	+11	−640	−353	−287	+69	+359	+223
Ireland	+0.16	0	+266	+105	+161	+98	+11	−375
Italy	+4.11	+3	−1,183	−1,349	+166	+343	+289	+554
Luxembourg	+0.02	0	−4	−10	+6	−1	+2	+3
Netherlands	+1.56	+14	−135	−168	+33	+27	+43	+79
UK	+2.80	−2	−927	−39	−888	+183	+192	+550
EEC	+19.72	−196	−5,072	−4,458	−614	+3,953	+1,201	−278
USA [c]	+23.89	−2,832	−25,081	+5,664	−30,745	+16,991	+2,589	+2,670
Canada	+3.31	+13	−673	+1,952	−2,625	−7,616	+772	+7,530

(B)	Popula-tion	Total land area	Agri-culture	Crop-land [a]	Pas-ture [a]	Wood-land	Urban land	Other land
	per cent [b]							
Belgium	+5.3	0.0	−4.8	−5.2	+0.4	+0.4	+0.8	+3.6
Denmark	+7.6	+0.1	−4.6	−3.4	−1.2	+0.4	+0.6	+3.7
France	+10.9	−0.4	−4.0	−4.5	+0.5	+6.1	+0.5	−3.0
W. Germany	+9.6	+0.1	−2.6	−1.4	−1.2	+0.3	+1.5	+0.9
Ireland	+5.7	0.0	+3.8	+1.5	+2.3	+1.4	+0.2	−5.4
Italy	+8.2	0.0	−4.0	−4.6	+0.6	+1.1	+1.0	+1.9
Luxembourg	+6.2	0.0	−1.6	−3.9	+2.3	−0.4	+0.8	+1.2
Netherlands	+13.4	+0.4	−4.0	−5.0	+1.0	+0.8	+1.3	+2.3
UK	+5.3	0.0	−3.8	−0.1	−3.7	+0.7	+0.8	+2.3
EEC	+8.5	−0.1	−3.4	−3.0	−0.4	+2.7	+0.8	−0.2
USA [c]	+13.3	−0.3	−2.7	+0.6	−3.3	+1.8	+0.3	+0.3
Canada	+18.1	0.0	−0.1	+0.2	−0.3	−0.8	+0.1	+0.8

[a] Subdivisions of 'Agriculture'
[b] As a percentage of the total land area or population in 1961 (1960 – USA)
[c] Changes between 1960 and 1970

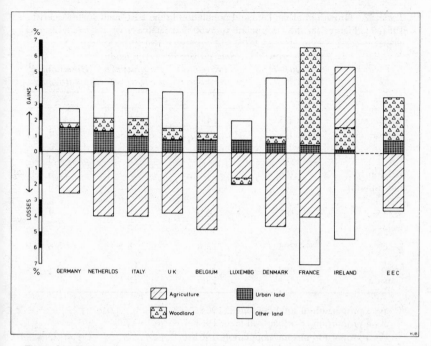

Figure 21 Changes in land use in the member countries of the EEC between 1961 and 1971. The countries are arranged in order of declining gain of land to urban use over this period

seen to have experienced an exceptional 31 per cent increase; but most other gains are considerable – usually at over 10 per cent. Evidently, there is no particularly close relationship to be seen between the rate of population growth in these countries and the rate of urban growth, and indeed this would not normally be expected in the short term (see Chapter 7).

In only one of the nine EEC member states – Luxembourg – is there a net loss of land from the forest and woodland area, though this is also true of Canada. In six of the other countries, the gain recorded is of a similar or lesser magnitude to the increase in urban land, whereas in Ireland and the USA the gain is of a considerably higher order. But the real exception is provided by France, where the growth in forest area at the expense of agricultural and other land is registered at more than 6 per cent of the land surface, or a 28 per cent rise over the area of woodland in 1961. Such a massive gain over so short a period must raise doubts about the validity of the

Table 32 Growth in urban land and population in the EEC and North America, 1961–71. Figures for the USA relate to 1960 and 1970

	Urban growth [a] 1961–71	Urban growth [b] 1961–71	Population growth [c] 1961–71	Urban area [d] 1971
	per cent			
W. Germany	1.5	14.4	9.6	11.8
Netherlands	1.3	9.3	13.4	15.0
Italy	1.0	31.0	8.2	4.2
UK	0.8	11.1	5.3	8.0
Belgium	0.8	5.7	5.3	14.6
Luxembourg	0.8	13.3	6.2	6.6
Denmark	0.6	7.5	7.6	9.2
France	0.5	10.9	10.9	4.9
Ireland	0.2	11.9	5.7	1.5
EEC	0.8	13.6	8.5	6.8
USA	0.3	10.2	13.3	3.0
Canada	0.1	18.0	18.1	0.6

[a] As a proportion of total land area, 1961
[b] As a proportion of urban land area, 1961
[c] As a proportion of total population, 1961
[d] As a proportion of total land area, 1971

figure, and warrants further investigation. Interestingly, if the French figure were to be excluded, the increase in woodland for the other eight EEC countries would amount to 0.8 per cent of their combined land surface (compared with 2.7 per cent for the whole EEC with France included), or the same figure as for the growth in urban land for the EEC as a whole. In considering Table 31 and Figure 21, therefore, the possibility of such a distortion must be borne in mind.

It has also been mentioned previously that the transfer of land in and out of the 'other land' category can cause serious statistical problems, as demonstrated in the United Kingdom. Five of the EEC member states show a percentage increase in other land which is more than the combined gain for urban and forest land in these countries. In most cases, this increase represents over 2 per cent of the land surface, and in Belgium and Denmark it is well over 3 per cent. Inevitably, this situation must again lead to some concern over statistical verisimilitude.

From the previous discussion, it can be seen that the interpretation of land conversions is fraught with difficulties and needs to be carried out with extreme care, and perhaps with an element of constructive scepticism as well. In the EEC as a whole, and in several of its member states, the net changes in land use over the decade appear to have affected something like 4 per cent of the total land area. It has been noted, however, that because of 'paper' rather than real transfers of agricultural land in the United Kingdom the actual area of its territory involved in land conversions has probably been nearer 2 per cent than the 3.8 per cent shown by the official statistics. A similar level of change may also apply to the entire EEC if possible exaggerations of land transfers to woodland are proved to be correct. For various reasons, the same may be true of some of the individual member states, especially those with large gains in the 'other land' area; but this is not to imply, of course, that all the countries concerned will necessarily have had a level of land transfers of around this magnitude. Nevertheless, certain of the overall shifts in land use that have been registered give the impression of being statistically excessive, and a more detailed investigation will be needed before they can be either confirmed or refuted.

A number of these reservations also apply to the figures for land conversions in the United States and Canada, though the far greater size of these two countries introduces a further possibility of potential inaccuracy into their statistics for land-use change.

EEC, USA and UK – some conclusions

This study has attempted, for the first time, to sketch the broad outlines of a comprehensive inventory of land use in the EEC and North America, but it makes no pretence at being more than an initial excursion into the subject. Even so, it is contended that the effort made to harmonise the statistics used has produced a more consistent and reasonable comparative statement of land-use structure and change than has previously been available.

Although there are clearly difficulties which arise in the interpretation of comparative land use and trends within the areas studied, several general conclusions may still be safely drawn. The information has a particular relevance to the British situation because it is now possible to set the detailed knowledge which exists on land-use structure and change in the United Kingdom and its component parts into the much wider perspective provided by the neighbouring countries of Europe and those across the Atlantic. The comment thereby provided on the United Kingdom is extremely illuminating and is likely to dispel or call into question many of the myths which have grown up and flourished in the emotional context surrounding British discussions on land use and land conversion.

The main conclusions to be drawn from this investigation of comparative land use are as follows:

(a) The rural sector of the land surface is well-documented in most European and North American countries, and this is particularly true with agricultural land use. Information about urban land use and changes between the major uses, on the contrary, is relatively poor and insufficient.

(b) Probably the most important single factor which limits the comparability and harmonisation of land-use data between countries is the lack of consistent definitions.

(c) The structure of land use in the individual countries shows considerable dissimilarities. Nevertheless, rural land uses predominate to a marked extent. In the EEC as a whole in 1971, agriculture took up some 64 per cent of the land surface, while forest and woodland occupied about 22 per cent, leaving only around 7 per cent in urban use and another 7 per cent of other miscellaneous land.

(d) Agriculture is invariably the largest single use of land in EEC countries (and the USA); but unexpectedly the United Kingdom has the highest proportion of all (78 per cent), though this figure contains much poor grazing of which a considerable amount is virtually unused. The large percentage of pasture land in the United Kingdom is offset by a very low proportion under forest and woodland (8 per cent) when compared with the EEC and North American averages.

(e) Urban land covers only a small proportion of the land surface in the twelve countries considered, with a maximum figure of 15 per cent in the Netherlands in 1971. The United Kingdom is appreciably lower, with no more than 8 per cent. Its urban land provision is also smaller (the density is higher) than in most of the other countries. Conversely, the United States and Canada have very large urban provisions but a low proportionate urban coverage (3 and 0.6 per cent, respectively).

(f) Statistical irregularities intrude severely into the assessment of correct rates of land-use change between 1961 and 1971, and the overall scale of conversion may, in some cases, be far less than the recorded figures suggest. In the United Kingdom, for instance, by far the greater part of the 550,000 ha loss of farmland to the category of 'other land' can be accounted for by the reclassification and redefinition of land in agricultural use.

(g) In spite of such constraints on interpretation, certain definite trends are evident. Nearly all EEC countries show a fairly substantial loss from the agricultural area, whereas woodland and particularly urban development show a persistent increase, though at variable rates. In contrast to North America, most of the agricultural loss is from the cropland sector, except in the United Kingdom where the decline in pasture land far outweighs the diminution in the area of crops, even when statistical reclassifications are allowed for. Three countries have urban gains of between 1 per cent and 1.5 per cent of the land surface over the decade, but the United Kingdom is noticeably lower at only 0.8 per cent.

Even this very brief summary of results, which may be filled out in more detail from the main text, begins to throw a new light on many of the contentious arguments surrounding British land use. Firstly, the extent of the urban area in the United Kingdom as a whole, and even in England and Wales alone, is in no sense disproportionate or excessive compared with other EEC countries, several of which have a distinctly greater coverage. Secondly, and perhaps still more surprising, the proportion of agricultural land in the United Kingdom is markedly larger than in the other countries. Thirdly, when considering changes in land use, the conversion rate of farmland to urban development is the same as the EEC average and noticeably lower than in some of the other member states. The gain in woodland area is also in no way unusual in the United Kingdom.

With this background information, it is not easy to subscribe to the widespread tendency in this country to regard British land-use structure and change as a very special combination of circumstances and events. Often, the British situation is even considered as being a unique cause for concern, particularly where urban growth and agricultural land loss are involved; yet it is now seen that, comparatively, the Netherlands, West Germany, Belgium and Italy all appear to have a far more impressive array of adjustments facing them. But whatever the difficulties involved, the downward trend of farm area and farm labour is not paralleled by declining agricultural output. On the contrary, whether in North America, Continental

Europe or the United Kingdom, the spectre of insufficient food supplies by the end of the century is largely a figment of the imagination. Indeed, the opposite circumstance more nearly applies, and one of the most serious problems facing North American and European agriculture, both now and in the future, is the predicament of surplus production and the related dilemma of too much farmland rather than too little.

References

1   This chapter is based on: Best, R.H. (1979) 'Land-use structure and change in the EEC', *Town Planning Review*, 50 (4), 395–411.
2   Rogers, A.W. (ed.) (1978) *Urban Growth, Farmland Losses and Planning*, Institute of British Geographers.
3   Stamp, L.D. (1968) *Our Developing World*, London, Faber & Faber.
4   Food and Agriculture Organisation (1979) *Production Yearbook, 1978*, 32, Rome.
5   *The Ecologist* editors (1972) *A Blueprint for Survival*, Harmondsworth, Penguin. Reproduced from Doane, R.R. (1957) *World Balance Sheet*, New York, Harper.
6   Clawson, M., Held, R.B. and Stoddard, C.H. (1960) *Land for the Future*, Baltimore. Johns Hopkins University Press.
7   Stamp, L.D. (1965) *Land Use Statistics of the Countries of Europe*, World Land Use Survey, Occasional Papers, No. 3, Geographical Publications.
8   Corver, H. and Kippers, M. (1969) *Changing European Land Use Patterns*, Food and Agriculture Organisation.
9   Best, R.H. and Mandale, M. (1971) *Competing Demands for Land in Technologically Advanced Countries*, SSRC Final Report, Wye College.
10 Organisation for Economic Co-operation and Development (1976) *Land Use Policies and Agriculture*, Paris.
11 The sources from which detailed statistical data on land use in the EEC have been drawn are given in full in Best, R.H. (1979) op. cit.
12 Hansen, J.A. (1981) 'A land-use study of Canada, the US and Britain c. 1951–71,' *Area*, 13 (2),169–71. See also: US Department of Agriculture (1973) *Major Uses of Land in the United States, Summary for 1969*, Agricultural Economic Report No. 247, Washington D.C.; and corresponding publication in 1962 (Summary for 1959); Hart, J.F. (1976) 'Urban encroachment on rural areas', *Geographical Review*, 66 (1), 3–17.
13 Statistics Canada (1973) *Canada Yearbook, 1971*, Ottawa; and corresponding publication for 1961. See also: Statistics Canada (1973) *Census of Agriculture, 1971*, Ottawa; and Gierman, D.M. (1977)

Rural to Urban Land Conversion, Occasional Paper No. 16, Lands Directorate, Canada.

14 National Central Bureau of Statistics (1980) *Swedish Experience in the Use of Particular Data Collection Techniques for the Compilation of Land Use Statistics*, Contribution to the ECE meeting on land use statistics, Geneva, March 1980.

15 European Documentation (1976) *The Agricultural Policy of the European Community*, Brussels.

16 Beresford, T. (1975) *We Plough the Fields*, Harmondsworth, Penguin. See also: Centre for Agricultural Strategy (1980) *The Efficiency of British Agriculture*, Report No. 7, University of Reading.

17 OECD (1976) op. cit.

18 Ministry of Agriculture, Fisheries and Food *et al*. (1978) *Agricultural Statistics, United Kingdom 1975, Agricultural Census and Production*, HMSO.

10
Land-use myths and reality

Rarely do the facts and the perceptions correspond.

(Eric Ashby: *Reconciling Man with the Environment*)

Are we running short of land or have we plenty? Is urban encroachment a serious threat to our countryside and food supplies or not? Do we have adequate living space in our towns and villages? Contradictory answers and attitudes to land-use questions like these abound: even the 'doctors' disagree over the symptoms and the prescriptions. In the present state of confusion, then, it is small wonder that few people have any coherent idea of whether the shifts taking place in the land-use structure of this country are critically important for us all, or whether they are largely immaterial.

Perhaps the chief trouble in getting somewhere near the truth of the matter is that the whole subject of land use is so charged with emotive overtones. Scratch the surface of any Britisher who lives in a city or town and, more often than not, you will find a countryman underneath. Suggest that the rural heritage is in any danger and he or she will fly to its defence with disquieting alacrity. Such fervour as this is hardly conducive to factual appraisal and objective evaluation.

Here, then, is the very essence of myth-making. To a disturbing extent, it has become apparent that land-use planning in Britain – and in most other countries as well – has been built on the extremely shaky and insecure foundation of illusion rather than that of reality. This book has tried to rectify this unsatisfactory situation to some extent by setting down, as far as is possible, a more quantified and carefully researched statement and appraisal of land-use structure and change than has previously been attempted. When this is done much of the conventional wisdom about land use can be shown to be incorrect or very suspect. If we simply record several of the more widespread and now almost traditional views which are held, it is not difficult to show, from information given in previous chapters, how inadequately they measure up to the real-world situation.

To begin with, we have what is a fundamental fallacy:

A vast expanse of our country is already sterilised by cities and towns which spread out at wastefully low densities.

Maybe it is because so many of us live and work in towns that, in the mind's eye, we seem inevitably to exaggerate the actual extent of urban land around us – often to as much as a quarter or even a third of the whole surface of the country. A few accurate figures can give a more correct perspective. In 1971, the urban area took up no more than 11 per cent of the total area of England and Wales, and only around 8 per cent of Britain or the United Kingdom as a whole. In sharp contrast, up to 78 per cent of the land area was still in some form of agricultural use. Another 7 or 8 per cent of forests and woodland has to be added into the rural sector, while a further few per cent should also be included to cover other rural land which has not been enumerated for one reason or another.

The relatively limited extent of urban land in so urbanised an economy as ours is further emphasised by the smallness of the land provision for urban use in cities and larger towns. The allocation is no more than 10 ha per thousand population for residential land, or only about a third of that in small towns and villages. New towns, so often criticised for their so-called 'prairie planning', are, in reality, not at all exceptional in the space standards they have adopted compared with other towns of the same population size. Indeed, the trouble with most of our larger towns, old and new, is not that they take up too much space, but that they occupy too little to provide adequate living conditions for their inhabitants. To quote from the author's booklet on *Land for New Towns*:

> because of limited space, Britain cannot reasonably hope to emulate in all new development the far more liberal space standards which are being adopted in many countries overseas. On the other hand, the country is certainly not so short of land that inferior space standards for housing or other urban uses should be imposed on any section of the community. There is enough room available, provided it is allocated sensibly, to allow every family that requires it a moderately spacious house-plot without detriment to agriculture or the countryside in general.

This is always assuming, it should be added, that planning control over the location of new development is allowed to continue in the effective way it has done since 1947, ensuring a contained but less constricted urban area in many places.

This comment leads on to what has become perhaps the most persistent myth of all:

Each year urban sprawl engulfs still greater amounts of good land so that, before long, most of our precious countryside will be completely submerged beneath bricks and concrete.

This is undoubtedly the most common and widespread belief in the land-use catalogue, and it is the one which lies at the root of many of the restrictive attitudes that are adopted in planning and conservation policies. It is certainly true that, although the urban area is far smaller than is generally recognised, its rate of growth in the past has been relatively fast. In the first half of this century, or thereabouts, urban land actually doubled its extent in England and Wales. But the high point in the conversion rate was not a recent event: it was reached as long ago as the 1930s when over 25,000 ha of farmland each year were being absorbed, particularly by the sprawl of unregulated suburbia.

At that time, the fortunes of agriculture were at a low ebb, and land could be bought easily and cheaply with hardly any constraints imposed by land-use planning. After the Second World War, however, transfers of farmland to urban use were cut back to less than 16,000 ha a year on average, largely through the operation of planning control under the Town and Country Planning Act of 1947 (and later legislation) and the persistent policy of urban containment.

Contrary to popular assumption, there has been no sustained increase in the urban growth rate since the early postwar years. If anything, the trend overall has been for a decline in urban demands and a tightening up in housing densities. Latterly, the deepening recession of the late 1970s has further restricted residential demand and house-building, along with other types of development, and this resulted by 1978 in the lowest level of annual land loss (about 8,000 ha) achieved in any year since the end of the war. At this rate, by the end of the century, no more than about 14 per cent of England and Wales will be covered by cities, towns, villages and transport facilities – definitely not a very substantial proportion of the land surface.

If the whole of Britain is considered, afforestation rather than urban growth is now the chief acquirer of farmland, although the land taken is of much lower quality than that normally used for urban purposes. Indeed, it is not generally realised how much poor land there is in the country; even in England and Wales it amounts to over a third of the farmed area (i.e. ignoring forested land) while in Scotland it is well in excess of 80 per cent.

Although it is now often appreciated that most of our afforestation takes place in the north and west of Britain, the regional distribution of urban growth is not nearly so well understood. Herein lies a third myth:

Across most of the country, encroachment by urban uses on to agricultural land is on a very large scale, and it is particularly excessive in south-eastern counties.

This concept is again completely fallacious, although certain parts of the country – not always the most expected areas – are being much more rigorously affected than others. At one extreme, as many as twenty-one counties in England and Wales in the 1960s had a rate of change from agricultural to urban use which was 0.05 per cent or less of the total county area per annum. In other words, no more than one hectare in every 2000 was affected each year: an extremely slow turnover by any measure. And what is more, these areas of sluggish urban expansion lay not only in the remote upland regions but also along the eastern side of England, particularly around the Wash, where agricultural output is high and farming among the most productive in the country.

On the other hand, fairly rapid urban growth is concentrated in two main groupings of counties, the so-called 'central urban region' (which comprises mainly the conurbations and urban areas of northern England and the west midlands) and the London region. These two regions have been separated by a band of only weakly urbanising country, but recent years have seen this rural divide increasingly impinged upon by large-scale developments on the fringe of the London region.

This regional configuration of urban growth has altered fundamentally in emphasis since 1945. At first, the counties at the core of the London region dominated the pattern of urban extension. By the 1960s however, there had been a radical turn-about and the most prominent areas of urban growth were now certain parts of the central urban region, where conversion rates reached up to 0.3 per cent annually – or about one hectare in 300 going urban each year. Conversely, the rate of change faded away in the home counties as near-saturation of development approached in some districts. Not only does this latest pattern of regional urban growth run counter to established preconceptions; it is also completely opposed to the trends in population geography, where a south-eastward emphasis is still apparent. It is, for instance, most unexpected to find that two counties with among the highest farmland conversion rates to urban use – Lancashire and Durham – actually had absolute decreases in population.

At first sight this appears contradictory, but the explanation of these seeming anomalies lies mainly in changing urban space standards. As the physical fabric of the cramped, northern industrial towns was renewed from the 1960s onwards, people moved from crowded central areas to lower density housing on the outskirts. These new estates on green-field sites had more open space and more spacious schools and shopping facilities, as well as far fewer houses to the hectare. Conversely, many lower density localities in the London region were being in-filled with more tightly-built residential developments (often utilising the gardens of large houses), so that more people were accommodated without absorbing any further agricultural land in the process.

If the strongly highland distribution of afforestation is also taken into account along with transfers of farmland to urban use, the north-west of England and parts of Wales stand out even more distinctly as the predominant areas of land-use change as against most of the south and east. It is, of course, this latter division of the country which is its most productive agricultural part; and this brings us to the fourth major myth:

> *Agricultural output will be gravely endangered, and food shortages a serious possibility, if continuing losses of productive farmland to urban use and afforestation are not soon reduced substantially.*

Again, this is not correct. About 180,000 ha of farmland are lost to urban growth each decade over the whole of Britain, while a larger area still is converted to forest and woodland. But authorities most closely associated with the agricultural industry are often the least worried on this score. This is not surprising when we look at land budget studies which have been carried out into the problem of the land requirements for agriculture in the United Kingdom up to the year 2000. Their conclusions are revealing.

The most important factors affecting the area of land needed for food production are: population growth and composition; alterations in real, personal incomes; changing productivity in agriculture; and the balance required between home-produced and imported food products. Models taking account of these factors have been constructed by Wye College and Reading University, and the results have been independently assessed by two investigators of the Agricultural Research Council. They conclude that the budgets provide a basically reassuring outlook, particularly when, with the wisdom of hindsight, it is now apparent that the magnitude of certain of the variables involved – like population growth and income – are likely to have been over-estimated by a not inconsiderable amount in the original calculations. What the Agricultural Research Council investigators regard as undeniable is that a reduction, or even the prevention, of further loss of farmland to urban use could not affect the land budgets to any notable extent. 'Therefore', they say, 'there appears to be little justification for . . . the suggestion that losses of agricultural land to the urban sector constitute a main threat to the UK food supply.' The reduction of losses to afforestation would be of even less moment because of the very poor quality and productivity of the land involved.

At first sight, then, there would seem to be no prospect by the end of the century of any real difficulty in making ends meet where competing land uses are concerned, particularly when we are an integral part of the EEC whose agricultural economy is dominated by surpluses. Yet, with future generations in mind, this is no reason for being prodigal with our land resources. There is, for instance, little sense in hindering rather than helping farming productivity by building on our relatively limited stretches of really fertile land when, as so often happens, alternative sites of poorer quality are readily available. Agriculture is still the most important use of rural areas, and planners therefore should certainly give a significant weighting to farming considerations in their decisions about the allocation of land.

Intense competition for land often seems to be a peculiarly British phenomenon. But is it? Do we really compare unfavourably with other countries in this respect? Here is our final myth:

Because of its small size and high level of urbanisation, Britain is unique in its pattern of land use and in the severity of land competition it experiences.

Not so. Far from taking up a much greater part of the land surface than elsewhere, urban land coverage in Britain and the United Kingdom (8 per cent) is well below that in several other

EEC countries, including the Netherlands (15 per cent) and West Germany (12 per cent). But on an international scale most of these European countries are fairly small in total area; with vastly larger nations, even though they may be basically urban-industrial in character, the urban proportion falls to a very low level. The United States and Sweden have only 3 per cent of urban land, for instance, while Canada has less than 1 per cent. When it comes to urban living space, the United Kingdom is somewhat deprived with only 34 ha/1000p, or one of the poorest provisions in the EEC – less even than in the Netherlands, though rather more than in Italy. In contrast, the United States is conspicuously different with four times as much urban space per head as in this country.

On the other hand, the United Kingdom has more agricultural land in percentage terms (78 per cent) than any other EEC country, although a good deal of it is poor land. Therefore, it is not farmland but forest and woodland that is deficient in area compared with many other western nations. We have only some 8 per cent in this use in contrast to an average of 22 per cent in the EEC. But all in all, for an industrial nation, it seems that Britain is not particularly exceptional in land use, or even in the provision of living space, compared with several of our European neighbours. Moreover, the agricultural/urban land conversion rate in this country of under 1 per cent a decade is well outpaced by countries like West Germany, the Netherlands and Italy. Britain's long-continued policy of urban containment, brought about largely by stringent planning control since 1947, appears to have been remarkably effective.

How do we sum up this information on the reality of land use as opposed to the mythical conceptions so often propounded? In the first place, it is evident that both land-use structure and the intensity of competition for land in Britain are far from unique: indeed, they are fairly unexceptional in comparative terms. Certainly, several other countries of equivalent socio-economic status have similar, or considerably greater, urban pressures on their rural land. Here in Britain, it seems likely that we shall be able to meet all reasonable demands on our land surface from urban growth and afforestation until the beginning of the next century without food supplies being affected in any serious way. Nor should it be necessary to restrict unduly the densities of urban development, and particularly houses and gardens, to a level which is inadequate to meet the legitimate aspirations for space of a twentieth-century society.

But such conclusions take little account of the impact of land-use change on environmental quality. Uninspired and poorly executed urban development and afforestion are only too frequent, while the mechanisation and intensification of farming is inflicting dramatic transformations on the rural scene. Rural uses themselves are increasingly in conflict with one another: agriculture, forestry, nature conservation and recreation all interact and clash to varying but growing degrees. Indeed, where once, in the 1930s, urban encroachment was indisputably the main threat to the countryside, now, some fifty years later, the menace of urban development has faded into a relatively subordinate position. This is compared with the damage to the landscape in general, and to other uses in particular, which can often be brought about by insensitive and aggressive agricultural, forest or recreational development.

From the point of view of resource utilisation alone, however, it appears from the evidence presented in this book that few grounds exist for becoming unduly worried about our land and food supplies, or certainly not by the end of the century. We should build enough decent homes in suitably spacious and attractive urban areas until all the population is adequately housed. But, while doing this, let us keep and improve our best and most productive farmland wherever possible; and let us plant more forest on some of our poorer lands and make reasonable and satisfactory provision for amenity and nature conservation requirements as well. If this should sound like wanting to have our cake and eat it, it has, on the contrary, been demonstrated in previous chapters that all these things are possible with present land resources, if only we plan, allocate and use these resources prudently. With sensible decision-making and an appropriate strategy of land use, as contained in county structure plans, we could achieve all of our land-use objectives. In other words, there is no real land problem in Britain at the moment. Most of the perceived problem is simply in the mind; it is not out there on the ground.

Appendix

Hectares/acres conversion table

hectares		acres
0.41	**1**	2.47
2.02	**5**	12.36
4.05	**10**	24.71
6.07	**15**	37.07
8.09	**20**	49.42
10.12	**25**	61.78
12.14	**30**	74.13
14.17	**35**	86.49
16.19	**40**	98.84
18.21	**45**	111.20
20.23	**50**	123.55
22.26	**55**	135.91
24.28	**60**	148.27
26.31	**65**	160.62
28.33	**70**	172.98
30.35	**75**	185.33
32.37	**80**	197.69
34.40	**85**	210.04
36.42	**90**	222.40
38.45	**95**	234.75
40.47	**100**	247.11
44.52	**110**	271.82
48.56	**120**	296.53
52.61	**130**	321.24
56.66	**140**	345.95
60.71	**150**	370.66

The centre column in bold figures represents either of the two columns beside it: e.g. 5 acres = 2.02 ha; 5 ha = 12.36 acres. The table also refers to provisions of land: e.g. 5 acres/1000p = 2.02 ha/1000p.

Index

abandonment of farmland, 113, 166, 174
afforestation, 36, 55, 84, 96, 102, 110, 111, 117, 118, 120, 186–91 *passim*
agricultural land: decline of, 50, 55, 89, 102, 113, 173, 181; extension of, 5, 10, 15, 45, 80; extent of, 45, 64, 102, 113, 152, 170–1, 180, 181, 185, 190; good quality, 91, 104, 139, 141–9 *passim*, 151–3, 159, 189, 191; medium quality, 141–9 *passim*, 153, 159; output, 2, 24–5, 26, 45, 49, 50, 102–3, 106, 109–14 *passim*, 141, 164, 171, 181, 187, 188; outside farms, 50–1; poor quality, 49, 55, 96, 113, 142–9 *passim*, 151–3, 159, 168, 186, 189, 190; quality classification of, 139–46, 149–53, 155, 159
Agricultural Research Council, 111, 188–9
agricultural returns, 24–7, 50, 51, 82, 84, 86–7, 120, 174
Agricultural Statistics, 23, 25–7, 31, 38, 39, 40, 43, 51, 54, 55, 56, 82, 83, 118
agricultural subsidies, 26, 48
Agriculture Act, 1947, 91
airfields, 29, 54, 60, 62, 82, 83, 90, 140, 168
allotments, 21, 41, 64, 82, 105, 107, 121, *see also* gardens
amenity land, 101, 102, 104, 149–60, 191
Anderson, Margaret, 44, 64, 112, 149, 150, 156
Anglo-Saxons, 12
Antartica, 163
arable land, *see* cropland

Areas of Outstanding Natural Beauty, 149–60 *passim*
axial belt, 9, 67, 77, 117, 133, 136

Barlow Committee, 39
Bath, 12
Belgium, 167, 170, 172, 178, 181
Beresford, T., 171
Best, Robin, 41–4, 65, 70, 84, 135, 146, 166, 185
Black Death, 13
Blacksell, Mark, 155
Blair, A.M., 84
Blake, R.N.E., 62
Boddington, Michael, 113, 141
Bournville, 81
Bracknell, 75
Brighton, 157
Bristol, 106
Buckinghamshire, 135
Burnham, Paul, 141

Canada, 4, 167, 172, 173, 175, 177, 179, 180, 189
Cardiganshire, 129
cemeteries, 64, 168
central areas of cities, 95, 101, 134, 188
Central Urban Region, 122–23 *passim*, 136, 187
Centre for Agricultural Strategy, 102, 111, 188
Champion, Tony, 63, 66–7, 73, 75, 131, 132–3, 135
'change in area' data, 27, 82–5, 96, 97, 120, 133
Channel Islands, 37
Cheshire, 7, 12, 118, 126, 127

193